RUMINATIVE THOUGHTS

Advances in Social Cognition, Volume IX

RUMINATIVE THOUGHTS

Advances in Social Cognition, Volume IX

Edited by

ROBERT S. WYER, JR.
University of Illinois, Urbana—Champaign

Lead Article by

Leonard L. Martin
Abraham Tesser

LAWRENCE ERLBAUM ASSOCIATES, PUBLISHERS
1996   Mahwah, New Jersey

Copyright © 1996 by Lawrence Erlbaum Associates, Inc.
All rights reserved. No part of this book may be reproduced in any form, by photostat, microform, retrieval system, or any other means without the prior written permission of the publisher.

Lawrence Erlbaum Associates, Inc., Publishers
10 Industrial Avenue
Mahwah, New Jersey 07430

Cover design by Gail Silverman

Library of Congress Cataloging-in-Publication Data

Ruminative Thoughts
Advances in Social Cognition, Volume IX

ISSN: 0898-2007
ISBN: 0-8058-1815-4 (cloth)
ISBN: 0-8058-1816-2 (paper)

Books published by Lawrence Erlbaum Associates are printed on acid-free paper, and their bindings are chosen for strength and durability.

Printed in the United States of America
10 9 8 7 6 5 4 3 2 1

Contents

Preface		vii
1	Some Ruminative Thoughts *Leonard L. Martin and Abraham Tesser*	1
2	Goal Engagement and the Human Experience *Charles S. Carver*	49
3	Restructuring and Realigning Mental Models: Ruminations as Guides to Cognitive Home Repair *Leslie F. Clark*	63
4	Ruminations on the Rebound *Ralph Erber and Daniel M. Wegner*	73
5	Some Thoughts About Thinking *Carol L. Gohm, Linda M. Isbell, and Robert S. Wyer, Jr.*	81
6	Thinking About Goals, Glue, and the Meaning of Life *Laura A. King and James W. Pennebaker*	97
7	Theories of Thought Flow: Points of Kinship and Fertile Contrasts *Eric Klinger*	107
8	Attention Inhibition: Does It Underlie Ruminative Thought? *Patricia Linville*	121

9	Chewing the Cud and Other Ruminations *Susan Nolen-Hoeksema*	135
10	Recurrent Thought: Implications for Attitudes and Persuasion *Richard E. Petty, W. Blair G. Jarvis, and Lisa M. Evans*	145
11	When Do Unconscious Goals Cloud Our Minds? *James S. Uleman*	165
12	Rumination: When All Else Fails *Michaela Wänke and Jeannette Schmid*	177
13	Clarifying Our Thoughts *Leonard L. Martin and Abraham Tesser*	189
Author Index		209
Subject Index		215

Preface

This is the ninth volume of the *Advances in Social Cognition* series. From its inception, the purpose of the series has been to present and evaluate new theoretical advances in all areas of social cognition and information processing. An entire volume is devoted to each theory, allowing the theory to be evaluated from a variety of perspectives and permitting its implications for a wide range of issues to be examined.

The series reflects two major characteristics of social cognition: the high level of activity in the field and the interstitial nature of the work. Each volume contains a target chapter that is timely in its application, novel in its approach, and precise in its explication. The target chapter is then followed by a set of companion articles that examine the theoretical and empirical issues that the target has raised. These latter chapters are written by authors with diverse theoretical orientations, representing different disciplines within psychology and, in some cases, entirely different disciplines. Target authors are then given the opportunity to respond to the comments and criticisms of their own work and to examine the ideas conveyed in the companion chapters in light of their own. The dialogue created by this format is both unusual and, we believe, extremely beneficial to the field.

Until recently, most theory and research in social information processing focused on the cognitive activity that underlies responses to stimulus information presented in the immediate situation being investigated. In contrast, people's thoughts outside the laboratory often concern life events that either have occurred in the past or are likely to occur in the future. Thoughts about such past and future events can be spontaneous and, once elicited, can affect the ability to respond effectively to demands of the present situation with which one is confronted.

The present volume focuses on this type of cognitive activity and examines both its determinants and its consequences. The lead article, by Martin and Tesser, develops a theoretical formulation of ruminative thinking. The authors conceptualize rumination as a class of conscious thoughts that have a common instrumental theme and recur in the absence of immediate environmental demands. Their theoretical analysis has obvious implications for thought processes that mediate responses to everyday life events. Although their general conception of rumination is broad in scope, the authors give particular attention to the ways in which people's perceptions of the consequences of past and present events for long-range goal attainment affect both controlled and uncontrolled thinking about these events. They also consider the implications of their theory for the ability to suppress unwanted thoughts, the interplay of emotion and cognition, and the cognitive consequences of rumination for the performance of daily life activities. Thus, the formulation integrates a number of cognitive phenomena that are not usually considered within a single theoretical framework.

The diverse implications of Martin and Tesser's work are also reflected in the companion chapters. These articles, many written by the field's foremost contributors to the literature on emotion and cognition, suggest important refinements and extensions of the conceptualization proposed in the target chapter. Moreover, they make important conceptual contributions in their own right, covering topics that include the role of mental models in cognitive functioning, the dynamics of thought suppression and attentional inhibition, stress and coping, personality correlates of ruminative thought, and attitudes and persuasion. As a result, the volume as a whole is a valuable contribution to research and theory not only in social cognition, but in numerous other areas as well.

In addition to the authors themselves, we want to acknowledge the invaluable assistance of Lawrence Erlbaum Associates. Their continued support and encouragement of the *Advances in Social Cognition* series, and their commitment to the publication of a high quality set of volumes, is deeply gratifying. It is a genuine pleasure to work with them.

—*Robert S. Wyer, Jr.*

Chapter 1

Some Ruminative Thoughts

Leonard L. Martin
Abraham Tesser
University of Georgia

Have you ever had recurrent thoughts about a former flame, experienced difficulty focusing on your work because you kept thinking about an upcoming vacation, or reminded yourself throughout the day to pick up a loaf of bread on your way home? If so, then you have experienced the type of thoughts we discuss in this chapter. We call these *ruminative thoughts*.[1] We use this term (or the term *rumination*) throughout this chapter to refer to a class of conscious thoughts that revolve around a common instrumental theme and that recur in the absence of immediate environmental demands requiring the thoughts. A more detailed discussion of the definition of rumination is presented later.

Rumination has several features that make it a particularly interesting and important topic of study. First, it is unintended and difficult to eliminate. As a result, it can be long-lasting and can dominate a person's mental life. For example, people may experience some ruminative thoughts for years despite their best attempts to rid themselves of these thoughts (Horowitz, 1986; Rachman & Hodgson, 1980; Silver, Boon, & Stones, 1983). Second, rumination has been found to be associated with a number of cognitive, affective, and behavioral phenomena. For example, the occurrence of repetitive, unwanted thoughts appears to be a major contributor to unhappiness (McIntosh & Martin, 1992) and depression (Beck, 1982; Ellis, 1962; Pyszczynski & Greenberg, 1987). Rumination may also influence

---

[1] Although we use the term ruminative *thoughts*, it should be noted that we do not restrict the referent of this term to verbal content. Ruminative thoughts can involve emotions, images, and bodily sensations as well.

people's abilities to solve problems (Carver, Scheier, & Weintraub, 1989; Taylor & Schneider, 1989), form impressions (Martin, 1986), and maintain attitudes (Lassiter, Pezzo, & Apple, 1993; Tesser, 1978).

Rumination is also interesting in that it is in some sense illogical. It often occurs in situations in which nothing can be done about the target of the thought or after the best chances for effective instrumental behaviors have passed. For example, it is only after we graduate from college that we begin to ruminate about how we should have studied much harder in school.

In this chapter, we propose a formal definition of rumination and a theoretical model. The model addresses the factors that initiate and terminate rumination as well as those that influence its content. The model also outlines some of the consequences of rumination for a variety of cognitive, affective, and behavioral phenomena. Some of these phenomena have been identified in the literature, whereas others have yet to be empirically addressed. Thus, we believe the model not only suggests a way in which to integrate what are currently separate yet related literatures on ruminative phenomena (e.g., meaning analysis, daydreaming, problem solving, reminiscence, anticipation) but also suggests directions for future research. After we discuss the model, we present evidence for some of the model's assumptions and then discuss some consequences of rumination.

VARIETIES OF CONSCIOUS THOUGHT

We begin with the classic Hollywood storyline: Boy meets girl, boy loses girl, boy meets girl again. What might pass through the mind of the boy over the course of this on-again/off-again relationship? Perhaps the boy starts with a *daydream* (Singer, 1966). He imagines being out with the girl, taking her to a nice restaurant, talking, having fun, perhaps even falling in love. The more he entertains these thoughts, the more positive his feelings become (*polarization*; Tesser, 1978). These feelings eventually motivate the boy to ask the girl out. As soon as he decides to do so, however, he begins to *worry* (Roemer & Borkovec, 1993). "What if she does not accept my offer? What if she does accept, but things do not go well?" Finally, the boy gets up enough courage to ask the girl out, and she accepts. Now the boy cannot stop thinking about the upcoming weekend. The *anticipation* (Martin, Tesser, & McIntosh, 1993) is so great that it *intrudes* (Rachman & Hodgson, 1980) upon the boy's other thoughts, making it difficult for him to get anything done at work.

When the weekend finally rolls around and the boy leaves work to get ready for the date, he remembers to phone ahead for a table at the restaurant (*current concern*; Klinger, 1977). The night turns out beautifully. The two fall in love, and the boy *basks* (Isen, Clark, & Schwartz, 1976) in the warm glow of this positive emotion. Later, however, the relationship takes a turn for the worse, and the boy finds himself trying to *make sense* (Horowitz, 1986; Janoff-Bulman, 1992; Silver et al., 1983) of this negative state of affairs. He wonders, "What did I do to bring the relationship to an end? Why did God allow this to happen?" He concludes that the problems began when he started flirting with that other woman. He *regrets* (Landman, 1987) having done this but realizes that things could have been worse. At least he did not "go all the way" with her (*counter-factual thinking;* Taylor & Schneider, 1989).

Soon, the boy begins to reminisce (Clark, Collins, & Henry, 1994) about the great times he had during the early days of the relationship and starts working on a plan to win back the girl's affections (*problem-solving;* Lazarus & Folkman, 1984). Eventually, the solution comes to him (*incubation;* Yaniv & Meyer, 1987). He will apologize, change his errant ways, and ask the girl back to the restaurant where it all started. He rehearses various versions of the apology in his head and imagines her response in each case (*simulation;* Taylor & Schneider, 1989). Finally, he feels confident that he has a strategy that will work (*optimism;* Perloff, 1983). He tries it, it works (*flow;* Csikzentmihalyi, 1975), and the boy wins back the girl's affections. All is right with the world.

How many different kinds of thought do we have here? Nominally, there are 16. The question, though, is whether each of these nominal categories represents a unique form of thinking or whether there are smaller subsets into which these different thoughts can be clustered. Alternatively, can all the thoughts be placed into one common category? Which, if any, of these thoughts can be considered rumination?

It is our belief that many of these thoughts belong in the general class we call rumination. More specifically, we believe that they reflect different modes of rumination. These modes are similar in the mechanism that generates them, but they differ in their content. What allows us to call one thought rumination and another not, and what distinguishes one mode of rumination from another? We address these questions by highlighting several theoretical models relevant to rumination and then attempt to extract their common and distinctive features.

WHAT IS RUMINATION?

Models of Recurrent Thoughts

Klinger (1975, 1977) suggested that conscious thoughts can be divided into two categories: operant and respondent. Operant thoughts are those that are under a person's control and are related to the person's current task; the person experiences a sense of trying to produce the thought. Respondent thoughts, on the other hand, are those that occur without premeditation or conscious purpose and involve shifts of attention away from immediate goal-directed tasks. Whereas operant thoughts are related to evaluating the success with which one is approaching a predetermined goal, respondent thoughts are only indirectly goal-related. According to Klinger, respondent thoughts are a function of people's current concerns. These concerns reflect the state of an organism between the time it commits itself to a goal and the time it disengages from that goal.

According to Klinger, the cognitive system must establish a way to determine which information it should process immediately and which it can safely ignore or save until later. It does this by tagging concepts associated with goal pursuit as having priority. As a result, environmental cues related to one's current concerns easily activate concern-related thoughts. This ease of activation persists from the time the person first commits to attaining a goal to the time the person either attains the goal or gives up the desire for it.

It should be noted that not all concerns activate their associated thoughts to the same degree. It is assumed that concerns influence processing only to the extent that their cues arouse emotions. To summarize, operant thoughts are those that are intentionally directed toward the completion of immediate tasks, whereas respondent thoughts are those that are recurrent, unintentional, off-task, and engendered by emotionally charged current concerns.

We proposed a model similar to Klinger's (Martin & Tesser, 1989). Like Klinger, we assumed that recurrent thoughts are related to unattained goals. However, we did not assume that goal-related concepts are tagged from the time of commitment forward, nor did we assume that goal blockage causes people to disengage from goal pursuit. Rather, we assumed that unexpected progress (more or less) toward a goal instigates rumination. In fact, if a person is committed to a goal but is making nonproblematic progress, then the person will experience little or no conscious thoughts about the goal (cf. Csikzentmihalyi, 1975; Wicklund, 1986). Rumination occurs only when the rate of progress is not what the person expects it to be (i.e., is faster or slower).

A somewhat different view of recurrent thoughts has evolved out of investigations of people's reactions to stressful life events. The models developed in this area (see Horowitz, 1986; Janoff-Bulman, 1992; Silver et al., 1983) share several common assumptions. They all assume that serious life events challenge people's mental models of themselves or the world and that people have a need, desire, or goal to integrate reality with their mental models. Together, these assumptions imply that stressful life events compel people to assess the meaning, interpretation, or implications of these events. Unfortunately, such assessments can be difficult and may take a while to accomplish. It is assumed that thoughts related to the discrepancy, as well as people's emotional reactions to the discrepancy, stay active in memory until the person successfully reaches closure. This means that people may experience long-term, recurrent thoughts.

Another view of recurrent thoughts was developed by Rachman (1981; Rachman & DeSilva, 1978; Rachman & Hodgson, 1980) in his explorations of intrusive thoughts. According to Rachman (1981), a thought is labeled intrusive if it is attributed to an internal origin, is difficult to control, and is perceived as interrupting an ongoing activity. Rachman acknowledged that there are positive (e.g., inspiration) as well as negative intrusive thoughts, but he restricted his discussion to negative or unwanted ones.

According to Rachman, the prime instigator of unwanted intrusive thoughts is stress. In the presence of stress, people experience intrusive thoughts; in the absence of stress, they do not (Horowitz, 1986). Although intrusive thoughts are those that seem to have an internal origin, they can, in fact, have external triggers. These triggers, however, are not sufficient to explain the repetitive quality of the thoughts.

The type of thinking described by Singer (1966, 1975) as daydreaming may also have a connection to rumination. According to Singer (1975), daydreaming represents "a shift in attention *away* from some primary physical or mental task we have set for ourselves, or *away* from directly looking at or listening to something in the external environment, *toward* an unfolding sequence of private responses made to some internal stimulus" (p. 3). Although the majority of people report that they enjoy daydreaming, daydreaming does not always reflect positive wish-fulfillment. It sometimes can involve negative emotions as well (e.g., daydreaming about your wife's reaction when she discovers you accidentally took the keys she needed).

Singer noted that it is difficult to determine a function for daydreaming. He described it as a capacity that is just there, like breathing. However, empirical studies have shown that the content of daydreams is primarily projections into the future of the fairly practical immediate concerns people have in their daily lives (Singer, 1975). Thus, at least some daydreams reflect attempts to explore the future in alternative ways. Daydreaming may not only provide people with momentary enjoyment through escapist fantasies but may also help people in their long-range planning.

A related form of recurrent thought was explored by Taylor and Schneider (1989) in their work on coping. They have investigated mental simulation, which they define as the cognitive construction of hypothetical scenarios or the reconstruction of real scenarios. Simulations can occur involuntarily, as when victims of stressful events replay the events over and over, or simulations can occur intentionally, as when one rehearses the speech he or she will use to ask the boss for a raise. Simulations may also predominate the kind of thinking people experience while performing mundane activities like driving, showering, or listening to a boring lecture. According to Taylor and Schneider (1989), simulations serve both a problem solving and emotion regulation function. They help people prepare for future events, interpret past events, and alter their emotional states.

Extracting the Common Features

Clearly, there are a number of differences among the various models of recurrent thought. Nevertheless, there are some commonalities as well. For example, each model was developed to account for a type of *conscious* thought. Although in any given model the underlying mechanisms may have been nonconscious, the actual experience of the thought was always considered to be conscious.

Another commonality is that each of the models is based on the assumption that recurrent thoughts arise from some sort of discrepancy. For Klinger (1977) and Martin and Tesser (1989), the discrepancy involved unattained goals. For Horowitz (1986), Janoff-Bulman (1992), and Silver et al. (1983), the discrepancy involved a lack of fit between mental models and reality. For Singer (1975), the discrepancy existed, at least for some forms of daydreaming, in a potential future. People simulate an activity to ensure a more effective performance when the time comes. The same is true for Taylor and Schneider's (1989) model when the simulation concerns the future. When the simulation concerns the past, the discrepancy is between the way things turned out and the way people wish they had turned out. In short, what we find is that in every case, the recurrent thoughts have the same function: They are instrumental to reducing some form of discrepancy.

A third commonality between the models is their assumption that the thoughts they address are persistent or recurrent. In all cases, the thoughts were assumed to remain easily activated until the instigating discrepancy was resolved. According to Klinger (1977), the person must attain his or her current goal. According to us (Martin & Tesser, 1989), the person must either attain his or her higher order goals or return to nonproblematic progress toward those goals. In the models of Horowitz (1986), Janoff-Bulman (1992), and Silver et al. (1983), the person must find meaning. In each case, the thoughts remain until the discrepancy is resolved. If this takes years, then the person experiences recurrent thoughts for years (Silver et al., 1983).

The last common feature between the thoughts described in the different models is that the thoughts were assumed to occur in the absence of immediate environmental demands to produce the thoughts. This idea is explicit in Klinger's (1977) definition of respondent thoughts and in Singer's (1975) definition of daydreaming. Both of these types of thoughts were assumed to reflect unintentional shifts in attention away from current tasks. This unintentionality is also explicit in Rachman's (1981) analysis of intrusive thoughts and in the meaning analysis formulations (Horowitz, 1986; Janoff-Bulman, 1992; Silver et al., 1983). Although Taylor and Schneider (1989) did not explicitly address this issue, the simulations they discussed are of events that exist in either the past or the future. Even in this model, the recurrent thoughts are not simply responses to immediate environmental demands.

Taking all of these features into consideration, we propose the following definition of rumination:

> Rumination is a class of conscious thoughts that revolve around a common instrumental theme and that recur in the absence of immediate environmental demands requiring the thoughts. Although the occurrence of these thoughts does not depend on direct cueing by the external environment, indirect cueing by the environment is likely given the high accessibility of goal-related concepts. Although the external environment may maintain any thought through repeated cueing, the maintenance of ruminative thoughts is not dependent upon such cueing.

Several aspects of this definition need to be elaborated. First, in assuming that rumination is not required by or directly cued by the immediate environment, we do not necessarily mean that rumination is solely a function of internal cues. It may be, but it need not be. For example, a woman may be contentedly focused on her grocery shopping when she strolls past the baby products. Here, she encounters the scent of baby powder, and this starts her ruminating about the child she will be giving birth to six months from now (cf. Clark, Henry, & Taylor, 1991). There was nothing in the scent that required the woman to think about her pregnancy. The scent did not demand any meaningful processing, nor did it in any way facilitate or inhibit the woman's plans with regard to her pregnancy. Nevertheless, its presence, in the context of the women's goal to have a baby, was sufficient to trigger rumination. In this way, the thoughts were not required by the environment, but they were not entirely internally generated either. Interestingly, the thoughts may be experienced by the woman as internally generated precisely because there is nothing in the environment demanding that she have the thoughts at this time.

We also note that although ruminative thoughts can recur unintentionally, they are not necessarily unwanted or disruptive (cf. Rachman, 1981). Whether a ruminative thought is unwanted or not depends on the context in which the thought occurs. A woman's rumination about her impending motherhood, for example, might be an interference at work but a welcomed diversion on her ride home.

Although ruminative thoughts are recurrent, they are not necessarily repetitive. For example, imagine two people waiting to see a dentist. One wonders why there are no good magazines in the waiting room, how long it will be before the dentist sees him, what he might have for dinner tonight, and how his favorite team will perform this season. The other person wonders whether he will have any cavities, whether he could have taken better care of his teeth, how competent the dentist is, and how great he will look after he has his teeth cleaned. Although both people are experiencing a constant stream of thoughts, we suggest that only the latter is actually ruminating. Only in the latter case do we see a recurrent theme. The asystematic switch in content experienced by the first person might best be described as stream of consciousness (see Wyer & Srull, 1989, for an interesting explanation of the free flow of thought).

The preceding example raises another question about the definition of rumination: How much of each defining feature does a stream of thought have to possess in order to be classified as rumination? If a person has 20 recurrent thoughts, for example, is this rumination? What if he has only 19? Similarly, what if one person has 20 recurrent thoughts over the course of a year, whereas another experiences 20 recurrent thoughts over the course of an hour. Are both ruminating, or is only one? We believe that questions like this cannot be answered. We suggest instead that ruminative and nonruminative thoughts are a function of the same mechanism (i.e., goal attainment) and that there is no qualitative demarcation between the two. This stance parallels that taken by Rachman (1981) in his explorations of obsessive thought. He suggested that normal rumination and clinical obsession are a function of the same mechanism and even revolve around the same kinds of topic. Similarly, researchers no longer conceive of thoughts as either automatic or controlled. Whereas before there was a dichotomy, there are now fuzzy categories (e.g., Bargh, 1989; Uleman, 1989). So it is with ruminative and nonruminative thoughts. They differ in terms of their recurrence and their relevance to a person's current processing objectives, but there is no precise dividing line between the two.

Even without an exact demarcation, however, we feel that our definition still allows us to make some categorizations. Going back to our opening boy-meets-girl scenario, for example, we find that our definition includes the following as modes of rumination: anticipation, basking, counterfactual thinking, current concerns, regret, simulation, working through, and worry. Excluded by our definition are momentary stimulus-driven thoughts (e.g., noticing the weather), thoughts in the immediate service of a temporary goal (e.g., choosing a shirt, calculating a tip), incubation (which is not conscious), consummatory daydreaming (in which people engage purely for pleasure), and stream of consciousness (which involves no recurrent content and is not instrumental).

Modes of Ruminative Thought

In deriving our definition of rumination, we focused on the features the various models had in common. We did not discuss the models' differences.

We turn now to those. Recall that in our definition, rumination is a class of thinking. As such, it contains several subclasses or modes. For example, people can ruminate about positive content or about negative content. They can ruminate about the past, the present, or the future. They can ruminate about an incompleted task (e.g., needing to lose 10 more pounds) or about a completed task (e.g., that winning season 20 years ago). In our view, any kind of content can be rumination as long as it involves the recurrence of a common instrumental theme in an environment that does not require the thought. The differences in valence, temporal orientation, and discrepancy focus can be used to create different modes of rumination and, in our opinion, help us to partition the phenomena currently being studied by different investigators. Table 1.1 presents some modes of rumination as organized according to valence, temporal orientation, and discrepancy focus.

According to this organization, a person who ruminates in a negative way about a future difficulty can be described as worrying (Roemer & Borkovec, 1993). A person who ruminates in a negative way about a past completed action can be described as engaging in regret (Landman, 1987). A person who ruminates in a positive way about the present can be described as basking (Isen et al., 1976). We assume that in the course of any given ruminative sequence, a person is likely to pass through a number of these modes. As in our earlier boy-meets-girl example, the boy's thoughts flitted from anticipation to worry to basking, and so on.

There are three aspects of this table that need further elaboration. First, there are two empty cells. We are not sure at this time whether this is of theoretical significance. For the most part, the empty cells reflect the difficulty we had in coming up with terms that refer to thoughts that are negative, focused on an attained goal, and oriented toward either the present or the future. We came to the tentative conclusion that, to the extent that such thoughts occur, they are brief. It may be that when people find themselves in situations that foster negative thoughts of this kind, they either engage in behaviors to change the situation or they experience other modes of rumination. For example, instead of thinking about the negative

TABLE 1.1
Modes of Ruminative Thought

	Negative			Positive		
	Past	Present	Future	Past	Present	Future
Discrepancy Focus	Working through	Current concerns	Worry	Downward counterfactual	Flow	Optimism
Attainment Focus	Regret	*	*	Reminiscing	Basking	Anticipation

implications of a currently attained goal, a person may begin to think of ways to change the situation (i.e., problem solving) or may think of how things could have turned out differently (i.e., counterfactual thinking). In fact, evidence consistent with this general hypothesis has been obtained in work on post-decisional dissonance (e.g., Walster, 1964).

Second, it appears, at least on the surface, that some of our modes of rumination fit with our definition better than others do. Working through, for example, is a prototypical form of rumination. It involves a problem the person is trying to come to terms with, and thinking about this problem continues until the person arrives at a resolution. But what about reminiscing and basking? In these modes, people think about what they have, not about what they do not have. Where is the initiating discrepancy? We suggest that in these cases, rumination is in the service of bolstering or maintaining, rather than attaining, the goal (Roney & Sorrentino, 1995). For example, people have a motive to maintain a positive view of themselves (Tesser, 1988). Thinking about one's successes (e.g., reminiscing about being captain of the football team in high school, basking in the joy of that standing ovation after your last talk) may not only bring a person with a negative self-view to the point of having a positive one but may also remind a person with a positive self-view that he has already made it. It is in this sense that basking and reminiscing are in service of a discrepancy. When recurrent thoughts do not directly address a discrepancy, they aid in reaffirming the lack of one.

A related point to keep in mind is that the nature of the instigating discrepancy is not always revealed in the content of the rumination. For example, suppose a person was extremely awkward and nervous in his first few dates, got anxious giving class presentations, and got tongue-tied while asking his boss for an extra day off. Although these events are unrelated in terms of their declarative features, each carries the implication that the person lacks social skills. Although the person may be totally satisfied with his current love life, he may nevertheless ruminate about his former flames because these flames are associated with the discrepancy the person feels regarding his social skills.

The third point needing elaboration is our treatment of depression and obsession. We did not include them in our table, even though there is some reason to believe that the parameters specified in our model could be useful in helping to understand these extreme modes of ruminative thought. For example, some theorists (e.g., Pyszczynski & Greenberg, 1987) have proposed that depression is instigated by a loss or a discrepancy and is maintained by rumination. Rachman (1981), moreover, suggested that normal rumination and clinical obsession are a function of similar conditions and center on the same kinds of topic. Despite these commonalities, we are hesitant to suggest that our model applies equally well to normal and clinical populations (cf. Coyne, 1994). It may. On the other hand, it may not. There may be qualitative differences between the two populations that are beyond the scope of our model (e.g., biological factors; Strauman, in press). Until we have strong reason to believe otherwise, we restrict the application of our model to normal rumination.

THE MECHANICS OF RUMINATION

In this section, we describe the assumptions of our model of rumination (Martin & Tesser, 1989; Martin, Tesser, & McIntosh, 1993). In the next section, we discuss evidence for these assumptions. The model begins with the assumption that most thoughts are goal-driven. They occur in the service of moving a person from point A to point B. These goals are not always conscious, however, and they do not always represent distinct end states. They might be as subtle, for example, as "encode these behaviors in terms of a trait," which people do in the course of forming an impression (Wyer & Gordon, 1982). People appear to perform this operation without a conscious intention of doing so and without awareness of having done so (Uleman, 1989). We know this operation is goal-dependent, however, because it occurs under some instructional sets but not others (e.g., impression set vs. memory set; see Wyer & Gordon, 1982).

More generally, we believe that rumination is a manifestation of people's tendency to persist in goal-directed action until they have either attained their goal or given up the desire for it (Carver & Scheier, 1981; Klinger, 1977; Lewin, 1951; Miller, Galanter, & Pribram, 1960; Powers, 1973; von Bertalanffy, 1968; Zeigarnik, 1938). This goal-directed nature of thinking is revealed rather clearly in a child's riddle:

Q. Why is it when you look for something, you always find it in the last place you look?
A. Because once you've found it, you stop looking.

Metaphorically speaking, rumination is a form of looking. It persists until people find what they are looking for (e.g., a way to attain their goal). It differs from nonruminative thought primarily in that it takes longer for people to find what they are looking for.

Rumination Is Instigated by Discrepancies in Goal Progress

Because rumination is goal-directed, it can be modeled in control systems terms (Carver & Scheier, 1981; Miller, et al., 1960; Powers, 1973; von Bertalanffy, 1968). From this perspective, when people have a goal, they take steps to achieve that goal. If the steps are successful, then people move on to other goals. If the steps are not successful, then people attempt to attain the goal in other ways. These alternative attempts continue until people either attain the goal or give up the desire for it. If the goal or a substitute is immediately attained or if the person immediately abandons the goal, then there is no rumination.

In other words, we follow Csikzentmihalyi (1975) and Wicklund (1986) in assuming that when people's abilities and motivations are in sync with the demands of their environment, people engage in little or no off-task thinking. They simply perform the activities needed to attain the goal. When the environment is too demanding or not demanding enough, then people experience off-task thoughts (e.g., Why can't I perform this task? Is there anything else I can do to make this task more interesting?). These kinds of thoughts persist until people get back into flow. The thinking we call rumination occurs when people are out of flow for a long period of time.

Consider this example: A person is building a model ship. Everything is going well until the person gets to the rigging. How should he adhere the rigging to the mast? With that thought, the person drops out of flow (Csikzentmihalyi, 1975; Wicklund, 1986) and begins to consider alternatives to his current reality (e.g., The rigging is not on the mast. How can I get it on the mast?). He quickly decides that gluing will get the job done. He gets some glue, adheres the rigging, and continues with the model building. Because his flow was interrupted for only a few seconds, his thoughts were not recurrent. These thoughts would not be considered rumination.

What would happen, however, if the person were unable to find the glue? In this case, he might wonder if he should run to the store to buy some, if he could find a substitute around the house, if perhaps gluing is not the best way to hold up the rigging, and so on. Without an immediate way to attain his goal, the person may continue to consider alternative strategies, and his flow would be interrupted for a longer period of time. This would be rumination. Of course, looking for glue is a very low-level goal. However, we believe that the mechanisms depicted in this example are the same as those operating in more meaningful settings (e.g., losing a loved one, getting raped).

We should make it clear that the goal progress we describe here is not always objectively defined. This assumption has two important implications. First, it implies that personal states or traits can influence assessment of progress. For example, negative moods can lead people to perceive themselves as falling short of their standards, whereas positive moods can lead them to feel that they are close to meeting their standards (Cervone, Kopp, Schaumann, & Scott, 1994). Because of this, people may be more likely to ruminate when they are in negative moods than when they are in positive moods (Pyszczynski & Greenberg, 1987). The same appears to be true of anxiety (Rachman, 1981). Anxiety may instigate rumination because it may cause the person to think that something is wrong even when the person is experiencing no actual threat.

The subjective nature of discrepancies also implies that objective completion of a task is not synonymous with subjective attainment of a goal. One person may enjoy the act of building a model ship, for example, whereas another may look forward only to the finished product. As a result, completion of the model represents goal nonattainment for the former, but goal attainment for the latter (see Marrow, 1938).

Hierarchy Assumption

Of course, people do not ruminate about every unattained goal. They are more likely to ruminate about the loss of a loved one, for example, than about their inability to find glue. On the other hand, there are times when people do ruminate about events seemingly as trivial as finding glue. Why is this the case? We believe the answer lies in people's goal hierarchies. More specifically, people ruminate about goals they perceive as central to their well-being, and this is more likely to be true for higher order rather than lower order goals (Beck, 1982; McIntosh & Martin, 1992).

However, people often pursue lower order goals in order to attain higher order ones. People may attempt to find glue, for example, because they wish to attach the rigging to the mast of a model ship. This, in turn, will help them to finish the model which, in turn, will help them to demonstrate their creativity. Under these conditions, finding glue is important to one's well-being. A person is more likely to ruminate about obtaining glue if his or her creative expression is at stake than if nothing more than merely adhering the rigging to the mast is at stake.

There is at least one other case in which a threat to a lower order goal can appear to initiate rumination—when the frustration of a series of lower order goals (none of which is sufficient to elicit rumination) summates to make the nonattainment of a higher order goal salient. For example, a person may fail to bring enough money to the grocery, forget to pick up a suit before the cleaner closes, and lock his or her keys in the car. When the person tries later that same day to ride a bicycle and finds a tire flat, he or she may begin to ruminate about having little control over his or her life. Although the rumination started when the person noticed the flat tire, we cannot really say that the tire was the cause of the rumination. The rumination was caused by the entire succession of events. Had the bicycle incident happened earlier in the day, it may not have triggered rumination. However, it might have contributed to the summation of frustration, making it likely that one of the other lower order frustrations (e.g., locking the keys in the car) would trigger the rumination.

Motivation Versus Content

As can be seen in the preceding example, there is no necessary correspondence between the occurrence of any given event and the onset or content of the subsequent rumination. An event that sets off rumination on one occasion may not do so on another occasion, and an event that on one occasion causes rumination about itself (e.g., finding the flat tire) may on another occasion cause rumination about a related goal (e.g., having little control over one's life). This lack of correlation between events and the content of rumination occurs, in part, because there is no one-to-one correspondence between the occurrence of any given behavior and the reason the behavior is performed. When we see someone ride past us on a bicycle, for example, we do not know if this person is riding for the exercise, the enjoyment, or for mere transportation. When this person is blocked from riding, it is difficult to know which of the person's goals has been blocked.

Interestingly, this loose connection between behaviors and the reasons they are performed may pose a problem not only for observers but also for actors. It means that actors, at least on occasion, may have to infer the reasons for their own behaviors (Bem, 1967). When they do so, they could be wrong (Nisbett & Wilson, 1977). In terms of rumination, this means that people may sometimes ruminate not about the actual goal toward which progress has been thwarted but about a goal they believe to be the one toward which progress was thwarted. If our bicycle rider, for example, cannot ride for a number of days, he or she may begin to ruminate. But will this person ruminate about not getting enough exercise, about missing the outdoors, or about losing a cheap, reliable means of transportation? Any of these could be the goal that was blocked by the person's inability to ride. None of these, however, may reflect the real goal that was thwarted. Perhaps the person rode the bike because it gave him or her a chance to flirt with that attractive neighbor down the street. This thought may even have crossed the person's mind, but he or she may have dismissed it as implausible. After all, the person may see him- or herself as happily married and happily married people do not flirt (at least not according to this person's implicit theory).

In short, we hypothesize that the content of rumination revolves around a goal that, according to a person's implicit theories (cf. Nisbett & Wilson, 1977; Ross, 1989), is the goal that has been thwarted. This may or may not be the actual goal. Nevertheless, this is what determines the content of rumination. When more than one goal can plausibly be the one that was thwarted, rumination revolves around the one that is most salient or most accessible (i.e., most easily retrieved).

Another factor that influences the content of rumination is the perceived degree of goal blockage. When goal progress is only slightly thwarted, people ruminate about goals lower in the hierarchy (Vallacher & Wegner, 1987). When goal progress is more severely thwarted, people ruminate about goals higher in the hierarchy (Wicklund, 1986). For example, if a guitarist has the initial goal of entertaining an audience and then breaks a string, he or she may focus immediately on the lower order goal of trying to find the needed notes on the remaining strings. If this proves too difficult, then the guitarist may change focus to higher order concerns such as "What else can I do to entertain these people? What impact will this poor performance have on my career?"

A third factor that influences the content of rumination is perceived movement relative to a goal. Movement toward a goal elicits positive affect, whereas movement away from a goal elicits negative affect, and the faster the movement, the stronger the affect (Carver & Scheier, 1990; Hsee & Abelson, 1991). Thus, nonattainment accompanied by perceived progress elicits positively toned rumination (e.g., anticipation), whereas nonattainment accompanied by perceived lack of progress elicits negatively toned rumination (e.g., worry).

How Does Goal Blockage Lead to Rumination?

We have suggested that problematic progress toward a goal is the instigator of rumination, but we have not yet suggested how this occurs. What is it about problematic progress that fosters recurrent thoughts? Our assumption is similar to Klinger's (1977). Concepts associated with unattained goals are tagged as having priority. In functional terms, this means that categorization can occur in terms of these concepts with less input, the range of input characteristics that will be accepted as fitting the concept will be increased, and it is likely that concepts providing a better or equally good fit for the input will be ignored in favor of the more accessible, goal-related concept (cf. Bruner, 1957). Phenomenologically, the result is frequent and unintentional thought related to the unattained goal. Presumably, the priority system is, at least in part, a function of the perceived consequences of attaining or not attaining the goal. The more extreme these consequences, the higher will be the priority granted to constructs related to that goal.

Stopping Rumination

We have suggested that, once instigated, rumination may recur effortlessly and without conscious intention. In fact, it may recur even in the face of attempts to stop it (Rachman, 1981; Wenzlaff, 1993). How, then, does rumination ever stop? We believe that there are two ways. One is permanent; the other is temporary. Given that rumination is instigated by problematic progress toward a goal, the best way (i.e., the permanent way) to stop rumination is to attain the goal. There are several factors, however, that make this difficult (Emmons & Kaiser, 1995). First, people may set goals that are difficult to reach. For example, the goals may take a long time to attain (e.g., lose 30 pounds, understand why my baby died), they may be so ill-defined that attainment is unlikely (e.g., be happy), or progress toward one goal may threaten attainment of another (e.g., getting a new job may mean leaving old friends behind). A second reason goals may be difficult to attain is that people may not know what they need to do to attain their goals. For example, most of us want to be happy. But do we always know what to do to attain happiness? Work by Csikzentmihalyi and LeFevre (1989) suggests not. They found that at least some people were happier at work than they were when engaged in leisure activities. Yet when asked, these people said they would rather engage in leisure activities than be at work. According to Csikzentmihalyi and LeFevre (1989), the people failed to detect their enjoyment at work because they based their answer not on introspection but on the culturally accepted theory that people do not like work. When these people were feeling unhappy, they may have engaged in leisure activities, even though the more effective strategy would be to return to work.

Temporary cessation of rumination is accomplished by thinking about something other than the ruminative thought (Nolen-Hoeksema, 1987; Wegner, Schneider, Carter, & White, 1987). This off-rumination thinking occurs either when another goal has become prepotent (e.g., learning that you have cancer is likely to minimize your concerns over grades) or when a person intentionally engages in distraction (e.g., getting drunk, watching TV). One reason people may seek distraction is that lack of progress toward an important goal is aversive (Carver & Scheier, 1990; Hsee & Abelson, 1991). Negative affect may initiate an attempt to distract one's self from anything associated with the unattained goal (Horowitz, 1986; Nolen-Hoeksema, 1987).

There are two problems with distraction. First, it can be very difficult to accomplish or maintain (Rachman, 1981; Wenzlaff, 1993). Second, it may not bring the person any closer to attaining the goal. As long as the goal remains desired yet unattained, the mental conditions that promote rumination will persist, and rumination will eventually and inexorably be seen.

Finally, to the extent that rumination has been instigated by one's affective state, it can be terminated when the affect dissipates. We suggest, however, that if there is a real discrepancy that has not been addressed by the reduction in affect, then the cessation of rumination is likely to be temporary.

Channelized Rumination

We have suggested that goal attainment can permanently eliminate ruminative thoughts. Although this is often the case, goal attainment actually eliminates the goal-based mechanism for rumination. It does not necessarily eliminate all recurrent thoughts related to the nonattained goal. If a person has experienced a thought a large number of times in a variety of circumstances, then the person will have established a rich associative network related to this thought. As a result, this thought can be readily activated in a number of contexts even when the goal-attainment motivation has been eliminated. We have termed this nonmotivated ruminative process *channelization*.

ADDITIONAL CONSIDERATIONS

We have now laid out the major assumptions of our model. Doing so, however, raises additional considerations. We consider these now.

The Relation Between Affect and Rumination

In our model, we emphasize the goal-based instigators of rumination. A number of researchers have noted a strong relation between affect and rumination (e.g., Horowitz, 1986; Klinger, 1977; Rachman, 1981). Namely, the more intense the affect (especially negative affect), the greater the rumination. How does our model account for this?

We believe that rumination and affect are correlated primarily because the two result from very similar causes. As Wyer and Srull (1989) noted, the intensity of the affect a person experiences when his or her goal progress has been interrupted depends on three factors: the importance of the goal, the psychological distance of the interruption from the attainment of the superordinate goal, and the degree of investment of time and energy that is expended in vain as a consequence of the interruption. Interestingly, these are the same three factors that Klinger (1977) pointed to as those that increase the likelihood that people ruminate about one of their current concerns. Thus, rumination and affect covary primarily because the two are influenced by many of the same factors.

This does not mean, however, that rumination can never give rise to an affective experience. It can when the ruminating person engages in what might be called a secondary appraisal (Lazarus & Folkman, 1984). After ruminating for some time, people may come to the conclusion that they are unable to control their thoughts, and this conclusion may be distressing.

It is also important to note that even though rumination does not generally give rise to affect, it can have a significant influence on people's existing affect. Nolen-Hoeksema (1991), for example, has shown that following the occurrence of a negative life event, people who ruminate about their negative emotions experience longer periods of depression than do those who distract themselves from these emotions (see also McIntosh, 1995). In a program of research specifically intended to address the question of how thinking affects affect, Tesser (1978; Tesser, Martin, & Mendolia, 1995) found that when people think about targets toward which they initially had mild affective inclinations, people develop more extreme affective reactions. In both of these cases, the affect is not initiated by the rumination. The rumination merely maintains or polarizes feelings that are already present.

What about the converse relation? Can affect cause rumination? Yes, indirectly. It does so by influencing people's perceptions of goal attainment. It appears that people often interpret their emotional states as information relevant to judging the status of their goals (Frijda, 1988; Cervone et al., in press; Schwarz & Bless, 1991). More specifically, people experiencing negative affect often infer that they are not making progress toward their goals, whereas people experiencing positive affect often infer that they are making good progress toward their goals (see Martin & Stoner, 1995, for a qualification to this generalization). Because of this, people in negative moods may perceive more discrepancies and hence experience more rumination than people in positive moods.

On the other hand, this relation does not always hold. Whether positive or negative affect leads to increased thinking depends on the context in which these feelings occur (Hirt, McDonald, & Melton, in press; Martin, Achee, Ward, & Harlow, 1993; Martin, Ward, Achee, & Wyer, 1993). Furthermore, negative affect does not always suggest goal nonattainment, nor does positive affect always suggest goal attainment (Martin & Stoner, 1995). Sometimes the reverse is true. For example, the tear-jerker movie that leaves us sad may be evaluated more positively than the intended tear-jerker that leaves us laughing. In the former case, our sad mood tells us that the movie, which was designed to make us sad, has attained its goal (Martin & Stoner, 1995). Similarly, a person who experiences positive affect after hearing of the tragic death of a close friend may experience considerable rumination trying to figure out why he is feeling so good in a situation in which he should be feeling sad. We suggest that positive and negative affect can initiate rumination, but only to the extent that they suggest problematic goal progress.

Does this mean that there are absolutely no differences between positive and negative affect in their effects on rumination? Not necessarily. In an actuarial sense, people may be more likely to seek out positively valenced rather than negatively valenced goals (Emmons & Kaiser, in press; Singer & Salovey, in press). More times than not, negative affect suggests that the person is having difficulty attaining the goal, whereas positive affect suggests non-problematic progress. Also, to the extent that positive affect arises as a result of goal progress that is greater than expected and negative affect arises from progress that is less than expected (Carver, Lawrence, & Scheier, in press; Carver & Scheier, 1990; Hsee & Abelson, 1991), then negatively toned rumination should last longer than positively toned rumination. In many, though not all, situations, greater than expected progress is relatively easy to lose but difficult to maintain, whereas lower than expected progress is relatively easy to maintain but difficult to lose. For example, to continue an extra high rate of publication a person has to continue to conduct studies, have significant and interpretable results, write the paper, and so on. To continue a low rate of publication, a person merely has to do none of these things. Under conditions like these, negatively toned rumination will last longer than positively toned rumination, even though both are a function of the same goal-discrepancy mechanism.

Individual Differences

We earlier noted our hesitancy in applying our model to clinical populations. But other than this, do we expect our model to apply equally to all people? We see no a priori reason to limit our model's generalizability. On the other hand, we do believe that there are individual differences in the extent to which people ruminate. How should we address such differences?

Some researchers have addressed differences in rumination by developing a self-report or behavioral measure of rumination (e.g., Isbell, Gohm, & Wyer, 1994; Horowitz, Wilner, & Alverez, 1979; Nolen-Hoeksema, 1991). With such measures, a researcher can determine the extent to which rumination co-occurs with other psychological traits (e.g., attributional style, neuroticism), follows certain kinds of events (e.g., natural disasters, loss of loved one) or predict other psychological states (e.g., depression). However, in this approach, the measurement technique need not address the causal dynamics underlying rumination. To be useful, the measures only need to reflect in a reliable way the extent to which people differ in their tendency to ruminate.

Our preference is to think of individual differences in terms of the parameters of our model. This leads us to expect, for example, that people will differ in their amount of rumination to the extent that they also differ in the extent to which they see their unattained goals as being higher or lower in their goal hierarchy, the extent to which they see alternative paths to their goals, the extent to which they are able to generate and make use of alternate thoughts, and the extent to which they are willing to give up the goal. From this perspective, an individual difference measure would include scales that reflect one or more of these parameters, and the goal would be to predict rumination (see McIntosh, 1995). Clearly, the extent to which such a measure behaves as predicted reflects on the theoretical integrity of the model, and we believe that this is a strength of this approach. Of course, both approaches have their strengths and weaknesses, and to the extent that our model is incomplete, then scales of the first type may capture aspects of rumination that are missed in our approach.

Is the Model Falsifiable?

We have assumed that people do not always have conscious access to the goals that are guiding their behavior. Does this assumption make our model unfalsifiable? Consider the following scenario: We run a study in which we give subjects feedback that they have attained an important goal, and we find that this does not turn off their rumination. Do we conclude from this that the ruminative thoughts were not the result of a goal discrepancy? We are not compelled to do so. We can simply assume that we had provided feedback about the wrong goal and that the rumination was actually being driven by an as-yet unidentified goal that has remained unattained. Obviously, if we adopt this research strategy, then our model is not falsifiable.

Needless to say, we do not recommend adopting such a strategy. We believe that the problems of falsifiability inherent in any goal-based model can be minimized when these models are tested in a controlled setting. As experimenters, we can set up specific goals and then control the degree to which the subjects attain or fail to attain these goals. We can also choose goals that are salient and have clear and important implications for our subject population. In our own work, for example, we have often presented subjects with feedback regarding their intelligence and have measured the subjects' thoughts about their intelligence. When the subjects' thoughts differed as a function of our manipulations and there were no other differences between conditions, we felt safe in concluding that the goals were important in determining the subjects' thoughts. In this setting, we can know what goals are influencing the subjects' thoughts, feelings, and behaviors even if the subjects cannot tell us what these goals are. Further, if, under these conditions, we repeatedly fail to obtain the predicted effects, then we would have to conclude that our hypotheses are wrong.

THEORY SUMMARY

In sum, the major assumptions of the present model of rumination are as follows. The term *rumination* refers to thoughts that are conscious, recurrent, instrumentally oriented, and not demanded by the immediate environment. Rumination occurs when people are out of sync with the demands of the environment and stops when a person either attains the goal that is driving the rumination, returns to flow toward goal attainment, finds that another goal has become prepotent, or actively attempts to think about something else. The content of rumination is determined by the cause that is most accessible and most plausible in terms of the person's implicit theories and movement relative to the goal. There are various modes of rumination (e.g., problem-solving, meaning analysis). What differentiates one mode from another is the content (e.g., valence, time orientation). The underlying mechanism is the same, namely problematic goal progress.

EVIDENCE

In this section, we consider data relevant to a number of the model's assumptions. First, we examine the assumption that rumination is instigated by problematic goal progress. Then we explore the assumption that rumination is related only to progress relative to higher order goals. After this, we address the body of research that has failed to find evidence that goal nonattainment can lead to thought perseverance. We note that there are parameters on the occurrence of thought perseverance following goal nonattainment: One has to be careful to maintain the distinction between objective completion of a task and subjective attainment of a goal; when subjects have control over their response output, they sometimes indicate that they are not thinking about unattained goals when in fact they are; and sometimes rumination is not seen because people distract themselves from unpleasant ruminative thoughts. We discuss the temporary and strategic nature of this distraction effect, the automatic nature of the cueing of ruminative thoughts, and the factors that influence the content of rumination. Finally, we compare our goal attainment mechanism with an associative mechanism as an explanation for the thought rebound that can follow attempted thought suppression.

Problems with Goal Attainment

Evidence that problematic progress toward one's goals can lead to rumination was obtained by Millar, Tesser, and Millar (1988). They reasoned that attending college for the first time causes changes in one's life, including leaving friends or loved ones behind and being unable to continue activities one used to enjoy. On the other hand, the move may also open the possibility for making new friends and engaging in new activities. As such, one's first year in college may reflect a trade-off in the extent to which one's important goals are frustrated or facilitated. If rumination is a function of problematic goal attainment, then college freshmen should ruminate about the people and activities they left behind but only to the extent that they have been unable to find any substitutes for these (cf. Mahler, as cited in Atkinson, 1964; Ovsiankina, 1928, cited in Atkinson, 1964).

To test this hypothesis, Millar et al. asked first-quarter freshman at the University of Georgia to identify the person with whom they were closest before coming to the university and then to list the activities in which they had regularly engaged with this person and to indicate which of these activities they had been able to resume after coming to the university. Millar et al. also measured the extent to which the freshmen were ruminating about the person they had left behind. They did this using an inventory developed by Horowitz, Wilner, and Alverez (1979). This inventory included items such as "Memories of things we did together popped into my mind when I was trying to study," "I spent time thinking about when we could see each other," and "Pictures about him/her popped into my mind." Each of these items was followed by a 4-point scale (*never, rarely, sometimes, often*).

Millar et al. assumed that the more activities the freshmen were no longer able to perform, the greater the threat to the freshmen's goals and thus the greater the rumination. On the other hand, the greater the number of resumed activities, the lower the threat and the less the rumination. These hypotheses were supported. When self-reported rumination was regressed simultaneously on the number of interrupted activities and the number of resumed activities, the former went into the equation with a positive coefficient, whereas the latter went in with a negative coefficient. In short, the results support our first assumption: Rumination was predicted by the degree to which subjects had difficulty attaining their goals.

Rumination is a Function of Higher Order Goals

Our model suggests that people do not ruminate equally about every unattained goal. Rather, rumination is instigated by problems with higher order goals. This means that two people can face the same degree of objective goal frustration, but one who interprets this in higher order terms is more likely to ruminate than is one who does not make this interpretation. This hypothesis was tested by McIntosh and Martin (1992, Experiment 2). They began by blocking subjects into *linkers* and *non-linkers* (for details of this measurement, see McIntosh and Martin, 1992). Linkers are those who interpret negative feedback about lower order goals (e.g., being one's ideal weight) as an indication that they cannot attain happiness (i.e., a higher order goal). Non-linkers do not make this interpretation. Thus, in the face of what is objectively the same degree of problematic goal progress, linkers should ruminate more than non-linkers should.

To test this hypothesis, McIntosh and Martin presented linkers and non-linkers with a brief survey about their love lives. The survey included questions such as "When was the last time you were on a date?" "Do you currently have a steady boyfriend/girlfriend?" and "How many times have you been in love?" This survey served two purposes—it allowed the experimenters to divide the subjects into those who were currently in a relationship and those who were not, and it made salient subjects' status with respect to their goal of being in a relationship.

Following the survey, subjects engaged in a 5-minute distractor task and then proceeded to the task in which rumination was measured. In this task, subjects were presented with a series of words on a computer screen. Each word appeared first as a string of asterisks. Then one by one the asterisks disappeared to reveal the letters of a word. The subject's task was to guess the word being presented before all of its letters had been revealed. Some of the words were related to relationships (e.g., romance), and some were not (e.g., adjective). The assumption behind this task is that the more subjects were ruminating about relationships, the faster they would be at recognizing words related to relationships.

Consistent with the hypothesis that rumination is a function of problems in the attainment of higher order goals, McIntosh and Martin found that linkers who wanted but did not have a romantic relationship were significantly faster at recognizing relationship words than were linkers who were currently in a relationship. There was no difference in the time it took non-linkers who were or were not in a relationship to recognize relationship words. In other words, the only subjects ruminating were those not in a relationship who interpreted this as a threat to their happiness. It is important to note that the crossover interaction in the reaction times was significant only for the words related to relationships. There was no difference in the time it took subjects to recognize the control words. This is consistent with the hypothesis that the rumination is goal-specific.

Of course, one could rightly question whether these results actually reflect rumination. After all, what we have here are millisecond differences in the time it took subjects to recognize words. There is no assumption that the reaction-time task reflected rumination per se. It reflected accessibility, the mechanism presumed to be underlying rumination. However, McIntosh and Martin obtained analogous results using a self-report measure of rumination. In this study, McIntosh and Martin measured the tendency of linkers and non-linkers to ruminate and the percentage of time they reported feeling happy, unhappy, and neutral. It was assumed that linkers would report ruminating more than non-linkers would. Moreover, if, as the earlier experiment suggested, linkers are ruminating about their unattained goals, then linkers should also report more unhappiness than should non-linkers. Rumination about unattained goals is unpleasant. McIntosh and Martin used the analysis suggested by Baron and Kenny (1986) to test for mediation. The specific hypothesis being tested was that linking the attainment of lower order goals to the attainment of happiness would cause people to ruminate and that this rumination, in turn, would make them unhappy.

Consistent with this mediational model, McIntosh and Martin found that the more subjects linked the attainment of goals to happiness, the more they ruminated. The more they ruminated, the more unhappiness they reported, and the more they linked the attainment of goals to happiness, the more unhappiness they experienced. When rumination was included with linking in the regression equation, the relation between linking and unhappiness was removed, whereas the relation between rumination and unhappiness remained significant. In short, the mediation hypothesis was supported.

To summarize to this point, we have presented evidence that problems in attaining goals can instigate rumination, but this occurs primarily when the goals are higher order ones. It also appears that the mechanism underlying this rumination involves an increased accessibility of goal-related concepts.

Problematic Attainment Does Not Always Lead to Rumination

It should be clear by now that our model relies heavily upon the perseverance of goal-related thoughts as the generative mechanism for rumination. Over the years, evidence for this mechanism has been mixed. On the positive side, there is the original experiment by Zeigarnik (1938) in which subjects were asked to perform a series of rather mundane tasks, such as stringing beads and enumerating the names of cities. Zeigarnik allowed the subjects to finish some of these tasks but interrupted them before they could complete others. Later, when the subjects were asked to recall the tasks they had performed, they were about twice as likely to recall the interrupted as the completed tasks. Zeigarnik took this as evidence that thoughts related to the uncompleted tasks had remained active in the subjects' cognitive systems (cf. Lewin, 1951). Conceptually similar results have been obtained by others (e.g., Cartwright, 1942; Marrow, 1938; Martin, 1986; Millar, Tesser, & Millar, 1988; Ovsiankina, 1928, cited in Atkinson, 1964; Wicklund & Gollwitzer, 1982).

Alongside of these positive instances, however, are a number of failures to replicate. Rosenzweig (1943), for example, had subjects perform a series of tasks as part of what they thought was an important intelligence test. Under these conditions, subjects reported remembering more completed than uncompleted tasks, a reversal of the Zeigarnik effect. Rosenzweig (1943) took this as evidence of repression following failure to attain an important goal (see also Atkinson, 1953; Eriksen, 1954; Glixman, 1948, 1949).

Given this checkered history, how is it we still consider goal-related perseverance to be a reliable mechanism for rumination? The answer is simple: The effect has parameters, and we are increasingly coming to understand what these are. One was noted earlier—goal attainment is subjective. This means, in part, that objective completion of a task is not synonymous with subjective attainment of a goal.

This distinction was demonstrated very nicely in a study by Marrow (1938). He noted that, operationally, the Zeigarnik effect had been defined as better recall of interrupted as compared to completed tasks. Theoretically, though, the effect reflects perseveration of thoughts related to unattained goals. In his study, Marrow was able to vary task completion orthogonally with goal attainment. He did this by asking subjects to perform a number of tasks and then telling half of the subjects that they should attempt to complete the tasks in the time allowed. The other subjects were told that they should attempt to master each task and that they would be stopped when their performance on each indicated proficiency. For subjects given the completion instructions, being stopped meant that they had not attained their goal. For subjects given the proficiency instructions, however, being stopped meant that they had attained their goal.

Marrow stopped the subjects in their performance of some of the tasks but not others. He then asked his subjects to recall all the tasks they had performed. Consistent with the reversal in meaning of task completion in the two groups, Marrow found that subjects asked to complete the tasks showed the usual Zeigarnik effect; they recalled more interrupted than completed tasks. Subjects told they would be interrupted when they had demonstrated proficiency, however, showed an apparent reversal. They recalled more completed than interrupted tasks. In both cases, the results reflected better recall of information related to unattained goals.

Whereas Marrow concentrated on people's interpretations of objective task completion, other investigators have concentrated on the ability of subjects to control their output. Greenwald (1982), for example, suggested that when tasks are ego-involving, subjects may attempt to protect themselves by recalling information consistent with a positive self-view. This means that subjects may indicate more successes than failures in their free recall, even when this might not reflect the actual accessibility of their successes and failures. Greenwald further hypothesized that this self-serving bias would be observed only when the motivation to protect the self was activated and the subjects had control over their output.

This self-protection/control hypothesis was tested by Beckmann (in press). He asked subjects to perform a series of complex analogy problems. For half of the subjects, these problems were portrayed as part of an intelligence test, and they were told that the experimenter would eventually talk to them about their performance. The other subjects were not told this. Thus, self-protective motivations were presumably higher in the former condition than in the latter. All subjects received feedback indicating that they had performed well on some analogies but not on others. Following this feedback, the subjects' thoughts about the analogy task were measured in two ways: first in a reaction time task (in which subjects presumably had little control over their output) and then in a free recall task (in which subjects presumably had more control over their output). In the reaction time task, subjects were presented with words on a computer screen and were asked to indicate whether or not the words had appeared in one of the analogies. The computer surreptitiously measured the time it took the subjects to make this decision. In the free recall task, subjects were asked simply to recall as many of the analogies as they could.

The results for the reaction time task reflected a classic Zeigarnik effect. All subjects were faster at recognizing words related to analogies on which they had received failure rather than success feedback. The free recall measure, however, reflected something quite different. When the subjects' self-presentation concerns were made salient (i.e., they were told that the experimenter would talk to them about their scores on the intelligence test), subjects recalled more solved than unsolved analogies. When the self-protective concerns were not made salient, the Zeigarnik pattern was again observed: Subjects recalled more unsolved than solved analogies. In short, the results support the self-protection/control hypothesis (Greenwald, 1982). There was an apparent reversal of the Zeigarnik effect only when subjects had activated their self-protection mechanisms and had sufficient control over their output (Greenwald, 1982). According to Beckmann (in press), an increase in the accessibility of thoughts related to nonattained relative to attained goals is the default effect. Special conditions are needed for this effect not to be observed.

The third reason there may be a reversal or nonoccurrence of goal-related perseveration is related to the self-protection hypothesis. Because nonattainment of an important goal can be aversive (Carver & Scheier, 1990), people may attempt to distract themselves from unpleasant goal-related thoughts (Horowitz, 1986; Nolen-Hoeksema, 1987). Distraction from such thoughts can be difficult, however. People can have trouble generating suitable alternatives to their unwanted thoughts (Rachman, 1981; Wenzlaff, 1993). Yet when people are presented with a ready alternative, they are able to turn away from their unwanted thoughts (Wegner et al., 1987).

We (Experiment 2, described in Martin et al., 1993) made use of this contingency to see if people attempted to distract themselves from ruminative thoughts immediately after receiving negative feedback about an important goal. Subjects were asked to make a series of business decisions with the goal of making money for a hypothetical company. Subjects were told that people who made money for their company were more intelligent than those who did not make money. The purpose of these instructions was to increase the perceived consequences of the subjects' performance.

The business problems were presented on a computer screen and were constructed so that there were no obvious right or wrong answers. Occasionally, though, instead of another problem coming up, the computer would present a *newsflash*. These newsflashes depicted events that caused the subjects either to make money or to lose money in ways that were totally beyond their control (e.g., a tariff is repealed, a competitor retires). The ostensible purpose of these newsflashes was to reflect more accurately the real business world in which money can sometimes be gained or lost outside of the control of the corporation president. The actual purpose was to allow the experimenter to control whether subjects did or did not attain the goal of demonstrating their intelligence.

More specifically, subjects in the *skill* condition received feedback indicating that their company had made money through their good decisions. Subjects in the *luck* condition received feedback indicating that their company had made money because of a series of lucky events (i.e., favorable newsflashes). Theoretically, then, all of the subjects attained the lower order goal of making money for the company, but only the skill subjects also attained the higher order goal of demonstrating their intelligence (i.e., they made money through their skillful decisions). Thus, the luck subjects should be more likely to ruminate than the skill subjects or, alternatively, should be more likely to attempt to distract themselves from ruminating.

We measured the accessibility of the subjects' thoughts using a word recognition task similar to that used by McIntosh and Martin (1992). Briefly, subjects saw a series of asterisk strings on the computer, and the asterisks disappeared one by one to reveal the letters of a word. The subjects' task was to recognize each word before all of its letters had been uncovered. Some of the words in this task were related to intelligence, some were related to making money for the company, and some were not related to either goal. The time it took subjects to recognize the words in each of these groups comprised the measure of accessibility. It was assumed that the more subjects were ruminating about the goal of demonstrating their intelligence, the more accessible words related to intelligence would be and the faster subjects would recognize these words. Conversely, the more subjects were distracting themselves from thoughts of intelligence, the less

TABLE 1.2
Latency in Seconds to Identify Intelligence-Related, Business-Related and Control Words as a Function of Feedback and Distraction

Feedback	Distraction	Intelligence Related	Business Related	Control Words
Luck	Absent	21.64	24.62	24.82
	Present	25.78	27.62	25.14
Skill	Absent	19.11	24.29	23.42
	Present	20.21	26.93	24.95

Note. Distraction absent conditions are pooled across Experiments 1 and 2.

accessible words related to intelligence would be, and the longer it would take them to recognize these words.

To allow the differences in distraction motivation to play themselves out, some subjects were allowed to perform the word recognition task without a suitable distractor presented to them, whereas for others, a tape recording was played as they tried to recognize the words. This recording conveyed a preview of what at the time was an eagerly anticipated movie (e.g., *Batman*). Subjects in the distractor condition were told that the experimenters were interested in the effects of distraction on performance, "much like what would happen at a loud, crowded party." It was emphasized, however, that their primary task was the word recognition task.

If subjects receiving luck feedback seek to avoid goal-related thoughts by distracting themselves, then their recognition of intelligence-related words should be slower than that of subjects receiving the skill feedback, and this should be particularly true when an interesting distractor has been provided for them (i.e., the recording). As can be seen in Table 1.2, this is precisely what happened. The slowest recognition times were observed in distracted subjects who had received luck feedback.[2] It is important to note that this effect was significant only for the words related to the unattained goal (i.e., intelligence). There were no differences in the time it took subjects to recognize the other words. As it was in the earlier studies, the accessibility effects appear to be goal-specific.

These results suggest that the perseveration of goal-related thoughts may sometimes not be seen after goal nonattainment because people block these thoughts by thinking about something else. As noted earlier, however,

---

[2]There were no differences in incorrect guesses as a function of either word or condition. For purposes of analysis, condition means were substituted for missing values. Also, the immediate feedback conditions of Experiments 1 and 2 were identical in procedure. To increase the reliability of our analyses, we collapsed across these experiments for the two immediate feedback conditions. This decision was supported by the fact that there were no significant effects of experiment in our analyses, all F's < 1.

distraction attempts do not necessarily move people any closer to attaining their goals. If, as we assumed, people are primed for rumination until they either attain their goals or abandon them, then the kind of distraction effect seen in this study should be temporary. With time, rumination should eventually surface. We tested this hypothesis in another study (see Martin et al., 1993).

In this study, subjects were again asked to make a series of business decisions in order to make money for their company and thus demonstrate their intelligence. Again, subjects were told that they had made money through either luck or skill. Half of the subjects performed the word recognition task immediately following the feedback, whereas half performed it 5 minutes later (after drawing a map of their campus).

It was expected that, in the luck condition, there would be immediate distraction away from goal-related thoughts followed by rumination (because the goal remains unattained). In the skill condition, there should be immediate thinking about the goal (because of basking in success) followed by a slowdown because there is no Zeigarnik charge to maintain the positive affect (Isen, et al., 1976). Operationally, this means that when subjects performed the word recognition task immediately after receiving feedback, those receiving luck feedback would be slower than those receiving skill feedback at recognizing the intelligence-related words. After a delay, however, subjects receiving the luck feedback would be faster than subjects receiving the skill feedback at recognizing the intelligence-related words.

As Table 1.3 shows, the results were as predicted. Subjects given luck feedback recognized the intelligence-related words faster following the delay than immediately after the feedback, whereas subjects given skill feedback recognized the intelligence-related words faster immediately following the feedback than following the delay.

Also as expected, the timing and type of feedback did not influence the speed with which subjects recognized words related to the lower order goal of making business decisions. No differences were expected on this dimen-

TABLE 1.3
Latency in Seconds to Identify Intelligence-Related, Business-Related, and Control Words as a Function of Feedback and Delay of Measurement

Feedback	Time	Intelligence Related	Business Related	Control Words
Luck	Immediate	21.64	24.62	24.82
	Delay	19.29	25.57	24.82
Skill	Immediate	19.11	24.29	23.42
	Delay	21.38	26.56	25.90

Note. Distraction absent conditions are pooled across Experiments 1 and 2.

sion because all subjects received feedback indicating that they had attained this goal. Some subjects attained it through luck, whereas others attained it through skill, and the main implication of this difference was for the subjects' intelligence.[3]

How Distractors Distract?

As we have seen, the presence of a distractor can help people to avoid their ruminative thoughts. But how does this work? Is it a passive effect in the sense that the unwanted thought simply gets pushed out of consciousness because the distractor takes up too much capacity (i.e., one thought pushes out another)? Or is it a more active process? Does a person have to make strategic use of the distractor? There is reason to believe that the effect is more strategic than passive.

Kuhl (1984) drew a distinction between action-oriented and state-oriented people. Action-oriented people are characterized by an ability to change the focus of their attention to whatever happens to be the most adequate action plan in a given situation. State-oriented people, on the other hand, are less flexible in their self-regulation. They have trouble maintaining intentions when these intentions are in competition with strong alternative action tendencies, and they have difficulty disengaging from goal pursuit when either the goal becomes unattainable or attainment of the goal requires a plan of action not automatically available in the current situation. These differences between action and state-oriented people are reflected in the way these people deal with unwanted thoughts. Action-oriented people try to replace thoughts with something else, whereas state-oriented people merely attempt to suppress thoughts (Baumann & Kuhl, 1994).

If the ability of a distractor to suspend rumination temporarily depends on strategic use, then action-oriented individuals should be able to make use of the distractor to turn away from their ruminative thoughts, but state-oriented individuals should not. This hypothesis was tested by Beckmann and Martin (1994). They asked state-oriented and action-oriented

---

[3]There was an unexpected influence of feedback and delay on the time it took subjects to recognize words unrelated to either goal. Specifically, there was a relative slowdown in recognition time after a delay for subjects who received the skill feedback. The other conditions did not differ from one another. Because this pattern does not parallel the crossover observed for the intelligence-related words, we assume that, at best, the slowdown merely reflects a performance motivation deficit. It is reasonable to believe that after the skill feedback subjects had demonstrated their intelligence on the first task, their motivation to try hard on the subsequent recognition task decreased and their reaction times slowed down. This decrease would reflect only on the control words because these were the only ones not activated in the previous task.

subjects to solve a number of complex analogies as part of what was ostensibly a very reliable intelligence test. Following each analogy, subjects were told that they had not found the optimal solution. Following these failure trials, half of the subjects were asked to sit quietly until the next part of the experiment, whereas the remaining subjects waited while watching some colorful geometric figures evolve and change shape on the computer screen. The question was whether this simple distractor would be enough to stop the subjects from thinking about their recent failures.

Accessibility of failure-related thoughts was measured in a word recognition task similar to those previously described. One by one the letters of various words were uncovered and the subjects' task was to name each word before all of its letters had been revealed. Some of the words were ones that had been included in the previous analogies; some were not. The prediction was that subjects still ruminating about the analogy task would recognize more of the words related to that task than would subjects who are not ruminating.

Consistent with the hypothesis that the effects of a distractor involve strategic rather than passive mechanisms, correct recognition of words related to the analogy task was lowest among action-oriented subjects who had been exposed to the distractor. Participants in the other conditions correctly recognized significantly more words related to the analogies task but did not differ from one another. Thus, the effect of the distractor does not appear to be passive. To avoid rumination, one must not only have a distractor ready but must also know how to make use of it.

Rumination is Not Demanded by the Immediate Environment

In line with Klinger (1977), we have assumed that the unintentional onset of ruminative thoughts occurs because, metaphorically speaking, information related to unattained goals has been tagged as having priority in processing. Although this hypothetical tagging mechanism cannot be observed directly, we can see effects that would follow if such a mechanism were operating. Specifically, if certain information is given priority, then it should be processed more easily than other information (Krull, 1993), and stimuli related to this information should be particularly attention grabbing (Schneider & Shiffrin, 1977). Evidence consistent with these hypotheses has been obtained.

Young (1987) presented subjects with a series of letter strings on a computer screen. Some of these strings represented real words; others did not. The subjects' task was simply to indicate whether each letter string did or did not spell out a real word. These strings were presented in the center of the computer screen. Off to one side, however, was another string of letters and symbols that was ostensibly computer garbage, an unavoidable by-product of the computer program. The subjects were told to ignore this garbage. Every so often, however, as the subjects were making their word/non-word decisions, the letters presented in the computer garbage would spell out a word, and occasionally, these words were associated with the subjects' unattained goals (subjects had indicated these goals prior to the experiment). Young (1987) found that subjects took longer to make their word–nonword decisions when the words in the computer garbage were related to their unattained goals than when they were not. In other words, stimuli related to the subjects' unattained goals attracted the subjects' attention, even though the subjects had been told to ignore these words. More generally, the results suggest that information related to unattained goals automatically attracts people's attention even when people are trying to focus on other tasks.

Further evidence for this conclusion has been obtained by Isbell et al. (1994) using a completely different methodology. They developed an inventory to measure various types of recurrent thoughts. These included positive thinking about the past, positive thinking about the future, negative thinking about the past, and negative thinking about the future. These dimensions were collapsed to yield two dimensions: one reflecting positive thinking about the past and future and one reflecting negative thinking about the past and the future. People scoring high on these dimensions are essentially ruminators. They experience a great deal of thoughts about the past or future. Those scoring low do not think much about their past or future.

Isbell et al. (1994) compared the subjects' scores on these dimensions with their scores on other scales reflecting either spontaneous or controlled thinking. They found significant positive correlations between the ruminative dimensions and scales reflecting spontaneous thoughts (e.g., impulsivity, intrusiveness) but not with scales reflecting controlled thought (e.g., planning, need for cognition). This pattern of results is consistent with the conclusion that the tendency to experience ruminative thoughts is a function of an automatic rather than a controlled process. In other words, people do not have ruminative thoughts on purpose. The thoughts are automatically cued by relevant stimuli.

The Content of Rumination is Determined by People's Theories

We have hypothesized that people are not always aware of the goals that are guiding their behavior. This occurs, in part, because very similar behaviors can be performed for very different reasons, and very different behaviors can be performed for the same reasons. When people have their goals blocked, they may experience no more than a rough sense that something is missing from their lives, but not know exactly what this is. In such situations, people may experience an instigation toward rumination yet not have an immediate content. What do people do in this case? They ruminate about the content that, according to their implicit theories, is the cause of their discontent.

Although we have no direct evidence for this hypothesis, there is some indirect evidence. For example, several studies have shown that people's attributions about the causes of events can be influenced by whatever is most accessible to them at the time. In one of these studies, Williams (1993) had subjects read 10 sentences in the context of a memory experiment. Eight of these sentences primed a particular type of cause. Some of the subjects read about events in which the protagonist was responsible for the outcome, but others read about events in which the protagonist was not responsible for the outcome. Then, in the context of an ostensibly unrelated second experiment, subjects were asked to read a paragraph and answer some questions about the causes of the events depicted. In the paragraph, a target person is in need of class notes, but the exact reason is not made clear. The results indicated that, compared to subjects exposed to the "unresponsible" primes, those exposed to the "responsible" primes accorded more responsibility to the target, indicated more anger and less sympathy toward the target, and indicated that they would be less willing to help the target out of his predicament. We conclude with Williams (1993) that "how a person attributes causality to another, and therefore how the perceiver feels and behaves toward the actor, can be determined in part by the accessibility in memory of selected poles of a given causal dimension" (p. 227).

Related results were obtained by Rholes and Pryor (1982). In the context of a color perception test, subjects were exposed to words depicting either actors (e.g., physician) or entities (e.g., movie). Then, in an ostensibly unrelated second experiment, subjects were exposed to scenarios incorporating synonyms of some of the previously presented words (e.g., the doctor liked the film) and were asked to indicate whether the actor or the entity was more responsible for the outcome. The results showed that subjects accorded greater weight to the cause for which they had been primed in the earlier task.

These studies suggest that momentary accessibility of a specific cause can prompt people to weigh those causes more heavily in their inferences. This, in turn, should influence the content of their ruminations. This accessibility, however, need not come from temporary priming by the environment. Chronic individual differences may produce the same effect (Higgins, King, & Mavin, 1982). When unable to get a date, for example, a person in high in self-esteem may ruminate about the lack of available partners, whereas a person low in self-esteem may ruminate about his or her lack of social skills.

Evidence that individual differences in implicit theories can influence the thoughts that come to people's minds has been obtained by Hong and Dweck (1992). They provided success or failure feedback to subjects who believed either that intelligence is a fixed entity or that it is a malleable resource. The former, called entity theorists, interpret negative feedback about their intelligence as a sign that they lack intelligence. The latter, called incremental theorists, interpret negative feedback about their intelligence as a sign that there is room for improvement. When they are confronted with objectively the same negative feedback about their performance on an intelligence test, entity theorists should be more likely than incremental theorists to conclude that they have failed to attain a higher order goal (i.e., being intelligent). As a result, they should be more likely than incremental theorists to attempt to distract themselves from intelligence-related thoughts immediately following negative feedback about their intelligence.

Hong and Dweck (1992) tested this hypothesis by providing entity and incremental theorists with either positive or negative feedback about their performance on an intelligence test. Immediately after this feedback, Hong and Dweck assessed the accessibility of the subjects' thoughts. This was done by measuring the time it took subjects to categorize a series of adjectives as person oriented or not-person oriented. Among the person adjectives were some adjectives related to ability (e.g., smart, capable). The assumption was that the more subjects ruminate about their intelligence, the quicker they will be to identify the ability-related adjectives. The more subjects distract themselves from thoughts of intelligence, the slower they will be to identify these adjectives.

Hong and Dweck found that, after receiving negative feedback, entity theorists took significantly longer to respond to the ability-related adjectives than did incremental theorists. No such differences were found when the subjects had received positive feedback, and there were no differences in the time it took the subjects to identify adjectives not related to ability. Thus, the implicit theories these subjects held prior to getting negative feedback influenced their interpretation of that feedback, and this, in turn, influenced what remained on their minds. So, although we have no direct evidence yet for our content hypothesis, we believe these data provide partial support.

Alternatives to Goal-Related Perseverance

So far, we have been presenting evidence for the role of problematic goal attainment in producing rumination. Although we believe that this is a powerful mechanism, we do not wish to suggest that it is the only mechanism that could cause thoughts to recur. In fact, other mechanisms have been suggested. According to Roemer and Borkovec (1993), for example, worry is sustained both by reinforcement and by an association-based rebound effect (Wegner et al., 1987). When people worry, they often make things out to be worse than they really are. When the dreaded event actually occurs, it may seem less threatening and may be easier to cope with. This increases the likelihood that the person will continue to worry in the future.

Roemer and Borkovec (1993) also suggested that people may attempt to suppress their worrisome thoughts because these thoughts are unpleasant. Attempted suppression, however, can lead to increased experiences of the thought through a mechanism specified by Wegner et al. (1987). These investigators suggested that in attempting to suppress a thought, people may attempt to think of a variety of substitute thoughts. Unfortunately, these substitutes do not totally eliminate the to-be-suppressed thought. For people to know if they are successfully suppressing, they need to activate the unwanted thought (e.g., Am I thinking about a white bear now? No. Good. Wait a minute . . . I just thought about a white bear . . .). As a result of these recurrences, the to-be-suppressed thought becomes associated with the various substitute thoughts, and when the person experiences any of these thoughts again, the person also cues the to-be-suppressed thought.

Given that several mechanisms could possibly be operating in any instance of a recurrent thought, it becomes important to establish which, or perhaps how much of each, of the possible mechanisms is operating in that particular instance. This issue was addressed by Martin and Tesser (described in Martin et al., 1993) in a follow-up to Wegner et al. (1987).

Wegner et al. (1987) told some subjects that they could think about anything they wanted, except a white bear. If they happened to think about a white bear they were to indicate this by ringing a bell. The subjects were then told that they should try to think about a white bear. Wegner et al. (1987) found that these suppression subjects reported more thoughts of a white bear in the second thought session than did subjects who had not previously attempted to suppress these thoughts. This so-called rebound effect was explained by Wegner et al. in terms of the previously described associative mechanism.

We speculated that a goal mechanism could produce a similar effect (Martin et al., 1993). From this perspective, subjects are given the goal of not thinking about a white bear, yet they do think about a white bear. This means that they did not attain their goal. This nonattainment could result in the perseverance of goal-related thoughts, which, in turn, would reflect itself in an increased accessibility of white bear thoughts. Therefore, the rebound effect after attempted thought suppression could reflect, at least in part, rumination as a function of goal nonattainment. If this line of reasoning is correct, then if subjects are led to believe that they have attained their goal of not thinking about a white bear, they should not experience rumination and hence should not show the rebound effect.

Following Wegner et al. (1987), we asked subjects to think about anything they wanted, including a white bear. The only stipulation was that if they thought about a white bear, they should make a note of it by placing a check mark on a sheet. Two other groups of subjects were asked not to think of a white bear. In one of these groups, the experimenter merely picked up the sheet on which subjects had indicated the number of times they had thought of a white bear and placed that sheet aside. These subjects then proceeded to the next stage of the experiment. For the other group of suppression subjects, the experimenter picked up the response sheet, noted the number of times the subjects had reported thinking about a white bear, and remarked that they had done much better than most of the other subjects at not thinking about a white bear. We then assessed the accessibility of various thoughts by means of the word recognition task. The words were divided into those related to white bears (e.g., iceberg, polar bear), those related to the experimental setting (e.g., psychologist, experiment), and those unrelated to either white bears or the setting (e.g., adjective, electricity).

Subjects who were asked merely to express their thoughts attained their goal. They were asked to think about a white bear, and they did. Hence, they should experience no rumination and no rebound. Suppression subjects who received positive feedback objectively failed to attain their goal. They thought of a white bear when they were instructed not to. However, they were also given feedback indicating that they had done well, so, in essence, they did not fail. As a result, these subjects, like the expression subjects, should experience no rumination, and should show no rebound. The suppression subjects who did not receive positive feedback, in contrast, failed to attain their goal and did not have this failure removed from them.

TABLE 1.4
Recognition Times as a Function of Type of Thought, Type of Feedback, and Dimension of Thought

Dimension	*Expression*	*Suppression*	
		Success Feedback	*No Feedback*
White bear	23.30	23.17	21.01
Experiment	31.82	30.60	29.74
Control	30.91	29.55	29.64
Number of white bear mentions	6.77	6.67	6.08

Note. Recognition times are recorded in seconds. The shorter the time, the greater the accessibility.

Hence, they should experience rumination and a rebound.

Table 1.4 shows, these hypotheses were supported. The suppression subjects not given the success feedback were significantly faster at recognizing white bear words than were either the express subjects or the suppress subjects given the success feedback. The latter two groups did not differ from one another. Furthermore, as in the earlier studies, these accessibility effects were content specific. There were no differences between conditions in the time it took subjects to recognize words related to the experimental setting or the control words.

Clearly, these results suggest that goal nonattainment can lead to the kind of thought rebound effects usually attributed to purely associative mechanisms. The results do not suggest, however, that all instances of the rebound effect are due to goal-based rumination. We believe that goal nonattainment is a powerful mechanism for producing recurrent thought and it should be tested as an alternative in conditions in which only reinforcement or associative rebound have previously been assumed to be operating.

SOME CONSEQUENCES OF RUMINATION

Given that people are ruminating, what are the consequences? We discuss two general classes: the effects of rumination on other thought processes (e.g., problem solving, attitude change) and the effects of rumination of feelings (i.e., depression, unhappiness).

Effects of Rumination on Other Thought Processes

Nolen-Hoeksema and Lyubomirsky (1994) suggested that people who respond to negative life events by ruminating have poorer problem solving skills than do people who react to negative life events by distracting themselves (see also Carver et al., 1989). On the other hand, Taylor and Schneider (1989) showed that at least some kinds of rumination (e.g., mental simulations) aid in problem-focused coping. Together, these findings suggest that the effects of rumination are more complex than can be captured by a simple main effect statement.

Direct evidence of this complexity was obtained by Rude, Zentner, and Morrow (1993). They provided subjects with positive or negative feedback about their intelligence and asked them to recognize words presented one letter at a time. The subjects' task was to say what word was being presented before all of its letters had been revealed. The words being uncovered were either related to intelligence or not. Rude et al. (1993) found that subjects given negative feedback were faster at recognizing words related to intelligence than were subjects given positive feedback, but there were no differences between groups in the time it took to recognize words unrelated to intelligence. Prior to performing the word recognition task, however, Rude et al. asked the subjects to read several short stories and, after the recognition task, tested these subjects for comprehension of the stories. Subjects given the negative feedback showed lower comprehension than did subjects given the positive feedback. In other words, those who were fastest at recognizing the words related to intelligence also performed the poorest on the reading comprehension task. In this one study, then, we have all possible outcomes. The rumination enhanced the subjects' performance of an easy, goal-relevant task (i.e., recognizing words related to intelligence), impaired their performance of a demanding, goal-irrelevant task (i.e., reading comprehension), and had no influence on their performance of an easy, goal-irrelevant task (i.e., recognizing the control words).

Rumination Maintains Goal-Related Thoughts

Is there any way to predict the effects of rumination on any given task? In a general sense, yes. Recall that one of the identifying features of rumination is that it involves the recurrence of thoughts related to an unattained goal. Generally speaking, then, we should see improved performance when an activity is facilitated by the maintenance of earlier information, but we should see problematic performance when the earlier information gets in the way.

Lassiter et al. (1993) found evidence that goal-related thought perseverance can prevent the decay of attitude change. In an extension of a study by Boninger, Brock, Cook, Gruder, and Romer (1990), Lassiter et al. brought subjects to a lab for what was ostensibly a study in communication. The subjects were randomly assigned to one of four groups. The *receiver* subjects were told that they would hear a message and would be asked to indicate their agreement with that message. The *unfinished transmitter* subjects were given a message and were told that they would later be transmitting it into a tape recorder. However, after they had finished indicating their opinions about the issues in the message, they were excused from the experiment (as in Boninger, Brock, Cook, Gruder, & Romer, 1990). Subjects in the *finished transmitter* group were treated the same as the unfinished group except that they were allowed to tape record their message before being excused. Finally, the control subjects merely indicated their opinions on the issues without receiving or transmitting any message.

In goal attainment terms, the unfinished transmitters did not attain their goal. They did not get to transmit the message as they had been told they would. This may have led them to continue thinking about the message. This should not have happened in any of the other conditions. Lassiter et al. tested for this by assessing the subjects' attitudes at two times. With immediate testing, the results were not particularly surprising. The three groups exposed to the message showed attitudes more congruent with the message than did the control subjects. The interesting results came when the subjects were contacted 10 weeks later and had their attitudes assessed in an unconnected context over the telephone. This time the results indicated that only the unfinished transmitter subjects still maintained the attitudes they had developed in the initial testing. Although the receiver subjects and the finished transmitter subjects differed from the control group at Time 1, they did not do so after 10 weeks. In short, the attitude change was sustained only in the subjects who had not initially attained their goal (i.e., transmitted the message).

Analogous persistence effects were demonstrated in a quite different context by Martin (1986). In this study, subjects were asked to categorize a series of behaviors in terms of one of two traits. For half of the subjects, the two traits were positive, whereas for half they were negative. The subjects were then asked to form an impression of a person described in terms that were ambiguous with respect to the previously presented traits. It has been shown (e.g., Higgins, Rholes, & Jones, 1977) that prior activation of a trait concept can increase the likelihood that people will use that concept in forming a subsequent impression and the size of this effect depends on the recency and frequency of activation (Srull & Wyer, 1979). If rumination increases the likelihood that people will maintain thoughts about a certain trait, then it may increase the likelihood that people will use this trait in forming an impression (at least to the extent that the trait is seen as relevant).

Martin (1986) tested for this by asking subjects to categorize either 12 or 8 behaviors in the initial task. However, all subjects were stopped after they had categorized eight; the subjects asked to categorize 12 had not completed their task, whereas the subjects asked to categorize 8 had. Thus, the former should have been ruminating about the traits more than the latter was. As expected, the interrupted subjects interpreted the subsequent paragraph in terms of the activated traits, whereas the subjects allowed to complete the categorization task did not. As it was in the Lassiter et al. (1993) study, those who had not attained their goal maintained thoughts related to the goal, and these thoughts influenced subsequent performance.

Effects of Rumination on Negative Affect

One of the identifying features of rumination is recurrence. A person may experience ruminative thoughts for days, weeks, even years (Silver et al., 1983). If these thoughts are negative, then long-term unhappiness or depression may arise (e.g., Beck, 1982; Ellis, 1962; Nolen-Hoeksema, 1987;

Pyszczynski & Greenberg, 1987). An interesting example of the ability of rumination to sustain negative affect was presented by Nolen-Hoeksema and Morrow (1991). They divided subjects into those who respond to negative life events with rumination and those who respond with distraction. This was done by providing subjects with 16 ruminative and 16 distracting responses and asking the subjects to indicate which they used when experiencing a negative or depressed mood. The ruminative responses included reactions such as "I isolated myself to think about how I was feeling" and "I thought 'I won't be able to get anything done if I don't snap out of this mood.'" The distracting responses included reactions such as "I did something fun to get my mind off how I was feeling" and "I talked with friends about something other than how I was feeling." Following this task, the subjects' levels of depression were measured.

Coincidentally, this experiment was done shortly before the 1989 Loma Prieta Earthquake. Ten days following the quake, Nolen-Hoeksema and Morrow (1991) were able to get another measure of depression, a measure of the amount of time the subjects had ruminated about the quake, and the amount of quake-related damage the subjects had witnessed. Subjects who had displayed a ruminative style of responding before the quake, were significantly more likely to be depressed in the followup measurement than were subjects who had displayed a distractive response style. These results were obtained even after the subjects' initial levels of depression and the amount of destruction they witnessed were taken into account. Similar results were found in a subset of subjects 7 weeks after the earthquake.

Nolen-Hoeksema (1991) speculated about three possible sources for the ruminative response style: (a) Children could learn it from observing their parents, (b) parents could fail to teach the children a repertoire of more adaptive strategies for handling negative affect, or (c) biological factors could be involved. Our goal-hierarchy assumption suggests a fourth alternative. As noted earlier, individuals who interpret threats to lower order goals as threats to higher order goals ruminate more than do individuals who do not make this link (McIntosh & Martin, 1992). Thus, linkers should show more and longer periods of depression than should nonlinkers.

This hypothesis was tested by McIntosh, Harlow, & Martin (1995). Because linkers are more likely than nonlinkers to believe that the failure to attain lower order goals implies the failure to attain higher level goals, small everyday stressors could represent greater subjective threats to linkers than to nonlinkers. This may make linkers more sensitive than nonlinkers to changes in the level of their everyday stressors and may make them more likely to ruminate when they are experiencing stress. Rumination should sustain the stress-induced negative affect, causing linkers to experience more depression and longer lasting depression than nonlinkers.

McIntosh et al. (1995) began by categorizing subjects as linkers or nonlinkers and measuring the amount of everyday stress they experienced (e.g., family arguments, increase in academic workload), the amount of rumination they reported, their level of depression, and the extent to which they were bothered by a number of physical symptoms (e.g., headache, dizziness). These measures were taken at two time periods, 2 weeks apart.

As expected, at Time 1, linkers reported more rumination, more depression, and more bother from physical symptoms than did nonlinkers. This was true even though there was no significant difference in the number of stressors reported by linkers and nonlinkers. More importantly, using Time 1 stress and linking measures as predictors, the researchers found that linkers who had experienced high stress at Time 1 were more likely to be depressed and report more physical symptoms 2 weeks later than were subjects in any of the other conditions (see Fig. 1.1). There were no differences between the amounts of depression and physical symptoms reported by subjects in the other conditions.

In short, the results are consistent with our goal hierarchy assumption. People with a tendency to interpret everyday stressors as threats to higher-order goals (i.e., linkers) are likely to experience more rumination, more depression, and longer lasting depression than are people who tend not to interpret everyday stressors as threats to higher order goals.

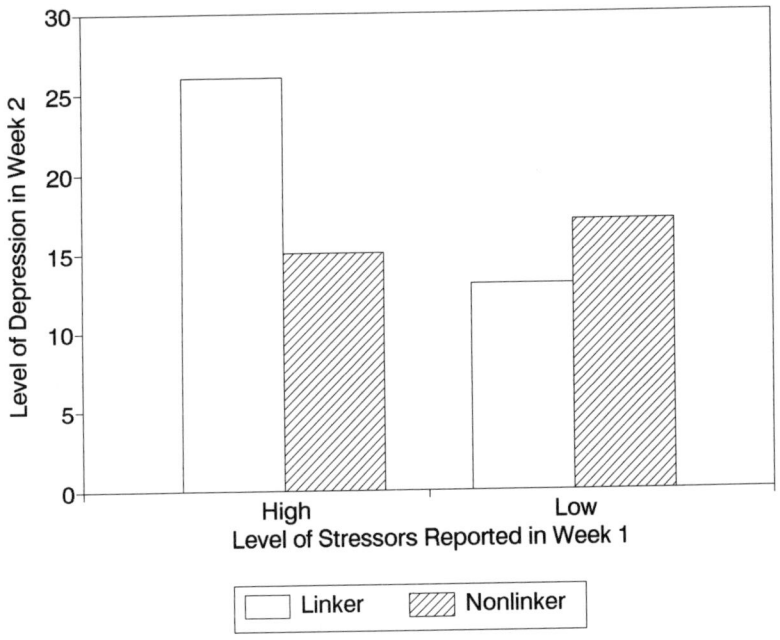

FIG. 1.1. Session 2 depression as a function of Session 1 linking and hassles.

CONCLUSION

As long as people are making nonproblematic progress toward their goals, they experience few off-tasks thoughts. People get out of sync when the environment is either too demanding (i.e., they have difficulty attaining the goal) or not demanding enough (e.g., they are bored). This lack of synchrony increases the accessibility of thoughts related to the threatened goal, which, in turn, makes it likely that goal-related thoughts will be experienced spontaneously and recurrently. Which specific thoughts become more accessible, however, depend upon an individual's a priori theories. It appears that only progress toward higher order goals is relevant for rumination, although frustration of lower order goals can cause rumination when these goals are subjectively linked to the attainment of higher order goals. Additionally, a person can temporarily suspend his or her ruminative thoughts by thinking about something else, but this diversion can be difficult. One needs to have an effective distractor available and to know how to make use of it. The best way to terminate rumination is to attain the goal that is driving the rumination.

We have couched our results in goal terms not only because goal attainment is a powerful mechanism for guiding thoughts, feelings, and behaviors but also because theorizing in terms of goals allows us to understand rumination in a more general context, namely a control systems or cybernetic view of self-regulating systems (e.g., Carver & Scheier, 1981; Miller, et al., 1960; Powers, 1973; von Bertalanffy, 1968). In this way, we not only tie together the various modes of rumination (e.g., problem solving, daydreaming, meaning analysis) but also tie rumination into a more general view of human behavior.

We close with one last example. For any readers who are still skeptical of the power of problematic goal attainment to induce recurrent thoughts, consider your reactions when you realize that the ending of this chapter....

ACKNOWLEDGMENTS

Preparation of this chapter was supported by grant No. 1021RR274100 from the National Science Foundation to the authors. The authors would like to thank Bob Wyer, Eric Klinger, Susan Nolen-Hoeksema, and Lie-jung Chang for their comments on an earlier version.

REFERENCES

Atkinson, J. W. (1953). The achievement motive and recall of interrupted and completed tasks. *Journal of Experimental Psychology, 46,* 381–390.

Atkinson, J. W. (1964). *An introduction to motivation*. Princeton, NJ: Van Nostrand.
Bargh, J. A. (1989). Conditional automaticity: Varieties of automatic influence in social perception and cognition. In J. S. Uleman & J. A. Bargh (Eds.), *Unintended thought* (pp.3–51). New York: Guilford.
Baron, R. A., & Kenny, D. A. (1986). The moderator–mediator variable distinction in social psychological research: Conceptual, strategic, and statistical considerations. *Journal of Personality and Social Psychology, 51*, 1173–1182.
Beck, A. T. (1982). *Depression: Clinical, experimental, and theoretical aspects*. New York: Harper & Row.
Beckmann, J. (in press). Self-presentation and the Zeigarnik effect. In T. Gjesme & R. Nygard, (Eds.), *Advances in motivation*. Oslo: Scandanavian University Press.
Beckmann, J., & Martin, L. L. (1994). *Distraction and disengagement: How people stop ruminating.* Manuscript in preparation.
Bem, D. J. (1967). Self-perception: An alternative interpretation of cognitive dissonance phenomena. *Psychological Review, 74*, 183–200.
Boninger, D. S., Brock, T. C., Cook, T. D., Gruder, G. L., & Romer, D. (1990). Discovery of reliable attitude change persistence resulting from a transmitter tuning set. *Psychological Science, 1*, 268–271.
Bruner, J. (1957). On perceptual readiness. *Psychological Review, 64*, 123–152.
Cartwright, D. (1942). The effect of interruption, completion and failure upon the attractiveness of activities. *Psychological Review, 48*, 425–442.
Carver, C. S., Lawrence, J. W., & Scheier, M. F. (1995). A control-process perspective on the origins of affect. In L. L. Martin & A. Tesser (Eds.), *Striving and feeling: Interactions between goals affect and self-regulation*. Hillsdale, NJ: Lawrence Erlbaum Associates.
Carver, C. S., & Scheier, M. F. (1981). *Attention and self-regulation: A control-theory approach to human behavior*. New York: Springer-Verlag.
Carver, C. S., & Scheier, M. F. (1990). Origins and functions of positive and negative affect: A control-process view. *Psychological Review, 97*, 19–35.
Carver, C. S., Scheier, M. F., & Weintraub, J. K. (1989). Assessing coping strategies: A theoretically based approach. *Journal of Personality and Social Psychology, 56*, 267–283.
Cervone, D., Kopp, D. A., Schaumann, L., & Scott, W. D. (1994). Mood, self-efficacy, and performance standards: Lower moods induce higher standards for performance. *Journal of Personality and Social Psychology, 67*, 499–512.
Clark, L. F., Collins, J. E., & Henry, S. M. (in press). Biasing effects or retrospective memory on current self-assessments. In N. Schwarz & S. Sudman (Eds.), *Autobiographical memory and the validity of retrospective reports*. New York: Springer-Verlag.
Clark, L. F., Henry, S. M., & Taylor, D. (1994). Examining one's motivation for childbearing and adjustment to infertility. In A. L. Stanton & C. A. Dunkel-Shetter (Eds.), *Psychological adjustment to infertility* (157–180). New York: Plenum.
Coyne, J. C. (1994). Self-reported distress: Analog or Ersatz depression? *Psychological Bulletin, 116*, 29–45.
Csikzentmihalyi, M. (1975). *Beyond boredom and anxiety*. San Francisco, CA: Jossey-Bass.
Csikzentmihalyi, M., & LeFevre, J. (1989). Optimal experience in work and leisure. *Journal of Personality and Social Psychology, 56*, 815–822.
Ellis, A. (1962). *Reason and emotion in psychotherapy*. Secaucus, NJ: Lyle Stuart.
Emmons, R., & Kaiser, H. (1995). Goal orientation and emotional well-being: Linking goals and affect through the self. In L. L. Martin, & A. Tesser (Eds.), *Striving and feeling: Interactions between goals affect and self-regulation*. Hillsdale, NJ: Lawrence Erlbaum Associates.
Eriksen, C. W. (1954). Psychological defenses and "ego strength" in recall of completed and incompleted tasks. *Journal of Abnormal and Social Psychology, 49*, 45–50.
Frijda, N. (1988). The laws of emotion. *American Psychologist, 42*, 377–399.
Glixman, A. F. (1948). An analysis of the use of the interruption-technique in experimental studies of "repression." *Psychological Review, 45*, 491–506.

Glixman, A. F. (1949). Recall of completed and incompleted activities under varying degrees of stress. *Journal of Experimental Psychology, 39*, 281–295.

Greenwald, A. G. (1982). Ego task analysis: An integration of research on ego-involvement and self-awareness. In A. Hastrof & A. Isen (Eds.), *Cognitive social psychology* (pp. 109–147). New York: Elsevier.

Higgins, E. T., King, G. A., & Mavin, G. H. (1982). Individual construct accessibility and subjective impressions and recall. *Journal of Personality and Social Psychology, 43*, 35–47.

Higgins, E. T., Rholes, W. S., & Jones, C. R. (1977). Category accessibility and impression formation. *Journal of Experimental Social Psychology, 13*, 141–154.

Hirt, E. R., McDonald, H. E., & Melton, R. J. (1995). Processing goals and the affect-performance link: Mood as main effect or mood as input? In L. L. Martin, & A. Tesser (Eds.), *Striving and feeling: Interactions between goals affect and self-regulation*. Hillsdale, NJ: Lawrence Erlbaum Associates.

Hong, Y., & Dweck, C. S. (1992, August). *Implicit theories as predictors of self-inference processes.* Paper presented at the annual convention of the American Psychological Society, Washington, DC.

Horowitz, M. J. (1986). *Stress response syndromes* (2nd ed.). New York: Aronson.

Horowitz, M. J., Wilner, N., & Alverez, W. (1979). Impact of event scale: A measure of subjective stress. *Psychosomatic Medicine, 41*, 209–218.

Hsee, C. K., & Abelson, R. P. (1991). Velocity relation: Satisfaction as a function of the first derivative of outcome over time. *Journal of Personality and Social Psychology, 60*, 341–347.

Isbell, L., Gohm, C., & Wyer, R. S. (1994). Unpublished raw data.

Isen, A. M., Clark, M., & Schwartz, M. F. (1976). Duration of the effect of good mood on helping: Footprints in the sands of time. *Journal of Personality and Social Psychology, 34*, 385–393.

Janoff-Bulman, R. (1992). *Shattered assumptions: Towards a new psychology of trauma*. New York: Free Press.

Klinger, E. (1975). Consequences to commitment to and disengagement from incentives. *Psychological Review, 82*, 223–231.

Klinger, E. (1977). *Meaning and void: Inner experience and the incentives in people's lives*. Minneapolis: University of Minnesota Press.

Krull, D. S. (1993). Does the grist change the mill? The effect of the perceiver's inferential goal on the process of social inference. *Personality and Social Psychology, 19*, 340–348.

Kuhl, J. (1984). Volitional aspects of achievement toward motivation and learned helplessness: Toward a comprehensive theory of action control. In B. A. Maher (Ed.), *Progress in experimental personality research* (Vol. 13, pp. 99–171). New York: Academic Press.

Kuhl, J., Baumann, N. (1995). *Rumination and personality: Negative affect, impaired accessibility, and inhibitory brain potentials*. Unpublished manuscript, University of Osnabrueck, Germany.

Landman, J. (1987). Regret: A theoretical and conceptual analysis. *Journal of the Theory of Social Behavior, 17*, 135–160.

Lassiter, G. D., Pezzo, M. V., & Apple, K. J. (1993). The transmitter-persistence effect: A confounded discovery? *Psychological Science, 4*, 208–210.

Lazarus, R. S., & Folkman, S. (1984). *Stress, appraisal, and coping*. New York: Springer-Verlag.

Lewin, K. (1951). *Field theory in social science: Selected theoretical papers*. New York: Harper & Row.

Marrow, A. J. (1938). Goal tension and recall. *Journal of General Psychology, 19*, 3–64.

Martin, L. L. (1986). Set/reset: Use and disuse of concepts in impression formation. *Journal of Personality and Social Psychology, 51*, 493–504.

Martin, L. L., Achee, J.W., Ward, D. W., & Harlow, T. F. (1993). The role of cognition and effort in the use of emotions to guide behavior. In R. S. Wyer & T. K. Srull (Eds.), *Advances in social cognition* (Vol. 6, pp. 147–157). Hillsdale, NJ: Lawrence Erlbaum Associates.

Martin, L. L., & Stoner, P. (1995). Mood as input: What we think about how we feel determines how we think. In L. L. Martin & A. Tesser (Eds.), *Striving and feeling: Interactions between goals affect and self-regulation*. Hillsdale, NJ: Lawrence Erlbaum Associates.

Martin, L. L., & Tesser, A. (1989). Toward a motivational and structural theory of ruminative thought. In J. S. Uleman, & J. A. Bargh (Eds.), *Unintended thought* (pp. 306–326). New York: Guilford.

Martin, L. L., Tesser, A., & McIntosh, W. D. (1993). Wanting but not having: The effects of unattained goals on thoughts and feelings. In D. M. Wegner & J. W. Pennebaker (Eds.), *The handbook of mental control* (pp. 552–572). New York: Prentice Hall.

Martin, L. L., Ward, D. W., Achee, J. W., & Wyer, R. S. (1993). Mood as input: People have to interpret the motivational implications of their moods. *Journal of Personality and Social Psychology, 64*, 317–326.

McIntosh, W. D. (1995). When does goal nonattainment lead to negative emotional reactions, and when doesn't it? The role of linking and rumination. In L. L. Martin & A. Tesser (Eds.), *Striving and feeling: Interactions between goals affect and self-regulation*. Hillsdale, NJ: Lawrence Erlbaum Associates.

McIntosh, W. D., Harlow, T. F., & Martin, L. L. (in press). Linkers and nonlinkers: The relation between goals beliefs, rumination, and depression. *Journal of Basic and Applied Psychology*.

McIntosh, W. D., & Martin, L. L. (1992). The cybernetics of happiness: The relation between goal attainment, rumination, and affect. In M. S. Clark (Ed.), *Review of personality and social psychology* (Vol. 14, pp. 222–246). Newbury Park, CA: Sage.

Millar, K. U., Tesser, A., & Millar, M. (1988). The effects of a threatening life event on behavior sequences and intrusive thought: A self-disruption explanation. *Cognitive Therapy and Research, 12*, 441–457.

Miller, G. A., Galanter, E., & Pribram, K. H. (1960). *Plans and the structure of behavior*. New York: Holt, Rhinehart, & Winston.

Nisbett, R. E., & Wilson, T. (1977). Telling more than we can know: Verbal reports on mental processes. *Psychological Review, 84*, 213–259.

Nolen-Hoeksema. S. (1987). Sex differences in unipolar depression: Evidence and theory. *Psychological Bulletin, 101*, 259–282.

Nolen-Hoeksema, S. (1991). Responses to depression and their effects on the duration of depressive episodes. *Journal of Abnormal Psychology, 100*, 259–282.

Nolen-Hoeksema, S., & Lyubomirsky, S. (1994). *Effects of ruminative and distracting responses on problem-solving and attributions*. Manuscript submitted for publication.

Nolen-Hoeksema, S., & Morrow, J. (1991). A prospective study of depression and posttraumatic stress symptoms after a natural disaster: The 1989 Loma Prieta Earthquake. *Journal of Personality and Social Psychology, 61*, 115–121.

Perloff, L. S. (1983). Perception of invulnerability to victimization. *Journal of Social Issues, 39*, 41–61.

Powers, W. T. (1973). *Behavior: The control of perception*. Chicago: Aldine-Atherton.

Pyszczynski, T., & Greenberg, J. (1987). Self-regulatory perseveration and the depressive self-focusing style: A self-awareness theory of reactive depression. *Psychological Bulletin, 102*, 122–138.

Rachman, S. (1981). Part I. Unwanted intrusive cognitions. *Advances in Behavior Research and Therapy, 3*, 89–99.

Rachman, S., & DeSilva, P. (1978). Abnormal and normal obsessions. *Behaviour Research and Therapy, 16*, 233–248.

Rachman, S., & Hodgson, R. J. (1980). *Obsessions and compulsions*. Englewood Cliffs, NJ: Prentice-Hall.

Rholes, W. S., & Pryor, J. B. (1982). Cognitive accessibility and causal attributions. *Personality and Social Psychology Bulletin, 8*, 719–727.

Roemer, L., & Borkovec, T. D. (1993). Worry: Unwanted cognitive activity that controls unwanted somatic experience. In D. M. Wegner & J. W. Pennebaker (Eds), *Handbook of mental control* (pp. 220–238). Englewood Cliffs, NJ: Prentice-Hall.

Roney, C. J. R., & Sorrentino, R. M. (1995). Reducing self-discrepancies or maintaining self-congruence? Uncertainty orientation, self-regulation, and performance. *Journal of Personality and Social Psychology, 68*, 485–497.

Rosenzweig, S. (1943). An experimental study of "repression" with special reference to need-persistive and ego-defensive frustration. *Journal of Experimental Psychology, 32,* 64–74.

Ross, M. (1989). The relation of implicit theories to the construction of personal histories. *Psychological Review, 96,* 341–357.

Rude, S., Zentner, M., & Morrow, D. (1993 August). *Building a model of attention regulation relevant to depressive memory impairments.* Paper presented at the annual convention of the American Psychological Society, Montreal.

Schneider, W., & Shiffrin, R. M. (1977). Controlled and automatic human information processing: I. Detection, search and attention. *Psychological Review, 84,* 1–66.

Schwarz, N., & Bless, H. (1991). Happy and mindless, but sad and smart? The impact of affective states on analytic reasoning. In J. P. Forgas (Ed.), *Emotion and social judgment* (pp. 55–72). Elmsford, New York: Pergamon.

Silver, R. L., Boon, C., & Stones, M. H. (1983). Searching for meaning in misfortune: Making sense of incest. *Journal of Social Issues, 39,* 81–102.

Singer, J. L. (1966). *Daydreaming.* New York: Random House.

Singer, J. L. (1975). Navigating the stream of consciousness: Research in daydreaming and related inner experience. *American Psychologist, 30,* 727–738.

Singer, J. A., & Salovey, P. (1995). Motivated memory: Self-defining memories, goals, and affect regulation. In L. L. Martin & A. Tesser (Eds.), *Striving and feeling: Interactions between goals affect and self-regulation.* Hillsdale, NJ: Lawrence Erlbaum Associates.

Srull, T. K., & Wyer, R. S. (1979). The role of category accessibility in the interpretation of information about persons: Some determinants and implications. *Journal of Personality and Social Psychology, 37,* 1660–1672.

Strauman, T. J. (1995). Self-beliefs, self-evaluation, and depression: A perspective on emotional vulnerability. In L. L. Martin & A. Tesser (Eds.), *Striving and feeling: Interactions between goals affect and self-regulation.* Hillsdale, NJ: Lawrence Erlbaum Associates.

Taylor, S. E., & Schneider, S. K. (1989). Coping and the simulation of events. *Social Cognition, 7,* 174–194.

Tesser, A. (1978). Self-generated attitude change. In L. Berkowitz (Ed.), *Advances in experimental social psychology* (Vol. 11, pp. 289–338). New York: Academic Press.

Tesser, A. (1988). Toward a self-evaluation maintenance model of social behavior. In L. Berkowitz (Ed.), *Advances in experimental social psychology* (Vol. 21, pp. 181–227). New York: Academic Press.

Tesser, A., Martin, L. L., & Mendolia, M. (1995). The impact of thought on attitude extremity and attitude–behavior consistency. In R. E. Petty & J. A. Krosnick (Eds.), *Attitude strength: Antecedents and consequences.* Hillsdale, NJ: Lawrence Erlbaum Associates.

Uleman, J. S. (1989). A framework for thinking intentionally about unintended thought. In J. S. Uleman & J. A. Bargh (Eds.), *Unintended thought* (pp. 425–449). New York: Guilford Press.

Vallacher, R. R., & Wegner, D. M. (1987). What do people think they're doing? Action identification and human behavior. *Psychological Review, 94,* 3–15.

von Bertalanffy, L. (1968). *General systems theory.* New York: Braziller.

Walster, E. (1964). The temporal sequence of post-decision processes. In L. Festinger (Ed.), *Conflict, decision and dissonance* (pp. 112–127). Stanford: Standford University Press.

Wegner, D. M., Schneider, D. J., Carter, S. R., III, & White, T. L. (1987). Paradoxical effects of thought suppression. *Journal of Personality and Social Psychology, 53,* 5–13.

Wenzlaff, R. M. (1993). The mental control of depression: Psychological obstacles to emotional well-being. In D. M. Wegner & J. W. Pennebaker (Eds), *Handbook of mental control* (pp. 239–257). Englewood Cliffs, NJ: Prentice-Hall.

Wicklund, R. A. (1986). Orientations to the environment versus preoccupation with human potential. In R. M. Sorrentino & E. T. Higgins (Eds.), *Handbook of motivation and cognition: Foundations of social behavior* (pp. 64–95). New York: Guilford.

Wicklund, R. A., & Gollwitzer, P. M. (1982). *Symbolic self-completion*. Hillsdale, NJ: Lawrence Erlbaum Associates.

Williams, C. W. (1993). The effect of priming causal dimensional categories on social judgments. *Social Cognition, 11*, 223–242.

Wyer, R. S., & Gordon, S. E. (1982). The recall of information about persons and groups. *Journal of Experimental Social Psychology, 18*, 128–164.

Wyer, R. S., & Srull, T. K. (1989). *Memory and cognition in its social context*. Hillsdale, NJ: Lawrence Erlbaum Associates.

Yaniv, I., & Meyer, D. E. (1987). Activation and metacognition of inaccessible stored information: Potential bases for incubation effects in problem-solving. *Journal of Experimental Psychology: Learning, Memory, and Cognition, 13*, 187–205.

Young, J. (1987). *The role of selective attention in the attitude–behavior relationship*. Unpublished doctoral dissertation, University of Minnesota.

Zeigarnik, B. (1938). On finished and unfinished tasks. In W. D. Ellis (Ed.), *A source book of gestalt psychology* (pp. 300–314). New York: Harcourt, Brace, & World. (Reprinted and condensed from *Psychologische Forshung*, 1927, *9*, 1–85.)

# Chapter 2

Goal Engagement and the Human Experience

Charles S. Carver
University of Miami

Martin and Tesser have presented what I think is an interesting and plausible account of rumination. That I find much to agree with in their chapter is not surprising. Many of the assumptions they make are the same as those that I make. Much of the conceptual structure of their analysis of rumination resembles closely the conceptual structure I have applied to other problems. My own interest focuses on the structure of behavioral self-regulation and on the origin and function of affect within that framework. I've devoted relatively little thought to rumination. Yet the principles I've relied on in sketching a picture of behavior and affect (e.g., Carver & Scheier, 1990a, 1990b, 1995) also appear to be useful in Martin and Tesser's attempt to conceptualize rumination.

I begin this comment by restating the broad underpinnings of Martin and Tesser's theory. Theirs is a theory about some of the manifestations of being committed to goals. It is also a theory in which the concept of discrepancy plays a critical role. That is, rumination is potentiated by discrepancies—more specifically, by *discrepancies that are not moving adequately toward their intended reduction*. This characterization of the origin of rumination is very similar to the Carver and Scheier (1990a) view of the origin of negative affect. (I focus here on rumination from inadequate progress toward a desired goal; I defer comments on rumination from unexpectedly quick progress to the end of this commentary.)

Discrepancies that prompt rumination sometimes exist between perceptions and mental models (e.g., when events are hard to interpret or to see meaning in). Mostly, though, discrepancies that lead to rumination are those that exist between desired rates of progress toward goals and current progress toward those goals. Goals vary widely, but a critical issue is their importance. Discrepancies lead to rumination only to the extent that the goals are important. Being important means that the goal is itself a high-level goal or exists in direct service of a high-level goal.

Thus the grounding themes behind this theory are the idea that goals determine the direction of people's actions, the idea that difficulty in moving toward goals leads to rumination, and the idea that this happens only when the forward movement pertains to an important or higher order goal. These themes are very much the same as those that underlie our analysis of behavior and affect (Carver & Scheier, 1990a, 1990b, 1995), though they play themselves out a bit differently in Martin and Tesser's analysis of rumination.

ISSUES

Martin and Tesser made a number of points about the conditions that elicit and prevent rumination. Along the way, they raised several issues concerning the nature of humans as self-regulatory beings. In what follows, I point to a few of these issues and say a little bit more about them. In the process of doing this, I'm going to un-make some of the distinctions that Martin and Tesser made in their chapter, in order to highlight some similarities of function that transcend the distinctions. This will permit me to ask from a different angle—an angle focusing on functional rather than descriptive properties—what each distinction implies.

Rumination as Problem Solving and Attempted Discrepancy Reduction

Martin and Tesser envision a system in which the thwarting of goal-directed effort recruits a set of cognitive processes that yield the phenomenology of rumination. The cognitive processes are aimed at unblocking the path to goal attainment, though they don't always do so directly or even successfully. Martin and Tesser see rumination as an attempt at discrepancy reduction. It's an attempt at problem solving—even when it isn't resolving the problem. The fact that it doesn't always have its desired effect should not be surprising, nor should this distract from rumination's purpose. Not every attempt at goal attainment is successful, nor is all problem solving successful. Not every instance of rumination lights a path to the goal. Yet the assumption that rumination is aimed at discrepancy reduction points to a functional similarity between rumination and goal-directed action.

2. GOAL ENGAGEMENT

Goal-directed action, which Martin and Tesser treat as distinct from rumination, is (obviously) also aimed at discrepancy reduction. Indeed, it is often aimed at the very same discrepancies to which rumination is directed. Action and the thoughts that accompany it dominate the overall discrepancy reduction effort when obstacles are not encountered or when they are minimal (see Fig. 2.1). In contrast to this, rumination dominates the overall discrepancy reduction effort when the action is thwarted.

Martin and Tesser distinguish rumination from the thoughts that accompany goal-directed action primarily on the grounds that rumination is recurrent, whereas the thoughts accompanying consciously mediated action are not. Although this is probably true, I think it is also misleading. When your efforts are moving you smoothly toward your goal, there is no need for the accompanying thoughts to be recurrent. Recurrence of the thoughts is necessary only when your efforts aren't moving you forward. Surely at a descriptive level a distinction between recurrence and nonrecurrence of the thoughts is useful. But emphasis on this distinction tends to obscure the fact that both kinds of thought have the same underlying purpose: moving the person toward the goal.

The recurrence criterion, then, seems to be an indirect reflection of the state of being "stuck" (cf. Shelby & Tredinnick, 1995). Recurrence of thought comes when progress is stifled. In contrast, there is little or no recurrence when there is smooth forward motion.

Rumination, Consciousness, and Prioritization

Martin and Tesser distinguish between rumination and incubation on the grounds that rumination is conscious, whereas incubation is not. Both, however, are presumably aimed at problem solving and, ultimately, dis-

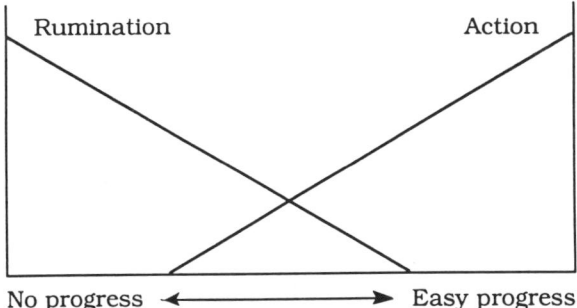

FIG. 2.1. When a person is self-regulating with respect to a goal and progress is relatively easy, action and the thoughts that accompany action dominate the discrepancy reduction effort. When progress is thwarted, rumination dominates. When progress is intermediate, both processes occur.

crepancy reduction. Thus, they have the same goals, but they differ with respect to the criterion of consciousness. What is the meaning or implication of this criterion?

I see the answer to this question as being bound up with the idea of prioritization. The idea that people prioritize among their goals comes up at several points in the Martin and Tesser chapter, but I think it deserves even more attention than it received there. As Martin and Tesser noted (in line with Klinger and others), keeping track of what information is more important to attend to and what is less important is a critical issue for a self-regulating organism (see also Lord & Levy, 1994). How does this issue of scheduling relate to consciousness?

One view is that the phenomenology of conscious experience reflects the end result of a great many implicit decisions (at preattentive levels) that some information matters more than other information. The information that matters most is what winds up in consciousness. According to this view, then, when rumination occurs, thoughts appear in consciousness unbidden; the information making up the rumination has been preattentively evaluated as important—indeed, more important than whatever the person was already doing. More specifically, the emergence of rumination seems to imply that some alternative goal is being judged as important enough that the lack of progress toward that goal is forcing a temporary shift in priorities.

Several aspects of the Martin and Tesser discussion fit this picture. For example, they say that rumination is more likely when the thoughts have affective connotations. This statement brings to mind Simon's (1967) argument about the nature and meaning of affect—that affect constitutes an internal call for reprioritization among goals. I think it may be reasonable to argue that the affect represents a call for reprioritization, and the rumination is the mental activity that follows from that priority shift (preattentive activity says that this matters most right now; therefore this is what you will think about now).

Similarly, Martin and Tesser emphasize that rumination is more likely to occur with respect to important goals than to unimportant goals. This is eminently consistent with a scheduling model such as Simon's. In his model, reprioritization isn't called for strongly whenever *any* goal is thwarted; such a call is strong only when an *important* goal is thwarted or threatened. The more important the goal, the stronger the affect generated, the stronger the call for reprioritization, and (as Martin and Tesser assert) the more likely it is that rumination will occur regarding the goal. As I noted earlier, though, this last step in the descriptive chain also assumes the unavailability of an action that would resolve the threat to the goal. If an action is available, everything follows up to the rumination, but the action would occur instead (cf. Fig. 2.1).

This general view implies that the human organism is pursuing a large—perhaps massive—set of goals in parallel. Some are accorded high priority by biological necessity, others by experience. None of these important goals disrupts the conscious pursuit of a currently focal goal with intrusion of ruminative thought (or action), however, until a relative lack of progress toward its attainment has been noted within the system. Thus, many pursuits must be monitored simultaneously, though a great deal of this happens outside consciousness (Carver & Scheier, 1990a, 1995).

Let me return to the difference between rumination and incubation, which prompted this detour into the realm of prioritization. The involvement of consciousness in the one type of event but not the other may be seen as indicating the place on the queue that is presently occupied by the goal involved. If its priority is high, the result is more likely to be rumination. If its place is lower, then its access to processing resources may be restricted to those available to incubation.

Rumination and Disengagement

I wrote a bit earlier that negative affect is more likely to result from disruption of movement toward important goals than less important ones. Thwarting of an important goal is more likely to prompt reprioritization—thus also rumination—than is thwarting of a trivial goal. This portrayal disregards one further point, however, which is important in its own right.

Sometimes when people are unable to move toward goals, they disengage from further pursuit of them (Carver & Scheier, 1990b; Klinger, 1975). A person who has disengaged from a goal (i.e., is no longer committed to its pursuit or attainment; Klinger, 1975) is not likely to ruminate about it. The goal is no longer relevant to the person. Thus, successful disengagement from a goal is another mechanism by which rumination can be prevented or stopped.

Why don't people always disengage from goals that they are unable to move toward? My usual answer (and the answer alluded to by Martin and Tesser) derives from the notion of hierarchicality (Carver & Scheier, 1990a, 1995; Carver, Scheier, & Pozo, 1992). People disengage readily from low order goals that don't matter much for the attainment of higher order goals (see Fig. 2.2). It's much harder, though, to disengage from low order goals that matter a great deal for the attainment of higher order goals. Giving up on such a low level goal means creating a discrepancy at the higher level, a discrepancy that may be hard to remedy. How hard it will be to remedy the higher level discrepancy depends on the availability of alternative paths to its attainment. If there are no alternative paths, it will be extremely hard

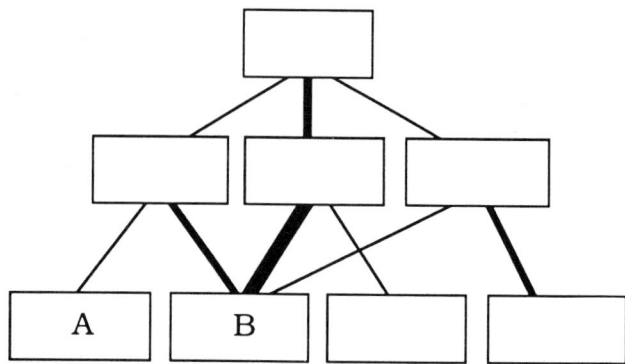

FIG. 2.2. Importance accrues to a lower order goal because its attainment contributes in a major way to attainment of a higher order goal (indicated here by a thicker line) or because its attainment contributes to several higher order goals at once (indicated here by multiple upward projections). On both of these criteria, lower goal A is relatively unimportant, and B is more important. Disengaging from A is relatively easy, because any discrepancy thus created at the higher level can be remedied in other ways. Disengaging from B is harder, because doing so creates higher level discrepancies at the higher level that are more difficult to remedy (from Carver & Scheier, 1995).

to remedy the discrepancy. As a result, it will be extremely hard to disengage from the lower level goal.

The main point at the moment is that some goals can be disengaged from easily, others not. A problem encountered with the former goal won't initiate much rumination because the person can simply disengage from the goal (as opposed to the fact that the goal would, in any case, be low in priority). A problem with the latter goal is more likely to prompt rumination because disengagement is so much more difficult. Given the inability to disengage and the apparent inability to move forward, the discrepancy-reduction system's remaining option is to ruminate.

Coping, Emotion, and Rumination

Discussion of rumination often leads to discussion of coping, because so much rumination derives from stressful events. Discussion of coping today tends to assume three classes of coping reactions (Holahan & Moos, 1987; Lazarus & Folkman, 1984). Problem-focused coping is doing something to remove the stressor or blunt its impact. Emotion-focused coping, a somewhat more controversial concept, is doing something to diminish the distress emotions that are being experienced. What makes this concept controversial is that emotion-focused coping is a diverse array of responses that often are at cross purposes to one another (Carver, Scheier, & Weintraub, 1989). A third class of responses is avoidance coping (sometimes also seen as emotion focused), which often has overtones of disengaging from the goal with which the stressor is interfering. In effect, problem-focused coping is explicitly problem solving; emotion-focused coping is problem solving that is more haphazard and superficially aimed (i.e., the goal is to reduce the feelings rather than to remove the conditions that produce the feelings); avoidance coping is refusing to problem solve.

Where does rumination fit into this scheme? I think rumination can potentially be classed as either problem-focused coping or emotion-focused coping, depending on the content of the rumination. Thinking about a blocked goal path (problem-focused rumination) may yield a way to remove the block. However, thinking about one's feelings (emotion-focused rumination), seems not to be a very good way to make them go away. Research by Nolen-Hoeksema (e.g., 1991), which makes this case, focuses on people who ruminate about their emotions. These people surely are ineffective copers. I want to caution, though, that this research does not show that rumination per se is invariably an ineffective response to distress. It shows that this particular focus for rumination is a poor choice. The distress won't go away and stay away (in theory) until something unblocks movement toward the goal. Other instances of rumination, with other focuses, may have such an effect, though emotion-directed rumination clearly does not.

Rumination Is Sometimes Unpleasant and Sometimes Not

Martin and Tesser noted that sometimes rumination is unpleasant and undesired and sometimes it isn't. What makes the difference between these cases? I suggest that the answer is partly a matter of <u>the person's expectations of eventually attaining the goal.</u>

Sometimes rumination is little more than the conscious anticipating of actions that are desired but can't be implemented at present for some reason. For example, the expectant mother can't yet play with her baby, but she can plan out and mentally rehearse some of the ways she will do so later on. This problem-solving activity (planning and rehearsal) is preparing her for an action that she thinks is very likely to take place in the future; it just can't take place yet. The act is presently thwarted, but the subjective probability of its eventual occurrence is quite high.

Often the problem-solving quality of rumination is focused explicitly on trying to find a way to remove an obstacle (e.g., the researcher needs a way to satisfy the reviewer of a rejected manuscript and ruminates over possible responses; a woman wants to convince a man she's right for her and ruminates over how to make him see the light). In such cases, an act (e.g., having the manuscript published, having a close relationship) is thwarted, and the subjective probability of its eventual occurrence may range from high to low.

Sometimes the problem solving in rumination is aimed at trying to create conditions that are extremely unlikely (e.g., yearning for a loved one to return from the dead or rescind a breakup). Sometimes it is aimed at trying to make sense of something that seems senseless (e.g., the family of the victim of a drunk driver may try to find meaning in the event for years afterward). In these cases, the act (raising the dead; finding meaning in the accident, putting it to rest, and moving on) is thwarted, and the subjective probability of its eventual occurrence is probably quite low.

I think that when rumination is occasioned by disrupted movement toward a goal, the unpleasantness and undesirability of the rumination will be proportional to the subjective probability of eventual forward movement. The more unfavorable the expectancy of forward movement, the more unpleasant and undesirable the rumination. Here, then, is another conceptual link between Martin and Tesser's analysis of rumination and our approach to action: subjective unpleasantness being related to unfavorable expectancies for eventual goal attainment (cf. Carver & Scheier, 1990a, 1990b).

Rumination Is Unintentional

Martin and Tesser argue that rumination is unintentional rather than planned, induced rather than directed. It may be cued by a stimulus in the environment or it may just appear in consciousness. In either case, however, it consists of mental activity that is not required by whatever action the person is performing at the present time. In Klinger's terms, it is respondent thought, not operant.

When I wrote earlier that a mechanism evaluates the priority to be accorded a particular goal, I had in mind a mechanism that operates outside consciousness. Only the results of its deliberations appear in consciousness. When this mechanism induces such an involuntary reprioritization, the change in the person's thoughts would probably feel respondent rather than operant, at least at first. If the person instead were facing a problem that had to be solved as part of the flow of a particular goal-directed action sequence (e.g., locking the keys in the car on the way to dinner), the problem-solving activity that resulted might well feel more operant. This wouldn't be rumination, however, because it is occurring as part of the effort to attain a focal goal.

How important is this respondent characteristic of rumination? I don't know. Clearly the two cases "feel" different. The operant feel is part of what gives people subjective cause to believe in free will. The operant quality feels volitional, self-directive, as though the person is in charge of mental content. The respondent quality can make a person feel out of control, as though his or her will might have lost its potency. But apart from the subjective sense, how does this difference matter?

I don't have much of an answer for this question, though I think it is an interesting one. I have long suspected that we make too much of this distinction. People assimilate countless numbers of unexpected, unplanned events into the flow of their experience, even in the midst of what they think of as self-directive activity. To put it differently, even fairly large parts of what we would tend to think of as operant thought are really respondent. The distinction may seem more pronounced in principle than it is in actuality. It may also feel more profound to the Western mind than it is in actuality. In many other respects the experiences are similar. Sometimes people surf in front of a wave that's pushing them; sometimes they're on the back side of the wave pushing to keep themselves on the source of power. The experiences aren't quite the same, but both are surfing.

Rumination and Positive Discrepancies

A final set of issues bears on the idea that rumination also occurs with respect to very good outcomes. Martin and Tesser assert that rumination does occur in such circumstances, though their terminology renders this assertion more than a little ironic. That is, throughout their chapter they say that "problematic" progress toward a goal leads to rumination, and "nonproblematic" progress leads to the absence of rumination. It is clear that their emphasis is on rumination that follows from things going badly. Yet Martin and Tesser also hold that rumination follows from things going unexpectedly well. How can this be? If rumination is problem solving, where's the problem in this situation?

For me to address this question requires me to say a little more about the relation between rumination and affect. Martin and Tesser suggest that the conditions leading to rumination are more or less the same as those that lead to affect. I agree. Their conditions for problem-produced rumination seem almost precisely those that we have argued underlie negative affect (Carver & Scheier, 1990a, 1995). If I pursue the parallelism between affect and rumination one step farther, I should accept a similarity between positive affect (which I think arises from unexpectedly quick progress) and some positive form of rumination (see Table 2.1, presented as a substitute for Martin and Tesser's Table 1.1, which I don't think fits their line of argument very well).

Positive rumination is exemplified by basking (rumination about the present) and reminiscing (rumination about the past). I certainly believe that both basking and reminiscing occur, but why? Do they have a function? If so, what is it?

TABLE 2.1
Modes of Ruminative Thought

Nature of "Problematic" Progress	Past	Present	Future
Negative discrepancy (no progress or too little progress)	Working through; regret	Current concern	Worry; doubt
No discrepancy (nonproblematic progress)	—	—	—
Positive discrepancy (better progress than needed)	Reminiscing	Basking	Anticipation; confidence

Note. Each cell assumes a desired endpoint, with perception of either inadequate progress or a high rate of progress, regarding an event in the past, present, or future (the middle row constitutes the condition in which rumination is expected to be minimal).

Positive affect, in my view, is a signal that you're making better progress at something than you expected (or needed) to do. I have also argued that (because progress is better than needed) positive affect typically leads to "coasting" with regard to that domain, and thus tends to be comparatively short-lived. If the conditions that produce affect also produce rumination, maybe rumination is simply the cognitive content that comes along with (or in response to) the affect. If so, positive rumination should be subject to the same constraints as positive affect. As one example, if my view of positive affect is right, positive rumination should be short-lived.

Basking reflects the fact that you have just done (or are presently doing) better than expected or needed. As Martin and Tesser said, it reaffirms the absence of a problematic discrepancy. It's not problem solving, because you don't have a problem. To the contrary, it's a continuing affirmation that you don't have a problem, that you're ahead of the game. Because you don't have a problem, you don't have to do anything. This characterization of basking leads me to suspect that it leads to coasting. If this were so (and I know of no information on the question), it would make the process behind basking look very much like the process behind positive affect as we have characterized it.

What of reminiscing? I think this case is more complicated. Reminiscing about a past success is sometimes prompted by having the same feeling in the present. Often, however, it is prompted by a current dissatisfaction. In such cases, reminiscence might well reflect problem solving.

There are several ways in which reminiscence might represent a problem-solving response to a current dissatisfaction. Reminiscence can create a primitive wish fulfillment, temporarily eliminating the current dissatisfaction by creating a mental image of success. As Freud pointed out, however, this solution is extremely limited. Reminiscence can also serve as an implicit—or even explicit—problem-solving tactic in a more reality-oriented fashion. Recalling a past success may suggest differences between how you dealt with the past situation and how you're dealing with the present one. Indeed, people sometimes even reminisce precisely in order to search for such differences. Another set of possibilities is suggested by the mood-altering effect of reminiscence. Thinking about a past success may make you feel more optimistic about enjoying a similar success now, by reinstituting the positive emotions associated with the past event. It may also yield better access to solution-relevant cues from the past event. In all these cases, reminiscence would be occurring in the service of problem solving.

Does Rumination Follow From Doing Unexpectedly Well?

One more question must be addressed in this context, concerning the evidence that basking or rumination actually is prompted by the condition of having done better than expected at something. Martin and Tesser presented a good deal of evidence from a variety of paradigms that failure to attain goals promotes ruminative thought. In contrast, they presented no evidence at all concerning the effects of doing better than expected.

Presumably the goal-attainment groups in the various experiments experienced nonproblematic progress toward their goal and therefore didn't ruminate. What would happen, though, to subjects who were told they had wildly exceeded their goals? According to Martin and Tesser's analysis, these subjects should display cognitive effects similar to those shown by subjects who failed to attain their goals. Maybe so. As suggested earlier, however, I would predict (along with Martin and Tesser) that if such effects occur, they will be shorter lived than those occurring among the failure subjects.

AN IMPLICIT WORLD VIEW

Martin and Tesser's chapter focuses on rumination as a particular set of phenomena. However, their picture of the dynamics of rumination has implications that go well beyond rumination per se. As I have suggested in this chapter, the picture they sketched has some things to say about the fundamental nature of the organism within which rumination occurs.

Most obviously, this is an organism in which goals—concrete and abstract, low level and high level—are intimately woven into the fabric of behavior, of existence. Everything the organism does seems to occur in service of attaining goals (though not necessarily attaining them more rapidly than necessary). When movement forward is smooth and relatively unimpeded, cognition is organized by what is needed in the course of preparing and executing action. When action is impeded, though, more cognitive activity is recruited, aimed at overcoming the impediments. It may be effective in doing so, or it may not. The point seems to be to try to undo the knot that prevents forward motion.

This implicit world view is one of an organism struggling forward toward survival and successful adaptation. As is true in many discussions pertaining to survival, there appears to be an asymmetry. Rumination seems to be largely an effort to fix problems, to open up clogged pathways for attaining goals. Relatively little rumination constitutes pure celebration of success. Several writers have noted that positive affect doesn't have nearly the survival value that negative affect has (e.g., Taylor, 1991). For survival per se, it is more important to notice and fix what's wrong than to be happy about what's right. Perhaps, then, positive rumination is similarly less important than rumination about problems. On the other hand, to say that negative affect is more demanding or more important than positive affect is not to say that positive affect doesn't matter at all. Experiences of positive affect and positive rumination may well be needed to develop the ability to recognize when things *are* right.

What experiences matter—and in what ways—for optimal survival and adaptation are questions that certainly bear further examination. As in all our explorations of human behavior, the theoretical models that we use are among our most important tools. I believe that the sort of model that's been employed by Martin and Tesser (and by Carver and Scheier) will remain a useful tool as we continue to ruminate about questions such as these and struggle toward our goal of better understanding.

ACKNOWLEDGMENT

The author's current research is supported by the American Cancer Society (PBR-82) and the National Cancer Institute (CA-64710).

REFERENCES

Carver, C. S., & Scheier, M. F. (1990a). Origins and functions of positive and negative affect: A control-process view. *Psychological Review, 97*, 19–35.

Carver, C. S., & Scheier, M. F. (1990b). Principles of self-regulation: Action and emotion. In E. T. Higgins & R. M. Sorrentino (Eds.), *Handbook of motivation and cognition: Foundations of social behavior* (Vol. 2, pp. 3–52). New York: Guilford.

Carver, C. S., & Scheier, M. F. (1995). *On the self-regulation of behavior.* New York: Cambridge University Press, in preparation.

Carver, C. S., Scheier, M. F., & Pozo, C. (1992). Conceptualizing the process of coping with health problems. In H. S. Friedman (Ed.), *Hostility, coping, & health* (pp. 167–199). Washington, DC: American Psychological Association.

Carver, C. S., Scheier, M. F., & Weintraub, J. K. (1989). Assessing coping strategies: A theoretically based approach. *Journal of Personality and Social Psychology, 56*, 267–283.

Holahan, C. J., & Moos, R. H. (1987). Risk resistance and psychological distress: A longitudinal analysis with adults and children. *Journal of Abnormal Psychology, 96*, 3–13.

Klinger, E. (1975). Consequences of commitment to and disengagement from incentives. *Psychological Review, 82,* 1–25.

Lazarus, R. S., & Folkman, S. (1984). *Stress, appraisal, and coping.* New York: Springer.

Lord, R. G., & Levy, P. E. (1994). Moving from cognition to action: A control theory perspective. *Applied Psychology: An International Review, 43,* 335–398.

Nolen-Hoeksema, S. (1991). Responses to depression and their effects on the duration of depressive episodes. *Journal of Abnormal Psychology, 100,* 259–282.

Shelby, J. S., & Tredinnick, M. G. (1995). Crisis intervention with survivors of natural disaster: Lessons from Hurricane Andrew. *Journal of Counseling and Development, 73,* 491–497.

Simon, H. A. (1967). Motivational and emotional controls of cognition. *Psychology Review, 74,* 29–39.

Taylor, S. E. (1991). Asymmetric effects of positive and negative events: The mobilization-minimization hypothesis. *Psychological Bulletin, 110,* 67–85.

Chapter 3

Restructuring and Realigning Mental Models: Ruminations as Guides to Cognitive Home Repair

Leslie F. Clark
Emory University

Eight years ago I had the good fortune of bringing together 14 social psychologists to talk about the definition of ruminations in a small conference at the University of Memphis entitled "Stress, Ruminations, and Self-Relevant Cognition." Some, such as Roxanne Silver, were invited because they had been collecting field data on the nature of ruminations due to loss. Others were invited because of their experimental lab work on obsessive thought, affect priming, construct accessibility, and the consequences of reminiscence. Some had theories centered on the functions of rumination. Still others were invited due to their theoretical work incorporating a place for intrusive thought. Theories represented included self-complexity, action-identification, self-discrepancy, and the role of expression in stress reduction. It was at this meeting that Martin and Tesser first described their model of ruminations resulting from blocked goals.

At that time a number of the people invited were confused about why they had been invited or about why others had been invited. At the end of the two days nearly all agreed that their work was relevant to this slippery concept of rumination. Several contributions to that conference were later published as a separate section in the well-received edited volume *Unintended Thought* (Uleman & Bargh, 1989). For a time, yearly conferences were established on the topic of mental control, and a recent handbook on this topic followed. Many of the participants are serving as commentators for this volume.

Overall, the goal of the original conference was to discover connections between the participants' work in order to illuminate the phenomenon of ruminative thought. The conference was intended to go beyond the antecdoctal and measurement approaches to post-traumatic stress syndromes. Martin and Tesser's work addressed one potential mechanism for ruminative thought: It is the consequence of blocked goals. Eight years after the initial presentation of their ideas I find I am less enthusiastic about such an explanation than I was at that conference.

Martin and Tesser's argument of goal blockage is a simple one, and simplicity is seductive. An elegant theory is much more appealing than a cumbersome one. However, utility is as important a criterion of theory evaluation as parsimony, and on this dimension what Martin and Tesser offer us falls short. Although they have done a commendable job of rounding up the usual suspects of related cognitive processes (e.g., counterfactual reasoning, basking, mental simuations) they fail to explain adequately how these processes are related to a goal blockage theory of rumination. The useful taxonomy of rumination types they offer may serve as a beginning step in this direction.

I have two particularly disturbing concerns with their goal blockage theory of rumination. The first is that the level of explanation for goals and goal blockage is so loosely articulated that it loses explanatory power. Second, the assumptions and evidence appear uninformed by the context surrounding the real-life experience of rumination, hence both the content of rumination and their implications for the individual are left largely unexplored. My concerns can be summed up in two questions: When is a goal more than a goal? What gets missed?

WHEN IS A GOAL MORE THAN A GOAL?

Reading Martin and Tesser's chapter I was reminded of a criticism Fiske and Linville (1980) made of schema theory, namely, that the schema concept had overextended itself. Many reseachers had used the term *schema* to refer to any form and level of knowledge structure and often used the term in isolation from any theoretical framework.

I fear that Martin and Tesser have not yet articulated the concept of goals sufficiently to make their theory testable in some cases. It is also a shame that they did not take this opportunity to relate a cybernetic model to the myriad works of goal theorists from cognitive science.

There are three features of cognitive science models that appear to be missing from the Martin and Tesser conceptualization of goals. First, goals are not seen as being represented only in terms of subordinate and superordinate relations but in horizontal relations as well. Yet little was said about the ramifications of competing, horizontally ordered sister goals.

Second, most cognitive science theories present goal structures as being embedded in a larger representational framework, as opposed to an isolated hierarchic order. The hierarchies themselves are related to other constructs such as the prerequisite physical, social, and emotional states for goal achievement (e.g., necessary skills, efficacy expectations, real-world constraints) as well as the consequences of goal completion and failure.

Third, the implication of such a grand cognitive scheme is that achievement of a goal affects the pattern as a whole. Hence the overall cognitive representation is constantly updating itself based on the rippling effects of changes in goals, goal achievement, constraining world events and states, and so on (see Graesser & Clark, 1985; Schank & Abelson, 1977, for examples of this approach). These systems theories are related to other cognitive processes such as comprehension, judgment, inference, memory, and the experience of affect. Martin and Tesser missed an opportunity to use such theoretical explanations as a way of exploring the relations among rumination-relevant cognitive processes.

WHAT GETS MISSED?

The model proposed by Martin and Tesser pays too little attention to the literature examining ruminations in real-world contexts. It is perhaps not by chance that of the eighteen studies described in the section on evidence for the theory, the vast majority are studies in which threats to IQ were invoked and intelligence tasks were used. These situations may adequately mirror the threats of self-esteem and needs for self-enhancement strategies experienced by victims of stressful life events (Taylor, 1983) but are probably inadequate for representing other aspects of victims' experiences that coincide with ruminations (e.g., suddenness of the threat, unknown future implications, the individual's inability to mount immediate coping responses).

There are several other aspects of the phenomenon that one misses by focusing on a goal/task perseverance explanation of rumination. Some of these include the dimensions on which ruminations may differ: vividness, duration, frequency, intrusiveness, or persistence (Tait & Silver, 1989), as well as the episodic nature of reliving the stressful event (Horowitz, 1982). These characteristics are defining features of ruminations, yet most of them do not receive much attention in Martin and Tesser's theory.

Determinants of the content of ruminations are also neglected in Martin and Tesser's model. They feel it is enough to cite two studies concerning the use of attributional processes for the comprehension of others' behaviors to illustrate how the content of ruminations is determined. Clearly clinicians and researchers of adaptation to stress feel that the determinants of ruminative content should not be given so little "air time" in a theory of rumination.

The goal concept also gives little attention to the overarching implications of a stressful event. Because in the current chapter Martin and Tesser largely ignored traumatic events, it leaves in the background issues such as adaptation tasks brought on by major shifts in role functioning, generalization of the conclusion of vulnerability, and phenomena akin to belief conversion that follow in the wake of traumatic life events. These consequences follow from the change inherent in the aftermath of such events and constitute major coping challenges for victims. How are these challenges met? Stress researchers highlight the link between the experience of ruminations and effortful cognitive processes used in understanding or mentally readjusting to the changes incurred from the experience of major life change. In the remainder of the commentary, I discuss the relation between rumination and meaning processes.

RUMINATION IN THE CONTEXT OF LIFE EXPERIENCES

Change occurs when people take stock, evaluate goal progress or priorities, and determine their satisfaction with themselves and their lives. However, the first reactions to life change may well be ruminations. More effortful constructive cognitive processes may follow afterward. The Millar, Tesser, and Millar (1988) study is the only example of this element of change in a real-life experience that Martin and Tesser discussed. It is unclear to me whether the resulting ruminations experienced by subjects in that study were due to a lack of goal progress or by the upheaval of normal daily activities and relationships. That is, it may be the change, and not goal progress per se that was responsible for the ruminations. Individuals may become aware of such a discrepancy in their lives when they experience goal blockage (see Clark, Henry, & Taylor, 1991, for an example in the area of infertility). However, external events (or internal events other than goal progress) may also trigger such a recognition of major change.

The construct of mental models has been used to refer to the stable representation of an individual's identity and aspirations as well as his or her views of the world. A mental models approach is more holistic than a goal blockage explanation and is better suited to the theories of mental representation from cognitive science discussed earlier in this commentary. Such mental models in the area of stress and coping have been called self- and world assumptions (Janoff-Bulman, 1989), life themes (Thompson & Janigan, 1988), and life perspectives (Collins, Taylor, & Stokam, 1990). An approach that focuses on the reparation of mental models speaks to the myriad ways in which people come to construe not only their goals and goal progress but also their self-views and world views. In short, a mental models aproach focuses on the evolving construction of one's reality.

REPARATION OF MENTAL MODELS

Victims of stressful events sometimes show dramatic changes in their basic beliefs about the world, beliefs that were unquestioned before the crisis situation arose. These changes in basic beliefs about the self and the world can endure for years after the event has occurred. Specifically, individuals who have experienced a traumatic event show a decrease in the belief that the world is a just and benevolent place and negative changes in their beliefs concerning self-worth (Janoff-Bulman, 1989).

There are two areas other than adjustment to traumatic stress that also discuss the relation among ruminative thought and the construction or reparation of mental models. These are *account building* in the close relationship area and *life review* among the elderly. Each of these three areas is discussed briefly in turn.

Adaptation to Trauma: Rumination and Making Meaning

Individuals under stress often experience thoughts dominated by themes and emotions related to the stressful event (Horowitz, 1982; Tait & Silver, 1989). These thoughts may intrude into one's awareness, taking the form of unbidden images or ideas, feelings that the individual has difficulty controlling, or some symbolic behavioral reenactment of a stressful event (Horowitz, 1982). According to Horowitz, intrusive thoughts (i.e., ruminations) are central to helping the individual to fit his or her understanding of a stressful event into the current mental models of the world (see also Silver, Boon, & Stone, 1983; Tait & Silver, 1989).

The difference in these approaches to rumination and the model offered by Martin and Tesser is not simply that the former are focused on adaptation to real-world traumas. In addition, they attempt to capture the coping and adjustment tasks that individuals undertake in the face of major life changes. These researchers have argued that ruminations serve as the triggers that prod individuals to reconsider life values, attitudes, and goals (see also Clark et al., 1991) as well as the data or building blocks used to reform one's mental models.

Adjustment to Relationship Break-ups: Rumination and Accounts

Researchers have documented that individuals can experience vivid and recurrent memories of past loves (Harvey, Flanary, & Morgan, 1986).

Collins and Clark (1989) found that even years after a relationship has ended, reports of a subjective sense of the relationship not really being over in the mind of the respondent was associated with a greater amount of rumination about the ex-partner and greater mental reliving of the episodic details of falling in love with that person. Although perhaps pleasant, the content of such rumination could be disturbing when compared to the actuality of the relationship loss. Yet it might be wrong to assume that such individuals hold the goal of reestablishing the relationship about which they are ruminating. How do people cope with such loss and their ruminative cognitive activity? Evidence suggests they often undergo a search for meaning much like victims of traumatic life events.

Research suggests that attributional activity is usually pervasive in close relationships but becomes particularly intensive during times of conflict (Harvey, 1987). Once a relationship is over the individuals involved may subject their memories to incessant causal analysis in a search for what happened and who was responsible (Bloom, Asher, & White, 1978). Answers to these questions impact on an individual's ability to cope with the changes and consequences inherent in relationship loss (Fletcher, 1983). The product of such endeavors to understand are referred to as *accounts* (Harvey, 1987; Harvey, Weber, Garvin, Huszti, & Garnick, 1986).

If individuals rejected by a past partner achieve a sense of understanding about what happened, they ruminate less about that ex-partner and less often experience a mental reliving of courtship details (Collins & Clark, 1989). Relationship accounts not only enhance self-esteem or increase feelings of mastery but also organize perceptions, plot the narrative of what happened, and serve as guidance to future decisions (Harvey, 1987). In short, the work of account-building is to repair and reconstruct one's mental models of the self and the (social) world.

Reminiscing Among the Eldery: Rumination and Life Review

Research on reminiscing activity among the elderly describes reminiscing as a reliving of the vivid details of a past life event (Molinari & Reichlin, 1985). Studies report that a high amount of reminiscing is associated with negative mood (Hyland & Ackerman, 1988) as well as positive mood (Havighurst & Glaser, 1972).

Reminiscing has also been examined for the role it plays in the life review process. Life review has been defined as cognitive activity that involves the interpretation and evaluation of past life events, including attempts to resolve past conflicts, an acceptance of the past, and psychological interpretations of the self (Coleman, 1974). The major goal of such an endeavor is to understand the causes of past life experiences in the hope of developing an integrative, coherent account of what happened and why it happened (Wong & Watt, 1991). The mental activity of life review involves the evaluative and integrative processes aimed at understanding past events and their implications for one's overall life (Coleman, 1974; Wong & Watt, 1991).

It is not clear how life review fits into the model proposed by Martin and Tesser. The mental activity involved appears to serve a holistic function. One might argue that life review occurs in response to ruminative activity that in turn accrues when the individual checks on the progress of high-level major life goals. Alternatively, ruminations may flow from the blocked superordinate goal of making sense of one's life. Such explanations miss the emphasis on the holistic and integrative nature of the product that ensues from life review and provide only simplistic explanations of the consequences for self and world views.

Expression as an Aid in the Reparation of Mental Models

By asking elderly individuals to talk about the past, Falot (1980) found that verbalizing reminiscences reduced depression and anxiety, whereas talking about present and future topics did not. There are also models of adjustment to stress that center on expression as a route to the reparation of mental models (Clark, 1993; Pennebaker, 1985; Pennebaker & Beall, 1986). These models focus on processes involved in the verbal labeling of events and the construction of a narrative for others; this may have beneficial effects on one's own adjustment to stress. In addition, Pennebaker (1985) documented the deleterious effects incurred by the inhibition of expression about stressors.

In a discussion of the adjustment benefits of expression, Clark (1993) described the cognitive processes involved in conversation. Specifically, ruminations ensue as a reaction to events experienced as distressing. However, when one enters into conversational interaction, he or she attempts to communicate a coherent explanation of the situation along with an account of his or her own reactions to it. The planful, creative nature of conversation may produce coherence, insights, emotional reactions, and a broadening of perspectives that directly enhances problem solving and interpretive coping. The understanding and adaptation that is facilitated by such conversational activity may in turn result in lowered rumination.

IS UNDERSTANDING NECESSARY AND SUFFICIENT FOR THE DISSIPATION OF RUMINATION?

The answer to this question is no. Clearly, ending mental perseverance regarding uncompleted tasks, as articulated by the studies described by

Martin and Tesser, does not require meaning processes or mental model reparation. In addition, even victims of traumatic stressful events can show adaptation over time without reporting lengthy or effortful attempts to find meaning or reconstruct mental models (see Wortman & Silver, 1989, for a review). Finally, even when individuals feel that they understand an event that required restructuring and realignment, they may still experience ruminations due to self-relevant implications of the understanding they achieved.

An example of this last point can be found in a study of the effects of understanding on rumination about a past lover (Collins & Clark, 1989). Specifically, for individuals who reported terminating a relationship in which they had made a large investment, those who claimed understanding of what happened ruminated more about the past relationship than did individuals who did not claim understanding. This higher level of rumination was comparable to that of the group of highly invested individuals who could not understand why their partners rejected them. In general, respondents who were experiencing greater rumination also felt more anger and depression after describing this relationship. In this case, understanding did not serve to lessen suffering over a past failed relationship. Collins and Clark argued that these individuals experienced more rumination because their action of terminating their own large investment invoked feelings of accountability that disallowed an easy sense of acceptance of the experience. Clearly the relationship between effortful cognitive reparations or explanations and the experience of rumination is an intriguing and complex one.

CONCLUSIONS

One may be able to translate specific research findings presented here in terms of goals and goal blockage. However, the question becomes, do we really learn something useful by doing so? What will we miss that could be gained by understanding humans not as actors pursuing discrete goals but as authors struggling to place ideas (ruminations) into their own evolving life narratives?

REFERENCES

Bloom, B. L., Asher, S. J., & White, S. W. (1978). Marital disruption as a stressor: A review and analysis. *Psychological Bulletin, 85,* 867–894.

Clark, L. F. (1993). Stress and the cognitive–conversational benefits of social interaction. *Journal of Social and Clinical Psychology, 12,* 25–55.

Clark, L. F., Henry, S. M., & Taylor, D. M. (1991). Cognitive examination of motivation for childbearing as a factor in and adjustment to infertility. In A. L. Stanton & C. Dunkel-Schetter (Eds.), *Infertility: Perspectives from stress and coping research* (pp. 157–180). New York: Plenum.

Coleman, P. G. (1974). Measuring reminiscence characteristics from conversations as adaptive features of old age. *International Journal of Aging and Human Development, 5,* 281–294.

Collins, J. E., & Clark, L. F. (1989). Responsibility and rumination: The trouble with understanding the dissolution of a relationship. *Social Cognition, 7,* 152–173.

Collins, R., Taylor, S. E., & Stokam, L. A. (1990). A better world or a shattered vision? Changes in life perspectives following victimization. *Social Cognition, 8,* 263–286.

Falot, R. D. (1980). The impact of mood on verbal reminiscing in later adulthood. *International Journal of Aging and Human Development, 10,* 385–400.

Fiske, S. T., & Linville, P. (1980). What does the schema concept buy us? *Personality and Social Psychological Bulletin, 6,* 543–557.

Fletcher, G. (1983). The analysis of verbal explanations for marital separatioon: Implications for attribution theory. *Journal of Applied Social Psychology, 13,* 245–258.

Graesser, A. C., & Clark, L. F. (1985). *Structures and procedures of implicit knowledge.* Norwood, NJ: Ablex.

Harvey, J. H. (1987). Attribution in close relationships: Research and theoretical developments. *Journal of Social and Clinical Psychology, 5,* 420–434.

Harvey, J. H., Flanary, R., & Morgan, M. (1986). Vivid memories of vivid lovers gone by. *Journal of Social and Personal Relationships, 3,* 359–373.

Harvey, J. H., Weber, A. L., Garvin, K. S., Huszti, H. C., & Garnick, N. N. (1986). Attribution in the termination of close relationships: A special focus on the account. In R. Gilmour & S. Duck (Eds.), *The emerging field of personal relationships.* Hillsdale, NJ: Lawrence Erlbaum Associates.

Havighurst, R. J. & Glaser, R. (1972). An exploratory study of reminiscence. *Journal of Gerontology, 27,* 245–253.

Horowitz, M. J. (1982). Stress response syndromes and their treatment. In L. Goldberger and S. Bresnitz (Eds.), *Handbook of stress: Theoretical and clinical aspects* (pp. 711–732). New York: Free Press.

Hyland, D. T., & Ackerman, A. M. (1988). Reminiscence and autobiographical memory in the study of the personal past. *Journal of Gerontology: Psychological Sciences, 43,* 35–39.

Janoff-Bulman, R. (1989). Assumptive worlds and the stress of traumatic events: Applications of the schema construct. *Social Cognition, 7,* 113–136.

Millar, K. U., Tesser, A., & Millar, M. G. (1988). The effects of a threatening life event on behavior sequences and intrusive thought: A self-disruption explanation. *Cognitive Theory and Research 12,* 441–457.

Molinari, V., & Reichlin, R. E. (1985). Life review reminiscence in the elderly: A review of the literature. *International Journal of Aging and Human Development, 20,* 81–92.

Pennebaker, J. (1985). Traumatic experience and psychosomatic disease: Exploring the roles of behavior inhibition, obsession, and confiding. *Canadian Psychology, 26,* 82–95.

Pennebaker, J., & Beall, S. (1986). Confronting a traumatic event: Toward an understanding of inhibition and disease. *Journal of Abnormal Psychology, 95,* 274–281.

Schank, R. C., & Abelson, R. (1977). *Scripts, plans, goals, and understanding.* Hillsdale, NJ: Lawrence Erlbaum Associates.

Silver, R. L., Boon, C., & Stone, M. (1983). Searching for meaning in misfortune: Making sense of incest. *Journal of Social Issues, 39,* 81–102.

Tait, R., & Silver, R. C. (1989). Coming to terms with major negative life events. In J. S. Uleman and J. A. Bargh (Eds.), *Unintended thought* (pp. 351–382). New York: Guilford.

Taylor, S. E. (1983). Adjustment to threatening events: A theory of cognitive adaptation. *American Psychologist, 38,* 1161–1173.

Thompson, S., & Janigan, A. (1988). Life schemes: A framework for understanding the search for meaning. *Journal of Social and Clinical Psychology, 7,* 260–280.
Uleman, J. S., & Bargh, J. (1989). *Unintended thought.* New York: The Guilford Press.
Wong, P. T. P., & Watt, L. M. (1991). What types of reminiscence are associated with successful aging? *Psychology and Aging, 6,* 272–279.
Wortman, C. B., & Silver, R. L. (1989). The myths of coping with loss. *Journal of Consulting and Clinical Psychology, 57,* 349–357.

Chapter 4

Ruminations on the Rebound

Ralph Erber
DePaul University

Daniel M. Wegner
University of Virginia

We believe that Martin and Tesser's theory is extremely useful and an excellent beginning, but it falls short of doing what a complete theory of rumination must do. What is missing is an *engine*, a causal mechanism that is sufficiently vigorous and well specified to create the most bizarre, oppressive, senseless, and unpleasantly repetitive ruminations of which the human mind is capable. Although Martin and Tesser seem to have crafted a fine automobile, the engine compartment is curiously empty.

Martin and Tesser hold that "rumination is instigated by discrepancies in goal process" (p. 11), or in other words, that goal blockage leads to rumination. This is a reasonable idea at its base, and it does a fine job of predicting some of life's most tragic cases of rumination. Thinking repeatedly about a loved one just after the person's death, for example, is a straightforward prediction from this theory, and it makes sense that the blocked goal of further interaction with the person could cause this rumination. Unfortunately, such straightforward cases are not the rule for ruminations. Why do some people obsess for years about cleanliness or about the organization of their sock drawer? Why do others keep thinking over and over about the possibility that they have run over someone with their car? Common yet hard-to-interpret cases require a mechanism that predicts both the *severity* of a particular rumination (i.e., its frequency of recurrence) and the seeming *senselessness* of the thought. When someone thinks for years about something that objectively should not matter, the blocked-goal theory is in serious trouble. In fact it is the most senseless ruminations that stand at the foundation of puzzling phenomena such as obsession, depression, and anxiety.

Martin and Tesser try to fix up the theory by adding some steps between the motive to ruminate and the topic of rumination. One possibility they suggest is that there are higher order goals that could power rumination about lower order goal objects. Another possibility they propose is that people start ruminating about things that they *believe* are blocked goals, even though these are not the real blocked goal. These attachments to the theory do not really do the trick, however, as they succeed only in introducing vagueness in how the topic of rumination is derived from the original blocked goal. The paths from a blocked goal to the ruminative thought topic become so convoluted as to rival even the most adventurous leaps of psychoanalytic interpretation. In fact, the path becomes so twisted that Martin and Tesser eventually end up saying that "there is no necessary correspondence between the occurrence of any given event and the onset or content of subsequent rumination" (p. 14). This is the squirrel-on-a-treadmill approach to a theoretical engine.

We would like to add to their auto the power of thought suppression. We believe that whereas incomplete goal attainment may *introduce* rumination and keep it running for some time, the mechanism that heightens rumination to pathological levels even in senseless cases is the person's attempt to suppress the initial ruminations. People try to suppress thoughts that are returning too often, and this effort ironically increases the frequency of the unwanted thought's return. Research has established that thought suppression increases the accessibility of suppressed thoughts (Wegner & Erber, 1992; Wegner, Erber, & Zanakos, 1993), that thought suppression leads to the rebound of suppressed thoughts once suppression is suspended (Wegner, Schneider, Carter, & White, 1987), that the suppression of emotional thoughts increases the strength of the emotional reaction (Wegner & Gold, 1995; Wegner, Shortt, Blake, & Paige, 1990), and that people who chronically suppress thoughts are susceptible to chronic rumination in the form of clinical obsessions, anxiety, and unwanted depressive thoughts (Wegner & Zanakos, 1994). There is good reason to believe, then, that this is a robust cause of rumination. It is powered by the deep and desperate desire people have to avoid the very thoughts about which they ruminate. Rather than echoes of incomplete goals, ruminations are continuously energized by the person's ongoing motive to eradicate them.

We think this is just the motor that belongs in Martin and Tesser's yawning engine compartment. It seems that Martin and Tesser are not interested in powering their vehicle this way, however, as they have conducted research in the specific attempt to explain suppression effects by means of their own rumination model. They conducted a replication of the Wegner et al. (1987) study in which one group of subjects received feedback indicating that they had succeeded at the task of suppressing thoughts of a white bear. As it turned out, these subjects were less susceptible to a subsequent rebound of white bear thoughts, as indicated by an accessibility measure, than subjects who had received no feedback regarding their suppression success. Martin and Tesser take this finding as evidence for a goal-blockage-based explanation of the rebound of thoughts following suppression. From their perspective, subjects who kept thinking of a white bear despite being asked not to think about it essentially failed to attain their goal of suppression. This nonattainment then leads to perseverance of goal-related (i.e., white bear related) thoughts, which is reflected in an increased accessibility of white bear thoughts. On the other hand, subjects who were told that they had succeeded at suppressing thoughts of a white bear attained their goal and thus should not ruminate. This is reflected in the decreased accessibility of white bear thoughts.

The findings of Martin and Tesser's white bear experiment create some problems for their theory of rumination. To begin with, the experiment shows that completing a goal of suppression can stop rumination. In a sense, the study thus rests on the assumption that suppression is what starts rumination in the first place. Although the study seems to have been intended as a challenge to the thought suppression theory, its message is that the self-perceived failure of thought suppression (rather than the nonattainment of just any goal) leads to rumination. People who fail to complete the goal of *suppression* are the ones who ruminate! It is possible to wonder whether the nonattainment of some other more mundane goal would regularly have the same effect.

There are further complications that prevent this experiment from speaking very clearly to the goal nonattainment theory. The theory allows, for example, that rumination could occur in the case of attainment as well as nonattainment of a goal. From this perspective, subjects in the success as well as in the failure condition might have been subject to rumination. What should have been different are the types of ruminative thoughts in which subjects engaged. Failure subjects with their hypothesized focus on discrepancies should have ruminated in a "current concerns" type of fashion, whereas success subjects should have ruminated by basking in the success of their goal attainment. Of course, it is not clear how the accessibility of white bear thoughts as a dependent measure could reflect the qualitative differences inherent in the different modes of ruminative thought.

One conclusion to be drawn, then, is that Martin and Tesser's white bear experiment has little or no bearing on the postulates of their theory of rumination. At the same time, the results *are* informative for understanding how and why the rebound following thought suppression occurs. We find this a most interesting set of findings, one that has implications for the two competing explanations currently available for the rebound effect. The first of these is the distracter/reminder explanation initially proposed by Wegner et al. (1987) and further elaborated by Wegner (1992). According to this explanation, suppressed thoughts become cognitively associated with the distracters people use in the service of suppression. When these distracters are later encountered, they serve as reminders of the thought once suppression is lifted. There is some evidence for this explanation. Specifically, rebound effects are strongest when people remain in the same context in which suppression took place and are somewhat ameliorated when the context is removed (Wegner, Schneider, Knutson, & McMahon, 1991; Wenzlaff, Wegner, & Klein, 1991).

The second explanation for the rebound following suppression is based on evidence that the unwanted thought becomes hyperaccessible to consciousness, especially when suppression occurs in the presence of cognitive load (Wegner & Erber, 1992; Wegner, Erber, & Zanakos, 1993). This seems to happen because when people attempt to suppress a thought, they employ a conscious, controlled search for distracters. At the same time, an automatic, ironic monitoring process checks for the recurrence of the suppressed thought. Cognitive load, such as distraction, time pressure, or another cognitively taxing task, infringes upon people's ability to search for distracters. At the same time, the automatic monitoring process is not influenced by load to the same extent, thus rendering the suppressed thought highly accessible to consciousness (Wegner, 1992, 1994).

It may be that this hyperaccessibility persists beyond the act of suppression, resulting in continued preoccupation with the suppressed thought. There are a couple of mechanisms that might account for this. One consequence of the ironic monitoring process may be that it primes the suppressed thought every time it is encountered (Macrae, Bodenhausen, Milne, & Jetten, 1994). Compared to subjects who are allowed to think about anything they want, subjects who are instructed to suppress a thought activate that very thought more frequently via the ironic monitoring process. There is ample evidence showing that the frequency with which a thought is activated is related to the speed with which the activation later decays (e.g., Higgins, 1989). The more frequent the activation, the less decay is to be expected. From this perspective, the rebound as a result of suppression may be an outcome of the increased activation of the suppressed thought, relative to people who were not instructed to suppress. Macrae et al. (1994) found evidence for this in a series of studies in which subjects were instructed to suppress thoughts of social stereotypes of a person. Relative to subjects who had been allowed to express their stereotypes, subjects who had been asked to suppress them subsequently reacted more derisively to a member of the stereotyped group. Furthermore, the applicable stereotype was more accessible to suppressors than nonsuppressors as assessed through response latencies on a lexical decision task. These findings, then, lend credence to the idea that the rebound following thought suppression may be an outcome of frequent priming caused by the ironic monitoring process.

The results of Martin and Tesser's white bear study create a problem for the priming/accessibility explanation of the rebound effect. If the rebound were simply caused by the frequency with which a thought becomes activated during suppression, then telling subjects that they succeeded should not attenuate the rebound because the decay of activation is not under conscious control. Instead, Martin and Tesser's findings suggest another way to understand the rebound effect. Like any other form of mental control, thought suppression is initiated and terminated through conscious intentions (Wegner, 1994). For example, self-imposed demands to stop giggling or being angry do not generally lead to immediate results. It may be that the process of suppression is similarly shut down in a gradual or incremental fashion despite the best conscious intentions. In other words, when experimenters terminate suppression by saying "stop suppressing," subjects may vary in the degree and the speed with which they turn off all the processes they employed in the service of suppression. This might be especially true for the ironic monitoring process because its automatic nature makes it less susceptible to conscious control than the controlled distracter search. From this perspective, the rebound following suppression may be due to the continued operation of the ironic monitoring process, which keeps detecting the suppressed thought in the absence of a conscious search for distracters.

It follows from this line of reasoning that anything that helps subjects to eliminate all processes involved in suppression also helps to eliminate rebound effects. When Martin and Tesser told subjects that they succeeded at suppressing thoughts about a white bear, they may have handed them the ticket to stop suppressing more completely than the subjects who received no feedback. As a consequence of a more thorough cessation of suppression, the ironic monitoring process set in motion by the intention to suppress is eliminated more effectively. After all, telling people that they succeeded at a task also informs them that no further energy needs to be expended toward its completion and that all previously employed strategies can now be abandoned. Simply telling people to stop doing something sends a more ambiguous message. For example, it could convey that they are to stop only temporarily or because they are presently doing something wrong. Either interpretation leaves open the possibility that the task may continue at some point in the near future and that the previously employed strategies may yet be needed.

From this point of view, telling people that they *failed* at suppression should have consequences similar to those when subjects are told that they succeeded. Either type of feedback sends the message that suppression can be turned off and that all the processes it entails can be terminated. This is an important point of divergence between Martin and Tesser's approach and ours. Martin and Tesser would predict that failure feedback would magnify the rebound because it implies nonattainment of the suppression goal. From the present perspective, failure feedback should attenuate the rebound because it tells people that they need not bother suppressing any further.

The present approach to explaining the rebound in terms of a gradual shutdown of suppression may also explain why the rebound is attenuated by a change in context (Wegner et al., 1987; Wenzlaff et al., 1991). It may be that a change in context upon the formal termination of suppression is functionally equivalent to the realization that one has succeeded or failed at the task. Switching to a different context may be a signal that the task is over. This, in turn, may help subjects terminate the ironic monitoring process they employed in the service of suppression more effectively than if they had remained in the same context. By remaining in the same context following suppression, subjects may not only be reminded of the distracters and their associations with the suppressed thought. The context may be a reminder of the very act of suppression along with the processes it entails. This, in essence, makes it harder to stop suppressing, and hence the rebound is observed.

In summary, we think there is something to be said for joining Martin and Tesser's theory with the thought suppression theory, rather than having them fight. People may begin ruminations because of unattained goals and then develop chronic unwanted thoughts because they attempt to suppress those ruminations. We believe that suppression may also exacerbate ruminations that stem from sources other than goal nonattainment, but it is probably the case that incompleteness is an important initial step, just as Martin and Tesser suggest. Although we were not impressed with the implications of Martin and Tesser's white bear study for this integration, we did learn something from these results about how the rebound effect occurs following suppression. It may be that people ruminate least when they truly stop suppressing their unwanted ruminations. Learning that their suppression is relatively successful may be the first step.

REFERENCES

Higgins, E. T. (1989). Knowledge accessibility and activation: Subjectivity and suffering from unconscious sources. In J. S. Uleman & J. A. Bargh (Eds.), *Unintended thought* (pp. 75–123). Englewood Cliffs, NJ: Prentice-Hall.

Macrae, C. N., Bodenhausen, G. V., Milne, A. B., & Jetten, J. (1994). Out of mind but back in sight: Stereotypes on the rebound. *Journal of Personality and Social Psychology, 67,* 808–817.

Wegner, D. M. (1992). You can't always think what you want: Problems in the suppression of unwanted thoughts. In M. Zanna (Ed.), *Advances in experimental social psychology* (Vol. 25, pp. 193–225). New York: Academic Press.

Wegner, D. M. (1994). Ironic processes of mental control. *Psychological Review, 101*, 34–52.

Wegner, D. M., & Erber, R. (1992). The hyperaccessibility of suppressed thoughts. *Journal of Personality and Social Psychology, 63*, 903–912.

Wegner, D. M., Erber, R., & Zanakos, S. (1993). Ironic processes in the mental control of moods and mood-related thought. *Journal of Personality and Social Psychology, 65*, 1093–1104.

Wegner, D. M., & Gold, D. B. (1995). Fanning old flames: Emotional and cognitive effects of suppressing thoughts of a past relationship. *Journal of Personality and Social Psychology, 68*, 782–792.

Wegner, D. M., Schneider, D. J., Carter, S. III, & White, L. (1987). Paradoxical effects of thought suppression. *Journal of Personality and Social Psychology, 58*, 409–418.

Wegner, D. M., Schneider, D. J., Knutson, B., & McMahon, S. R. (1991). Polluting the stream of consciousness: The effect of thought suppression on the mind's environment. *Cognitive Therapy and Research, 15*, 141–152.

Wegner, D. M., Shortt, J. W., Blake, A. W., & Paige, M.S. (1990). The suppression of exciting thoughts. *Journal of Personality and Social Psychology, 58*, 409–418.

Wegner, D. M., & Zanakos, S. (1994). Chronic thought suppression. *Journal of Personality, 62*, 615–640.

Wenzlaff, R. M., Wegner, D. M., & Klein, S. B. (1991). The role of thought suppression in the bonding of thought and mood. *Journal of Personality and Social Psychology, 60*, 500–508.

Chapter 5

Some Thoughts About Thinking

Carol L. Gohm
Linda M. Isbell
Robert S. Wyer, Jr.
University of Illinois, Urbana-Champaign

Until recently, the dynamics of everyday thought was a neglected area of social cognition research. However, our awareness of the need to understand information processing in natural settings has stimulated an emergence of concern with this topic by both cognitive and social psychologists. Research stimulated by this concern has taken many directions, including a consideration of the thoughts that are spontaneously elicited by a persuasive message (McGuire & McGuire, 1991; Petty & Cacioppo, 1986), the role of personal stories and narratives in comprehension and communication (Schank & Abelson, 1995), the effects of unintended thoughts on cognitive and social behavior (Uleman & Bargh, 1989), the persistence of thoughts that one consciously attempts to suppress (Wegner, Schneider, Carter, & White, 1987), and the interactive effects of cognition and emotion on task performance (Clore, Schwarz, & Conway, 1994; Dweck & Leggett, 1988).

There is nevertheless a need to develop a theoretical formulation of the thought processes that surround daily life activities and that can conceptually integrate the implications of this diverse body of research. Such a formulation could provide an understanding of the types of thinking that mediate individuals' behavior in situations both in and out of the laboratory. For this reason, Martin and Tesser's conceptualization is potentially very important.

At the same time, conceptual ambiguities are inevitable at this early stage in the theory's development. Without diminishing the importance of Martin and Tesser's work, we identify some of these ambiguities and, in doing so, suggest ways in which future iterations of the formulation might fruitfully be refined and extended. Our comments focus on a general concern, namely, that the authors' definition of rumination may be too broad to be useful in conceptualizing the types of thinking that occur both spontaneously and intentionally in the course of daily life activity. We personally prefer an approach that more explicitly recognizes the multidimensionality of thinking and the possible independence of different types of rumination that Martin and Tesser place under a single heading. Such an approach might lead more easily to a general conceptualization of thought processes that specifies the similarities and differences between thinking styles and their determinants as well as their effects.

Our argument can be conveyed in general terms. Suppose a construct, X, is defined as the disjunction of two variables, A and B, that are independent of one another. That is, $X = A \cup B$. Suppose further that the determinants of A (s_B) are independent of the determinants of B (s_B), and that A and B themselves have effects on quite different subsets of outcome variables (r_A and r_B). These conditions are shown in Fig. 5.1a. Under such conditions, a conceptualization of A and B as components of a single construct could lead to misleading conclusions. (For example, one might

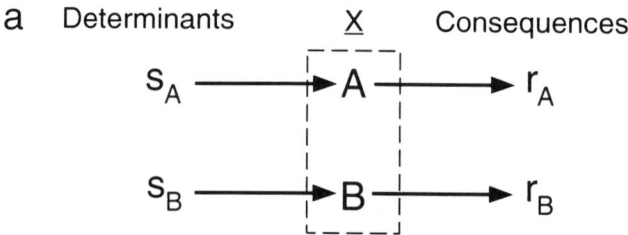

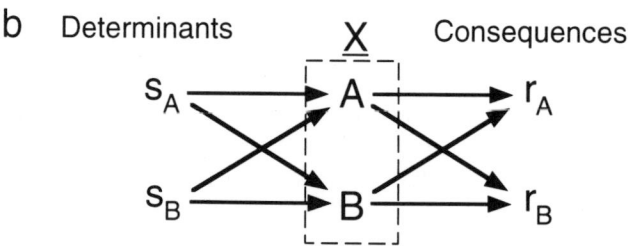

FIG. 5.1. Hypothetical relations between antecedents of variable X and consequences of X, where X is composed of two independent subfactors, A and B. (a) Each set of determinants and consequences are unique to one component of X (i.e., to A or B but not both). (b) Determinants and consequences are associated with both components of X.

infer that because s_A influences X and X affects r_A, s_A has an impact on r_B, but this is not the case.) The utility of conceptualizing A and B as components of X is predicated on the assumption that A and B have at least some determinants and consequences in common, as shown in Fig. 5.1b. Then, the conclusion that s_A has an influence on r_B might be appropriate.

In Martin and Tesser's conceptualization, the construct rumination presumably occupies the position of X in our abstract example. That is, it lumps together several different types of thinking. If these types of thinking are actually independent and if they have different antecedents and consequences, Martin and Tesser's present conceptualization of rumination could ultimately create confusion. We elaborate on this argument in the sections to follow. First, we consider the dimensions along which styles of thinking may vary. Then, we discuss antecedents of these thinking styles that Martin and Tesser have not explicitly considered. Finally, we briefly describe two experiments bearing on the effects of different styles of thinking to which Martin and Tesser's construct of rumination is relevant.

DIMENSIONS OF THINKING STYLE

Intentionality and Temporal-Situational Focus

Martin and Tesser define rumination as "... a class of conscious thoughts that revolve around a common instrumental theme and that recur in the absence of immediate environmental demands requiring the thoughts" (pp. 1, 7). They go on to state that "Although the occurrence of these thoughts does not depend on direct cueing by the external environment, indirect cueing by the environment is likely given the high accessibility of goal-related concepts. Although the external environment may maintain any thought through repeated cues, the maintenance of ruminative thoughts is not dependent upon such cueing" (p. 7).

This definition makes salient two important dimensions along which thoughts can vary. One dimension is temporal-situational focus. Thoughts can sometimes be stimulated by proximal stimuli in the immediate situation in which one finds oneself. In other cases, however, they can be stimulated by previously formed cognitions about other, distal stimuli (e.g., memories of past events or imagined future experiences) that come to mind in the situation at hand.[1] The second dimension is intentionality. Thoughts

---

[1] Distal stimuli can also include people and events that exist in the present but are in different physical locations from the cognizer. That is, a person taking an exam might wonder what a friend is doing or might think about who is winning the football game being played in another city. Nevertheless, because most distal events one thinks about are likely to be in the past or future, our discussion generally is directed to these types of distal events.

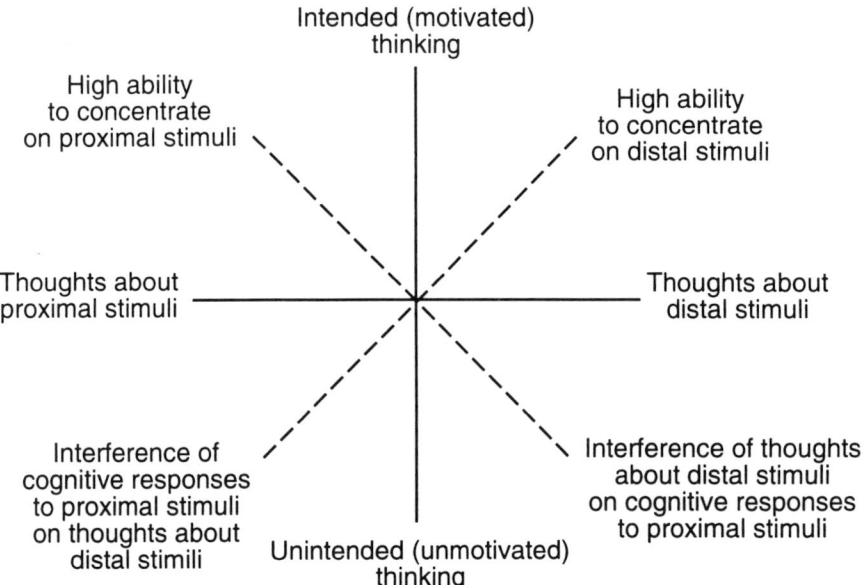

FIG 5.2. Two sets of orthogonal dimensions along which thoughts can vary. One set, represented by the horizontal and vertical axes, pertains to the temporal–situational focus and intentionality of thoughts, respectively. The second set, represented by dashed lines, concern the extent to which cognitive responses to proximal stimuli interfere with thinking about distal thinking (e.g., past and future events) and the extent to which thoughts about distal stimuli (e.g., the past or future) interfere with thinking about proximal stimuli (e.g., immediate situational demands).

are often controlled, intentional responses that are stimulated by the desire to attain a specific objective to which they are relevant (e.g., to solve a problem, to communicate information or ideas, or to perform a task.) Others, however, can be uncontrolled, spontaneous cognitions that intrude on other, motivated cognitive activity.[2]

These dimensions are embodied in Martin and Tesser's definition of rumination, and many of the specific types of thinking they identify can be conceptualized as exemplifying combinations of values along these dimensions. However, a consideration of the two dimensions in combination raises further issues that have not been fully explored. This can be seen from Fig. 5.2. The horizontal and vertical axes in this figure correspond to the

---

[2]In conceptualizing differences along these dimensions, Martin and Tesser make an implicit but important distinction between motivated thought and goal-relevant thought. Although rumination often concerns the failure to attain a desired goal and the consequences of this failure, it is not necessarily motivated. That is, these goal-relevant thoughts could occur spontaneously despite attempts to suppress them.

two dimensions noted previously. However, a rotation of these axes yields two other dimensions that may be equally fundamental. One concerns the extent to which unintended thoughts about distal stimuli (e.g., past and future events) intrude on motivated thinking about stimuli in one's immediate environment (e.g., a communication one is receiving or a task one is performing). The second concerns the extent to which stimuli present in the immediate situation spontaneously elicit unintended thoughts that interfere with attempts to concentrate on distal stimulus events (e.g., long range goals or the consequences of one's present behavior for future events). More simply, these composite dimensions reflect two different types of controllability: control over thoughts about proximal stimuli versus control over thoughts about distal ones (e.g., past and future events).

The relative utility of conceptualizing thinking styles along one set of dimensions or the other is not obvious. On one hand, general individual differences in distractibility might exist that generalize over the different types of stimuli that produce the distraction. Thus, those individuals who are distracted by proximal stimuli in their immediate surroundings when they are motivated to think about distal ones might also be distracted by thoughts about distal events while attempting to respond to demands imposed by the immediate situation. On the other hand, individual differences could also exist in "stimulus boundness," a tendency for thoughts to be governed by proximal stimulus objects or events rather than distal ones independently of whether these responses are motivated or unintended. In fact, neither of these possibilities may be true. Rather, the tendency to be distracted by thoughts about the past and future while attempting to respond to immediate situational demands could be quite independent of the tendency to be distracted by stimuli in one's immediate stimulus environment while attempting to think about distal events.

A theory of rumination must ultimately specify which of these possibilities is most likely. That is, one's conceptualization of the determinants and effects of rumination is likely to depend on (a) whether individuals vary systematically in distractibility regardless of whether the distraction is produced by immediate stimulus events or by memories of the past, or alternatively, (b) whether individuals differ more generally in the stimulus boundness of their thoughts regardless of whether these thoughts are controlled or not.

Valence

Martin and Tesser's conception of rumination potentially takes into account both the intentionality of thoughts and their temporal–situational focus. However, Martin and Tesser fail to consider the valence of these thoughts and of the persons, objects, and events to which the thoughts pertain. It seems intuitively unlikely that differences in the intentionality and focus of thoughts are completely independent of their pleasantness and the affect that they elicit. Indeed, Martin and Tesser's hypothesis that rumination is contingent on the perception that past or present setbacks are relevant to long-range goal attainment is obviously more pertinent to thoughts about unpleasant events than to thoughts about pleasant ones. It seems likely that thoughts about desirable experiences are more controllable than thoughts about undesirable ones.

Some preliminary data we have collected (Isbell, Gohm, & Wyer, 1994), cited briefly by Martin and Tesser, suggest the desirability of distinguishing between thoughts about positively valenced events and thoughts about negatively valenced ones and also between the tendency to think about these events and other styles of thinking. In this research, subjects reported their agreement with 68 questionnaire items concerning both the tendency to engage in different types of thinking and the motivation to do so. These items were divided on a priori grounds into nine subscales pertaining to positive thoughts about the future, negative thoughts about the future, positive thoughts about the past, negative thoughts about the past, planning, distractibility, nonsocial impulsiveness, social impulsiveness, and the motivation to think about the past or future. Representative items on these scales are shown in Table 5.1, along with scale reliabilities (Cronbach's alpha). (The low reliability of the social impulsiveness scale likely results from the fact that it contains only three items.)

Scale scores were computed for each subject separately, and these scores were then exposed to a principle components factor analysis. This analysis yielded three varimax-rotated factors with eigen-values greater than 1.0. Loadings on these factors are shown in Table 5.2. (An oblique rotation yielded similar results.)

Several aspects of the results are provocative. First, tendencies to think about the past and tendencies to think about the future are strongly related. However, thinking about positive events and thinking about negative ones load on different, independent factors. Moreover, the third factor, which could reflect a tendency for thoughts and behaviors to be governed by proximal stimuli (as evidenced by loadings of distractibility, nonsocial impulsiveness, and a failure to plan ahead), is independent of both positive and negative thinking per se. As noted earlier, Martin and Tesser's conceptualization of rumination does not distinguish between the types of thinking implied by these factors.

Second, motivation to think is more strongly associated with thoughts about positively valenced stimuli than with thoughts about negatively valenced ones. This suggests that whereas negative thoughts may be governed in large part by uncontrolled processes, positive thinking is more

TABLE 5.1
Reliabilities and Representative Items for Scales Assessing Different Styles of Thinking

1. Positive thinking about the future (.84)*
   a. I often think about happy events in the future (parties, vacations, etc.).
   b. I often imagine good things that might happen to me many years from now.
2. Negative thinking about the future (.85)
   a. I often find myself imagining bad things that might occur in the future.
   b. I often think about unhappy events in the future (exams, accidents, illnesses, etc.).
3. Positive thinking about the past (.86)
   a. I often find myself reminiscing about good times I have had in the past.
   b. When I have done something I am proud of, I think about it for a long time afterwards.
4. Negative thinking about the past (.82)
   a. I often find myself ruminating about about times I have had in the past.
   b. When I have done something I regret, I think about it for a long time afterwards.
5. Planning (.77)
   a. I make a list of things I want to do.
   b. (reverse scored) I usually don't think about the things I have to do until the time comes to do them.
6. Distractibility (.63)
   a. When I am reading or studying, I am easily distracted by thoughts about other things.
   b. (reverse scored) I have no trouble focusing all of my attention on one thing.
7. Nonsocial impulsiveness (.79)
   a. I have trouble resisting my cravings.
   b. (reverse scored) I seldom give in to my impulses.
8. Social impulsiveness (.53)
   a. I often say things without thinking.
   b. (reverse scored) I am always able to keep my feelings under control.
9. Motivation to think (.64)
   a. (reverse scored) I don't like to think about the future.
   b. It is important to set goals and work toward them.

Note. From Isbell, Gohm, and Wyer (1994)
*Numbers in parentheses are scale reliabilities (Cronbach's alpha).

likely to be motivationally rooted. To this extent, positive thinking is less likely to meet Martin and Tesser's conception of rumination as unintended thought (see p. 7, this volume).

Third, social impulsiveness, which could reflect a tendency for social behavior to be governed by proximal stimuli without thinking about its potential consequences, is positively associated with negative thinking. This suggests that tendencies to ruminate about the past are in part a result of a failure to think extensively about the future consequences of events at the time these events occur.

TABLE 5.2
Factor Loadings of Types of Thinking Identified by Isbell et al. (1994)

	Factor 1 (Negative Thinking)	Factor 2 (Positive Thinking)	Factor 3 (Distractibility)
Negative thinking about the future	.68	-.38	.04
Negative thinking about the past	.87	-.04	.10
Positive thinking about the future	-.19	.83	.06
Positive thinking about the past	.13	.75	-.08
Planning	.08	.07	-.82
Distractibility	.18	-.11	.77
Nonsocial impulsiveness	.65	-.01	.16
Motivation to think	-.47	.69	-.10

In any event, these data suggest the desirability of distinguishing between at least three different styles of thinking rather than combining them into a single construct. This is particularly true if these thinking styles have different antecedents and consequences. Martin and Tesser focus much of their discussion on thoughts that result from perceptions that an unpleasant event is detrimental to the attainment of some long-range, more general goal (e.g., happiness). This suggests that rumination consists primarily of negatively valenced thoughts. Elsewhere, however, the authors postulate that rumination results from perceptions of the *change* in rate of progress toward an external goal (pp. 11–13). This change could presumably be either an increase or a decrease in one's rate of progress and therefore could elicit either positive or negative thoughts. Finally, it is not clear that spontaneous thoughts about favorable past events (e.g., early childhood experiences) are related to maintenance goals of the sort that Martin and Tesser discuss (p. 10). Yet, these thoughts also fit their conception of rumination. In summary, the authors appear to view rumination as multiply determined. To this extent, the type of rumination that occurs could depend substantially on its antecedents. A conception of rumination that does not specify these differences might then be of limited utility.

INDIVIDUAL DIFFERENCES IN THINKING STYLE

A very positive feature of Martin and Tesser's analysis lies in its attention to both situational and individual difference factors that contribute to ruminative thought. The authors demonstrate, for example, that differences between "linkersm" (i.e., persons who perceive immediate outcomes as related to long-range goal attainment) and "nonlinkers" (i.e., persons who do not make this connection) generalize over domains of experience and produce differences in rumination in a variety of different situations. However, other chronic individual differences in thinking style could be independent of the goal-relevance of these thoughts. Moreover, these differences could be associated with more general differences in personality that have previously been identified in the literature.

Physiological Bases of Thoughts and Behavior

It is particularly interesting to consider differences in thinking style in the context of a conceptualization proposed by Gray (1987). Gray postulates that two independent biological systems underlie conditioned responses to one's immediate stimulus environment. One, the *behavior activation system* (BAS), is sensitive to stimuli associated with rewards (e.g., positively valenced stimuli) in the immediate environment and elicits behaviors that are associated with the acquisition of these stimuli. The second, the *behavior inhibition system* (BIS), is sensitive to cues that are associated with punishment (e.g., negatively valenced stimuli). This system elicits anxiety and inhibits behavior that might lead to punishment. These two systems operate independently, and a given individual can potentially be described by any combination of values along the dimensions that define them.

Gray has related differences in the strength of these two systems to extraversion and neuroticism, as shown in Fig. 5.3. Thus, extraversion is

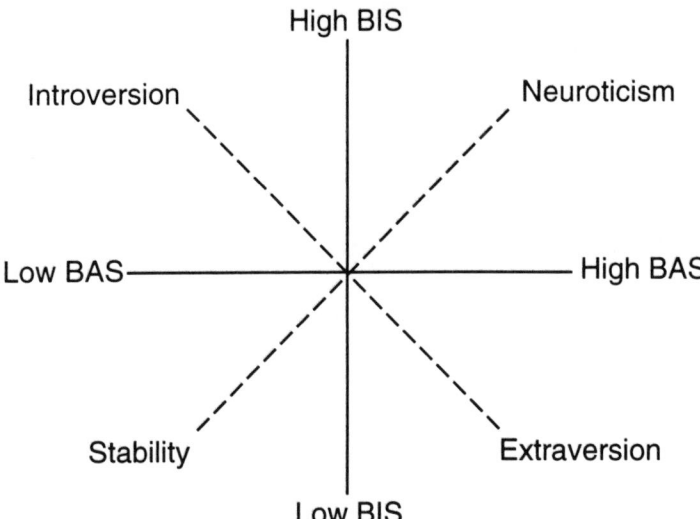

FIG. 5.3. Theoretical relation of extraversion–introversion and neuroticism–stability to differences in the intensity of the behavior activation system (BAS) and behavior inhibition system (BIS) proposed by Gray (1987).

characterized by a strong behavior activation system coupled with a relatively weak behavior inhibition system (i.e., a tendency to respond to positively valenced stimuli in one's immediate environment while being relatively insensitive to punishment cues). In contrast, neuroticism is characterized by high responsiveness to both reward and punishment cues in one's immediate environment.

Although Gray's theory focuses on overt behavior, it seems likely that the cognitions that mediate this behavior are subject to similar mechanisms. Indeed, the three factors identified by Isbell et al. (1994) and shown in Table 5.2 are reasonably consistent with this possibility. For example, the independence of thoughts about negatively valenced events (Factor 1) and thoughts about positively valenced events (Factor 2) is compatible with the assumption that different systems govern responses to these two types of stimuli. On the other hand, Gray's conceptualization also suggests that stimulus boundness, or the tendency for thoughts and behavior to be controlled by stimuli in the immediate environment rather than distal stimuli (e.g., remembered past events or imagined future ones), can often be restricted to stimuli of a given valence (e.g., either stimuli associated with reward or those that signal punishment) and might not necessarily generalize over stimuli of different types. The tendency to ruminate spontaneously about unpleasant past and future events and the tendency to have intrusive thoughts about pleasant ones could likewise be governed by different physiological systems.

The theoretical link between the behavior activation and inhibition systems that Gray postulates and thinking styles must obviously be established more firmly. Moreover, there are undoubtedly types of thinking to which Gray's theory does not directly apply. Nevertheless, his work clearly raises the possibility that an important source of variance in thinking style is physiologically rooted and is not captured by the situational factors to which Martin and Tesser have directed their attention.

Personality Correlates of Thinking Style

The relation of different styles of thinking to more traditional indices of personality is also worth noting. In the aforementioned study by Isbell et al., subjects also completed measures of extraversion (Goldberg, 1992), neuroticism (Goldberg, 1992), anxiety (Spielberger, 1983), and need for cognition (Cacioppo & Petty, 1982). These variables were each correlated with scores on the three factors defined in Table 5.2: positive thinking, negative thinking, and distractibility.[3] These correlations are shown in Table 5.3. Thinking about pleasant past and future events is positively associated with extraversion but is inversely related to both neuroticism and anxiety. In contrast, thinking about unpleasant events is associated positively with both neuroti-

TABLE 5.3
Correlations Between Styles of Thinking and Personality Indices

	Extraversion	Neuroticism	Anxiety	Need for Cognition
Positive thoughts about past and future	.41*	-.34*	-.40*	.18
Negative thoughts about past and future	-.26	.65*	.63*	-.21
Distractibility	.05	.25	.27	-.44*

*$p < .05$.

cism and anxiety but is nonsignificantly related to extraversion. Finally, distractibility is not significantly related to either extraversion or neuroticism but is inversely related to need for cognition (i.e., an index of the intrinsic enjoyment obtained from engaging in cognitive activity).

Although these results are intuitively not surprising, they do suggest that the different types of thinking are systematically related to more traditional indices of personality and motivation. To this extent, a question arises as to which set of variables is more fundamental. Is extraversion, which could have physiological roots (Gray, 1987; see also Eysenck, 1967), a pervasive aspect of personality that is manifested in thinking style as well as in overt behavior? Or is the tendency to think extensively about positively valenced past and future events a determinant of extraversion? To the latter extent, an additional question arises concerning how the factors postulated by Martin and Tesser to affect rumination are related to those that underlie extraversion, neuroticism, and other personality variables. These questions are worth considering in future research and theorizing.

CONSEQUENCES OF DIFFERENCES IN THINKING STYLE

We have argued for a clearer distinction between different styles of thinking. This argument is based primarily on the evidence that several styles of thinking that fit Martin and Tesser's definition of rumination load on independent factors and are likely to have different antecedents. A similar argument can be made with respect to the consequences of different thinking styles.

A very attractive aspect of Martin and Tesser's theory is the wide range of empirical phenomena that can be interpreted within its framework.

---

[3]Scores on Factor 1 were computed by summing scale scores for negative thoughts about the past and negative thoughts about the future. Scores on Factor 2 were computed by summing scale scores for positive thoughts about the past and positive thoughts about the future. Scores on Factor 3 were based on the difference between scores on the distractibility scale and scores on the planning scale.

However, it is not clear that the same thinking styles subsumed under the heading of rumination underlie each phenomenon. Our own work in this area is still preliminary, and any conclusions drawn from it should be treated as very tentative. However, two early studies suggest the need to make greater distinctions among thinking styles than Martin and Tesser's definition of rumination implies.

In one study, we were interested in the extent to which different general styles of thinking might influence task performance under conditions in which either thoughts about distal stimuli would be potentially disruptive or thoughts about proximal stimuli would interfere. Subjects performed two tasks in counterbalanced order. One, a section of the Remote Associates Test (Mednick & Mednick, 1967), required subjects to relate sets of stimuli in terms of a single, superordinate concept. The second required subjects to memorize a set of 25 behavior descriptions. We assumed that when the behavior memory task was performed last, subjects' recall of the behaviors would be poor if they continued to think about items on the preceding Remote Associates Test while trying to learn these behaviors. When the behavior memory task was performed first, subjects' recall was expected to be poor to the extent that the second (remote associates) task spontaneously captured their attention despite their efforts to keep the to-be-remembered behaviors in mind. Thus, we anticipated that general individual differences in the tendency to ruminate about distal events, or alternatively, to be distracted by proximal stimuli while attempting to concentrate on distal ones, would produce differences in memory performance under the two conditions.

Memory was expected to be generally affected by need for cognition, which reflects the intrinsic motivation to think about the tasks being performed. However, we expected that general dispositions to think about distal versus proximal stimuli might influence performance over and above this motivational factor. We considered four possible reflections of these dispositions, based on indices of a tendency to think spontaneously about past events, a tendency to think about the future, planning, and a self-report measure of impulsiveness.[4] As we expected, these variables had quite different effects on memory.

Perhaps the most interesting effect involved impulsiveness, which interacted significantly with both need for cognition and task order. These results are shown in Table 5.4. The simplest interpretation of these results

---

[4]These measures were based on a questionnaire constructed prior to the study by Isbell et al. (1994). Although differences in positive or negative thinking could not be distinguished clearly with this questionnaire, most items concerning thoughts about the past implicitly concerned unfavorable events, whereas those contained in the index of thoughts about the future concerned happy ones. Thus, these factors are not inconsistent with those obtained in the later study.

TABLE 5.4
Mean Number of Behaviors Recalled as a Function of Task Order,
Impulsiveness, and Need for Cognition

	Low Impulsiveness		High Impulsiveness	
	Low Need for Cognition	High Need for Cognition	Low Need for Cognition	High Need for Cognition
Behavior memory task first	8.8	11.3	10.9	11.0
Behavior memory task second	13.1	10.0	11.3	11.0

is that subjects with high need for cognition thought relatively more extensively about the first task they performed regardless of which task it happened to be, and their thoughts about this task persisted during the task they performed subsequently. Consequently, these subjects had better recall of the behaviors than subjects with low need for cognition when the behavior memory task was first. When the Remote Associates Test was first, however, subjects with high need for cognition persisted in thinking about it, and these thoughts interfered with their learning of items in the memory task they performed later.

As shown in Table 5.4, however, these motivational effects were evident only among subjects who were low in impulsiveness. Highly impulsive individuals remembered the same number of behaviors in each condition regardless of their need for cognition. This finding provides indirect evidence that impulsiveness is a general dispositional tendency that can override differences in the motivation to think about prior events.

On the other hand, other indices of thinking style were related to task performance in different ways. For example, behavior recall was marginally ($p < .10$) greater among persons who typically thought about past life experiences than those who did not (11.1 vs. 16.4), but this difference did not depend on either task order or need for cognition. In contrast, dispositions to think about the future and planning had no relation at all to behavior memory.

A second study also provides some insight into the behavior correlates of different thinking styles. In this study, subjects were asked to form an impression of a target person who was described by a series of behaviors. In some conditions, favorable behaviors were presented before unfavorable ones. In other conditions, the presentation order was reversed. Later, subjects evaluated the person described along a 0–10 scale of likableness and recalled the behaviors they had read.

The effect of information presentation order on judgments was significantly contingent on differences in thinking about the past. Specifically, subjects with a disposition to think extensively about past events evaluated the target more positively when the favorable behaviors were presented last than when they were first (4.99 vs. 4.42), indicating a recency effect of the information on judgments. In contrast, subjects with little tendency to dwell upon past events evaluated the target more positively when the favorable behaviors were first (4.96 vs. 3.55), indicating a primacy effect. Moreover, the former subjects recalled significantly more behaviors than the latter (7.0 vs. 5.9). These results, like those of the first study, suggest that individuals who have little tendency to ponder the past are also less inclined to think extensively about new information they receive. Thus, in the situation we constructed, they based their decisions on the first pieces of information they encountered and recalled the information less well overall. Although this interpretation is plausible, similar intuitions imply that need for cognition and impulsiveness also influence judgments and recall. This, however, was not the case; no other factor we considered was relevant to either memory or judgments in this study.

Any conclusions to be drawn from this research clearly need to be treated with caution pending replication with more refined indices of thinking style. However, the results serve to confirm the suspicion that the different thinking styles that Martin and Tesser have lumped under a common heading of rumination might be better considered as separate constructs that have both different determinants and different effects on cognitive processing. This is particularly true in the case of thoughts about positive stimuli and thoughts about negative ones, which loaded on different factors and, moreover, appeared to have different antecedents and consequences.

CONCLUDING REMARKS

In this chapter, we have attempted to consider three related issues surrounding the conceptualization of rumination that Martin and Tesser propose. First, the conceptualization may not adequately distinguish between different styles of thinking that are, in fact, independent. Second, these different thinking styles seem likely to have different antecedents, some of which may be physiologically rooted. Third, the different styles of thinking may influence behavior in different ways. To the extent these conclusions are valid, they suggest that Martin and Tesser have been somewhat overzealous in lumping together many different types of thinking under a single conceptual label. Rather, a conceptualization that takes into account the different dimensions along which styles of thinking can vary and specifies the determinants and consequences of differences along each dimension will ultimately be of greater value.

This observation, however, does not seriously diminish the importance of Martin and Tesser's work. Rather, it points out the directions that further refinements of their formulation might take. Even in its present form,

Martin and Tesser's conceptualization provides an integration of theoretical and empirical issues that have not previously been considered in combination and raises new questions. It therefore promises to broaden substantially our understanding of cognition in everyday life situations. This understanding is essential for meaningful progress in the area of social information processing. We therefore look forward to witnessing the impact that Martin and Tesser's work will inevitably have on this area.

ACKNOWLEDGMENT

This chapter was written with partial support of National Science Foundation grant SBR 94-07058. Appreciation is extended to Joseph Forgas, Michaela Wänke, and the University of Illinois Social Cognition Group for stimulating many of the ideas conveyed and to Rashmi Adaval for helpful comments on an earlier draft of this chapter.

REFERENCES

Cacioppo, J. T., & Petty, R. E. (1982). The need for cognition. *Journal of Personality and Social Psychology, 42,* 116–131.

Clore, G. L., Schwarz, N., & Conway, M. (1994). Affective causes and consequences of social information processing. In R. S. Wyer & T. K. Srull (Eds.), *Handbook of social cognition*: (Vol. 1 2nd ed., pp. 323–417). Hillsdale, NJ: Lawrence Erlbaum Associates

Dweck, C. S., & Leggett, E. L. (1988). A social-cognitive approach to motivation and personality. *Psychological Review, 95,* 256–273.

Eysenck, H. J. (1967). *The biological basis of personality.* Springfield IL: Thomas.

Goldberg, L. R. (1992). The development of markers for the big-five factor structure. *Psychological Assessment, 4,* 26–42.

Gray, J. A. (1987). The neuropsychology of emotion and personality. In S. M. Stahl, S. D. Iverson, & E. C. Goodman (Eds.), *Cognitive Neurochemistry.* Oxford: Oxford University Press.

Isbell, L. M., Gohm, C. L., & Wyer, R. S. (1994). Unpublished data, University of Illinois at Urbana-Champaign.

McGuire, W. J., & McGuire, C. V. (1991). The content, structure, and operation of thoughts systems. In R. S. Wyer & T. K. Srull (Eds.), *Advances in social cognition: Vol. 4. The content, structure and operation of thought systems* (pp. 1–78). Hillsdale, NJ: Lawrence Erlbaum Associates.

Mednick, S. A., & Mednick, M. T. (1967). *Examiner's Manuel: Remote Associates Test.* Boston: Houghton Mifflin.

Petty, R. E., & Cacioppo, J. T. (1986). The Elaboration Likelihood Model of persuasion. In L. Berkowitz (Ed.), *Advances in experimental social psychology* (Vol. 19, pp. 123–205). New York: Academic Press.

Schank, R. C., & Abelson, R. P. (1995). Knowledge and memory: The real story. In R. S. Wyer (Ed.), *Advances in social cognition*: Vol. 8 (pp. 1–85). Hillsdale, NJ: Lawrence Erlbaum Associates.

Spielberger, C. D. (1983). *State-trait anxiety inventory manual.* Palo Alto, CA: Consulting Psychologists Press.

Uleman, J. S., & Bargh, J. A. (Eds.). (1989). *Unintended thought.* New York: Guilford.

Wegner, D. M., Schneider, D. J., Carter, S. R., & White, T. L. (1987). Paradoxical effects of thought suppression. *Journal of Personality and Social Psychology, 53,* 5–13.

Chapter **6**

Thinking About Goals, Glue, and the Meaning of Life

Laura A. King
James W. Pennebaker
Southern Methodist University

Martin and Tesser build a compelling case for their model of rumination as a function of problematic goal pursuit. This theory of ruminative thought is both creative and persuasive. It is thorough and well-supported by empirical research. Importantly, rumination is placed within currently recognized modes of thought. They have allowed their definition of rumination to be general enough so that it applies not only to unwanted negative thoughts but to positive, though "off task," thoughts as well. The model makes an excellent first step in placing rumination into the larger picture of the person's life. In this commentary, we explore more fully some of the issues that occurred to us as we read the chapter. Some of these issues can be incorporated into the model; others are simply extensions of Martin and Tesser's approach. We are also interested in synthesizing this approach to rumination with research on the benefits of writing about traumatic experience.

Throughout the chapter, Martin and Tesser assert that the microcosmic examples used pertain to the macrocosm of human experience, so that ruminating about lost glue is analogous to ruminating about lost love. In this commentary, we hope to place the model within the context of the big picture, to elaborate on the model with real-world examples. We address four main issues. First, Martin and Tesser's model brings a new perspective to the issue of broad high level life goals. Enduring life concerns are, by nature, unattainable because they are not terminal goals with clear end-states. The relations of these types of goals to rumination warrant further discussion. Second, Martin and Tesser's model has implications for the role of major life events (i.e., powerful emotional experiences) in perseverative thought. How can we explain the thoughts of a person when a goal object is irrevocably lost? How does the magnitude of a life experience fit into the present model? Third, in thinking about Martin and Tesser's approach, it is important to consider the social context of rumination. What does the process and content of rumination indicate about the individual's social world? Finally, we examine the relevance of Martin and Tesser's model to research on the psychological and physical benefits of writing and talking about traumatic life events. How does the current model of rumination relate to the benefits of writing the story of one's experience?

THE UNATTAINABLE QUALITY OF LIFETIME GOALS

Martin and Tesser assert that all rumination is the result of problematic goal pursuit. Unattained goals haunt us until they are attained, replaced, or forgotten. Furthermore, Martin and Tesser wisely acknowledge the importance of the hierarchical organization of goals in determining which goals become the subject of rumination. For instance, low-level goals are more likely to be ruminated about if they exist in service of some larger enduring life goal that is higher on the hierarchy. Thus, rumination plays a role in the self-regulation of action (Carver & Scheier, 1982; Powers, 1973). Although it is important to acknowledge the existence of a motivational hierarchy, the implications of this hierarchy can be more fully explored. High-level goals are closest to the self and are most imbued with emotion (Carver & Scheier, 1981). Several issues with regard to these high-level goals deserve attention.

First, high-level goals are often truly unattainable. Further, these unattainable goals may be considered chronically accessible. Are they accessible simply because they are unattainable? Attaining these goals would not stop our ruminations about them. For example, Martin and Tesser refer to an individual who is building a model boat. The lost glue looms large in the person's mind because the model building is being done in order to satisfy a higher goal, to appear creative. So far so good. But imagine that the individual is interrupted in the search by a phone call informing the individual that she has been awarded top prize in a worldwide competition for creativity. Would creativity-relevant rumination cease forever? No. Although the news is good, the goal is not attainable. It is a motive that remains unsatisfied, the pursuit of which is in and of itself satisfying (cf. Aronoff & Wilson, 1985; Emmons & King, 1989). By definition, motives give rise to motive-relevant thought, even as an individual enjoys success at a motive-relevant pursuit (McClelland, 1985).

Another example highlights this point. Imagine an individual who is committed to the social cause of ending homelessness. She works tirelessly at homeless shelters and toils at political causes. Sooner or later, she will realize that no matter how hard she works her goal will never be attained. There will always be homelessness and hunger in her world. Martin and Tesser assert that in this example the options are to distract oneself or pursue some other goal. Yet individuals persist at such unattainable goals and continue to ruminate about these problems, regardless of the probability of goal attainment.

Essential to the perspective suggested by Martin and Tesser is that attainment of a goal and thoughts about the goal are inversely related. As long as things are going well, or at least as expected, the individual has little need to think about the goal. Thoughts and effective goal action are portrayed as at odds. Thoughts about a goal are assumed to be symptomatic of some irregularity in goal pursuit. In keeping with these assertions, Klinger and colleagues (Klinger, Barta, & Maxeiner, 1980) found that current concerns were more likely to appear in thought if they were not routine, if the action regarding the concern met with unexpected difficulties, and if little time remained for action toward the goal. In addition, Emmons and King (1988) showed that conflicting goals are more likely to appear in spontaneous thought but less likely to be acted upon. However, obstacles, conflict, and unexpected difficulties are not the only goal characteristics that have been found to relate to naturally occurring thought. Goals that are highly valued and to which a person is strongly committed (Klinger, Barta, & Maxeiner, 1980) are also likely to be thought of, regardless of these other issues.

For some goals it might be true that once attained we can forget them, but goals at the highest level of the hierarchy have an enduring influence on behavior and thought. In discussing goals that exist at the top of the goal hierarchy, discrepancy reduction may not suffice to explain the relation between attainment and thoughts. Fulfillment may lead to greater striving and greater thought about the goal. It may be possible to retain the discrepancy-reduction perspective, with the added provision that the discrepancy, with regard to lifelong goals, refers to one's minimally acceptable level of progress rather than attainment of a goal. On the other hand, it may be reasonable to assert that at the highest level of the individual's goal hierarchy, goals or motives may be based on incentives rather than deprivation (cf. McClelland, 1985).

Throughout the chapter, the authors assert that individuals enjoy "flow" until some problem emerges in goal pursuit. At this point rumination may begin. Unfortunately, this gives the impression that thought and productive goal activity are necessarily at odds. Although flow may be characterized as unself-conscious unity between the actor and the demands of the environment (Csikzentmihalyi, 1990), it is not necessarily thoughtless. A person can be full of thought and flowing. Thoughts are not always symptomatic of trouble in action. Indeed, given the broad definition of rumination used by Martin and Tesser, we can conclude that the operation of motives on thought processes is, by definition, ruminative.

In a sense, this argument leads to another ambiguity in the model. Martin and Tesser accurately assert that rumination is not by definition a negative experience. Rumination can be associated with either pleasurable or painful experiences, with celebration or defeat. However, thought processes that indicate a disruption of flow might well be judged negatively. In addition, at various places throughout the chapter, ruminations are described as thoughts that are difficult to eliminate and unwanted. Clearly, ruminations are not simply thoughts but thoughts that are noticeably off task. Is thinking about attaching the ship mast to a model boat while in the process of building a boat off task? Not necessarily. Is thinking about attaching the mast to a model boat while having sex off task? Yes. Ruminative thought is best conceptualized as thought that interrupts goal pursuit, rather than thought that emerges about and around goal interruption.

THE ROLE OF POWERFUL EMOTIONAL EXPERIENCE IN RUMINATION

Boy meets girl, man finds glue: Do the processes exemplified by these relatively low-level ends generalize to more magnificent obsessions? What happens when the model described by Martin and Tesser is applied to larger life dilemmas? The mechanisms are assumed to be the same in more meaningful settings. Do they readily generalize? Is it true that the level of discussion is irrelevant to an understanding of rumination? In other words, does it matter if an individual is ruminating about lost glue or lost love? We think it might. Throughout the chapter, Martin and Tesser reveal an assumption about the form of ruminative thoughts. In the example of the lost glue, the person is, presumably, thinking, "Where is that glue? Where is that glue? Is the glue here?" Consideration of less linguistic thought might give a more accurate picture of rumination. Ruminating about lost love or a traumatic experience might be experienced as images and replaying of scenes, more like a movie than a news report (cf. Tomkins, 1992).

Consideration of emotion in the model is limited to evidence showing that depressive affect seems to promote rumination and rumination seems to promote depressive affect. There is more to be explored with regard to the relation between intense emotional experience and rumination. For example, imagine a person who has just fallen madly in love, who at the same time has an article to write or a book editor's deadline to make. She is able to do some writing, but every once in a while she finds herself smiling and feeling really great. The article is not going that well, so why is she so happy? Feeling ecstatically happy without clear provocation from the environment, she is left to search for a reason for her emotion (Martin, Ward, Achee, & Wyer, 1993). Rumination kicks in when she finds, looking inward, the joy of a new love. Emotion may be the distractor that provokes ruminative thought. Martin and Tesser refer to this sort of experience as a function of basking or goal maintenance. Certainly, the emotion in the example might be a reminder that the woman has attained an important end in her life. However, it does not do justice to the emotion she experiences to relegate it to such a superfluous task. It seems more likely that her affective reactions are gloriously out of sync with her rational cognitive processes.

This example demonstrates that rumination may reveal times when the heart and mind work on different timetables. Although one might think that a particularly strong emotional experience can be set aside and even momentarily forgotten about, the intense emotion associated with the experience remains.

Importantly, rumination may be goal relevant without necessarily being centered on goals. For instance, any significant life change may have implications for many goals. Ruminative thoughts share a common thematic thread. However, that unifying thread may be provided not by a goal but by a loss that unites these goals or a life experience so dramatic that it disrupts an entire class of goals (e.g., divorce, death, rape). Martin and Tesser are right in asserting that rumination is a form of looking. But what happens when one is looking for something that is lost forever, such as a person who has lost a dear friend to a terminal illness. Martin and Tesser state that such an individual has few options. He or she can find an appropriate distractor (unlikely), or another goal may become prepotent. The prognosis is not a rosy one. Klinger (e.g., 1975, 1977, 1987) has presented an impressive examination of disengagement from unattainable goals. He suggested that failure to disengage from unattainable goals is linked to depressive symptoms. Although this distress is considered a normal part of the process of letting go of valued goals, Klinger (1977) suggested that reduced daily goal functioning and increased psychological distress may result from expending daily thought and emotion toward unfulfilled goals. Kuhl and Helle (1986) experimentally demonstrated that individuals who failed to disengage from unattainable goals tended to show depressive symptoms and limited opportunities for new goals.

Consider an individual who has experienced an event so disruptive and complete that previously held goals are no longer viable, such as an individual who has lost a lover to AIDS. This person is likely to ruminate about the loss and how much he or she misses the dead individual. Many of the survivor's previous goals were tied to the lover's care and health. A preponderance of the goals may have been shared goals. The individual is likely to ruminate on this loss and on feelings of grief, sorrow, and anger. In addition, however, rumination may also reveal the search for new goals and a new place in the world. We suggest that one possibility that remains for this individual is resolution of the loss. Rumination may serve to provide closure and, perhaps, lead to personal growth. Rumination may reveal not only effort to close an existing gap in one's goal pursuits but also the search for a purpose toward which to strive. It may be that the person is able to accommodate the change in a way that leads to a more complex relationship with the environment (Block, 1982). Perhaps ruminative thought reveals an effort to grow through major life changes. Later we discuss this possibility with regard to writing about traumatic events.

THE SOCIAL PSYCHOLOGY OF RUMINATION: IS RUMINATION A SUBSTITUTE FOR TALKING?

One of the more interesting aspects of rumination is the issue of what people ruminate about and the relation of rumination to the social world. In two studies, Pennebaker and Harber (1993) were able to identify a pattern of thinking and talking in response to major events (e.g., the Loma Prieta earthquake and the Persian Gulf War). Shortly after the events, people who had been affected were likely to think and talk a great deal for about two weeks. Next, these individuals reported little interest in hearing about others' experiences, although they were still interested in telling their own stories. During this inhibition phase, individuals persisted in ruminating about the event for about 6 weeks after social interactions were no longer welcome. Rumination continued in place of talking. Interestingly, indicators of distress such as hostility and dreaming about the event peaked during the inhibition phase.

This social stage model of collective coping may help bring specific mechanisms into the rumination model presented by Martin and Tesser. It is possible to interpret these results in terms of frustrated goals, in that people may be assumed to have the goal of talking about the event. In addition, it is possible to assume that thinking and talking serve the same function of working through the event.

In terms of more general processes, however, we can see that ruminative thoughts about the event belong in the same category as dreams and other aspects of residual coping that occur after talking about the event is no longer possible. In this case, thoughts about the event indicate an imbalance—a discrepancy in the larger system of which the individual is a part. Thoughts about the event only become problematic when they are no longer accompanied by the opportunity to talk.

THE HEALING POWER OF WRITING AND TALKING ABOUT TRAUMA

In the remainder of this commentary we address the implications of the rumination model proposed by Martin and Tesser for research on the psychological and physical benefits of confronting traumatic experience through writing. A large body of evidence has established that writing about emotional upheavals in brief sessions over three or four days is associated with a wide range of positive benefits, including fewer physical illnesses (Pennebaker & Beall, 1986), heightened immune system function (Pennebaker, Kiecolt-Glaser, & Glaser, 1988), improved academic performance (Pennebaker, Colder, & Sharp, 1990), and even employment after being laid off (Spera, Buhrfeind, & Pennebaker, 1994). In all of these studies, subjects had thought about their traumas quite a bit, yet writing about the experiences proved valuable. In other words, ruminating about the traumatic experience was not productive, but writing about the trauma was. Why should writing have benefits that thinking lacks? What is writing if not ruminating on paper?

One important and obvious difference between thinking and writing is that ruminations need not be linguistic. We can ruminate in images, and images of trauma may be particularly disturbing. Recurrent memories of the smell of a particular cologne or the sight of a particular room may be more haunting than a verbal label. Writing, in contrast, is tied to language. Writing about traumas allows linguistic labels to structure and limit memories of traumatic events. In addition, writing over a period of time almost compels an individual to elaborate on the issues addressed. Ruminating, the individual can engage in similar repetitive thoughts without necessarily feeling obligated to be productive. Rumination about traumatic life events is piecemeal. Indeed, the ephemeral nature of thought prevents the individual from being able to reflect back with certainty on what has been thought previously. Short term memory is, after all, short. Writing, in contrast, has permanence, and we are accustomed to writing in ways that lead from one point to the next. Perhaps ruminating on paper allows the individual to ruminate in ways that are productive. Research has begun to address this possibility.

Originally, it was assumed that the beneficial effects of writing occurred because individuals had been actively holding back talking about traumatic events. This inhibition was thought to lead to chronic autonomic arousal, which would presumably lead to eventual vulnerability to disease (Pennebaker, 1989). Recently, research has looked at mechanisms other than disinhibition to explain the salubrious effects of writing about trauma. In particular, studies have examined the importance of the actual content of what people write to their responses to writing about traumatic experiences. Pennebaker (1993) examined essays written by subjects who seemed to benefit most from the writing paradigm. A variety of content analytic procedures identified a pattern of writing associated with psychological and physical benefits. First, subjects who improved tended to express more emotions in their trauma essays. Second, these subjects tended to grow in insight over the course of writing. In these essays subjects tended to draw more causal links and mention coming to understand aspects of their trauma. More recent data have supported the notion that individuals who grow in insight over the course of writing are likely to benefit from writing about trauma (Pennebaker & Francis, 1995).

Thus, writing about traumatic events seems to foster cognitive change. Subjects who benefit from writing write essays that become more story-like and more linear—less like movies and more like stories. Writing differs from thought in that writing requires us to go on whereas ruminating allows us to remain. Writing may represent a complete form of rumination.

AREAS FOR FRUITFUL FUTURE WORK

Martin and Tesser have constructed a thorough model of rumination that is theoretically important and supported by solid empirical research. We have a few suggestions for future work, avenues that we look forward to seeing investigated from this perspective. First, what is rumination like for the ruminator in the natural world? Is rumination, as we have assumed, more imagistic and less linear than writing? Second, the role of emotion warrants further exploration. Can emotion serve to propel an individual to ruminate? Finally, although Martin and Tesser prefer to separate their model from the clinical realm, clinical issues certainly bear further exploration. The model may have important implications for symptoms of intrusive thoughts, obsessions, and so on that should not be dismissed out of hand. In addition, the role of interpersonal conflict and experience in rumination may provide a fascinating area for future exploration.

TOWARD A SYNCHRONY THEORY OF THOUGHTS, FEELINGS, AND GOALS

In discussing the issues in this commentary, we have begun to look at rumination in a different way. From Martin and Tesser's perspective, rumination occurs when the individual is out of sync with or disengaged from the environment. Rumination is rooted in the discrepancy between one's current goal progress and some optimal or expected level of progress. Martin and Tesser place rumination within a hierarchy of control and tie their model to systems theory. A provocative extension of their perspective is to place that hierarchy of goals into a broader general system (von Bertalanffy, 1968). Rumination is interconnected with the wider system of the person, who is connected to the still broader system of the social and physical environment. Considering rumination from this perspective, we have come to wonder if rumination is not likely to occur when aspects of this system are out of sync. Rather than focus on a single goal or a goal hierarchy, we might approach the person's life as a collection of interconnected systems. Not all of these subsystems are on the same time table. Recall the examples we have used. Rumination may occur when the mind races ahead of the heart, such as when an individual must focus on work even as he or she is occupied emotionally by an exciting new love. Rumination may occur when social convention dictates that an event has ended before one is prepared to move on, such as when an individual continues to grieve over a loss long after friends and family feel it is appropriate (Wortman & Silver, 1988). Rumination may occur when members of a group tire of listening to others talk about an event, even as they continue to wish to talk (Pennebaker & Harber, 1993). Rumination may occur when the individual's behavior demonstrates that all is well, even as an undisclosed trauma presses for expression (Pennebaker & Susman, 1988). In a sense, then, rumination may occur when the world continues to go around even when one feels as though the world has stopped.

All these examples imply discrepancies. These discrepancies do not concern a single goal, however, but rather they concern goal-relevant functioning across and within the subsystems of a person's life. Rumination indicates a lack of balance in a broad system. Rumination truly becomes the object of preoccupation, revealing much about the person's relation to his or her world, when placed in this larger tapestry.

ACKNOWLEDGMENT

Preparation of this chapter was made possible by a NIMH FIRST Award (R29 MH54142) to Laura King and by NSF grant SBR9411674 to James Pennebaker.

REFERENCES

Aronoff, J., & Wilson, J. P. (1985). *Personality in the social process*. Hillsdale, NJ: Lawrence Erlbaum Associates.

Block, J. (1982). Assimilation, accomodation, and the dynamics of personality development. *Child Development, 53*, 281–295.

Carver, C. S., & Scheier, M. F. (1982). Control theory: A useful conceptual framework for personality-social, clinical, and health psychology. *Psychological Bulletin, 92*, 111–135.

Csikzentmihalyi, M. (1990). *Flow*. New York: Harper & Row.

Emmons, R. A., & King, L. A. (1988). Conflict among personal strivings: Immediate and long-term implications for psychological and physical well-being. *Journal of Personality and Social Psychology, 48,* 1040–1048.

Emmons, R. A., & King, L. A. (1989). On the personalization of motivation. In R. Wyer & T. Srull (Eds.), *Advances in Social Cognition.* Hillsdale, NJ: Lawrence Erlbaum Associates.

Klinger, E. (1975). Consequences of commitment to and disengagement from incentives. *Psychological Review, 82,* 223–231.

Klinger, E. (1977). *Meaning and void: Inner experience and the incentives in people's lives.* Minneapolis, MN: University of Minnesota Press.

Klinger, E. (1987). The interview questionnaire technique: Reliability and validity of a mixed idiographic-nomothetic measure of motivation. In J. N. Butcher & C. D. Spielberger (Eds.), *Advances in personality assessment* (Vol. 6, pp. 31–48). Hillsdale, NJ: Lawrence Erlbaum Associates.

Klinger, E., Barta, S. G., & Maxeiner, M. (1980). Motivational correlates of thought content, frequency, and commitment. *Journal of Personality and Social Psychology, 39,* 1222–1237.

Kuhl, J., & Helle, P. (1986). Motivational and volitional determinants of depression: The degenerated-intention hypothesis. *Journal of Abnormal Psychology, 95,* 247–251.

Martin, L. L., Ward, D. W., Achee, J. W., & Wyer, R. S. (1993). Mood as input: People have to interpret the motivational implications of their moods. *Journal of Personality and Social Psychology, 64,* 317–326.

McClelland, D. C. (1985). *Human motivation.* Glenview, IL: Scott, Foresman.

Pennebaker, J. W. (1989). Confessions, inhibition, and disease. In L. Berkowitz (Ed.), *Advances in experimental social psychology:* Vol. 22 (pp. 211–244). New York: Academic Press.

Pennebaker, J. W. (1993). Putting stress into words: Health, linguistic, and therapeutic implications. *Behavior Research and Therapy, 31,* 539–548.

Pennebaker, J. W., & Beall, S. K. (1986). Confronting a traumatic event: Toward an understanding of inhibition and disease. *Journal of Abnormal Psychology, 95,* 274–281.

Pennebaker, J. W., Colder, M., & Sharp, L. K. (1990). Accelerating the coping process. *Journal of Personality and Social Psychology, 58,* 528–537.

Pennebaker, J. W., & Francis, M. E. (1995). *Cognitive, emotional, and language processes in writing: Health and adjustment to college.* Manuscript submitted for publication.

Pennebaker, J. W., & Harber, K. D. (1993). A social stage model of collective coping: The Loma Prieta earthquake and the Persian Gulf War. *Journal of Social Issues, 49,* 125–145.

Pennebaker, J. W., Kiecolt-Glaser, J. K., & Glaser, R. (1988). Disclosure of traumas and immune function: Health implications for psychotherapy. *Journal of Consulting and Clinical Psychology, 56,* 239–245.

Pennebaker, J. W., & Susman, J. (1988). Disclosure of traumas and psychosomatic processes. *Social Science and Medicine, 26,* 327–332.

Powers, W. T. (1973) *Behavior: The control of perception.* Chicago: Aldine.

Spera, S., Buhrfeind, E., & Pennebaker, J. W. (1994). Expressive writing and job loss. *Academy of Management Journal, 37,* 722–733.

Tomkins, S. S. (1992). Script theory. In R. A. Zucker, A. I. Rabin, J. Aronoff, & S. J. Frank (Eds.), *Personality structure in the life course* (pp. 152–217). New York, NY: Springer.

von Bertalanffy, L. (1968). *General systems theory.* New York: Braziller.

Wortman, C. B., & Silver, R. L. (1988). The myths of coping with loss. *Journal of Consulting and Clinical Psychology, 57,* 349–357.

Chapter 7

Theories of Thought Flow: Points of Kinship and Fertile Contrasts

Eric Klinger
University of Minnesota

Martin and Tesser have produced a significant contribution to the understanding of thought flow. This commentary focuses on identifying the most important original elements of this formulation, both theoretical and empirical; indicating some necessary conceptual corrections; and exploring relations and some central contrasts between the theory and the current-concerns theory from which it has diverged.

ORIGINAL CONTRIBUTIONS

Theoretical Contributions

Martin and Tesser's chapter is intended to provide a theory of rumination, the delineation of which constitutes a significant theoretical advance. As I argue, however, the insistence on a separate theory of rumination is at best a minor theoretical gain, one with some advantages for articulation and application but also some offsetting conceptual costs. Rumination can fruitfully be viewed as one variety of the multidimensional general phenomenon of thought flow and can be accounted for by the laws that govern it. Nevertheless, in addressing this special region of the thought-flow hyperspace, the authors and their collaborators have achieved a number of impressive contributions.

Applications of Goal Hierarchies and Linkage Concepts. The most original theoretical contribution appears to be the detailed account of how rumination is influenced by the ruminator's goal hierarchies and especially by the linkages that the ruminator perceives to exist among the goals in each hierarchy. The idea that people are most likely to ruminate when they perceive unattained and especially threatened low-level goals to be linked to higher level goals—along with related propositions—provides both predictions regarding the goals that individuals will ruminate about and predictions regarding individual differences in rumination.

The precise mechanism by which linkage increases rumination is, in this model, presumably largely cognitive: realization that low-level failure leads to high-level consequences, thereby raising the stakes for failure, and enlarged associative nets for goals that are linked to others, thereby increasing accessibility. A possible mechanism seemingly left out of this model is that when the stakes for goal attainment go up, so does the intensity of emotional response to goal-related cues. The latter mechanism becomes important in the context of current-concerns theory, which postulates that thought segments are launched by and with emotional responses.

The notion that people vary in the extent to which they perceive linkages among their goals—which then in turn influences their risk for depression—raises a question about how perceiving linkages may be related to existing concepts in cognitive theories of depression. For example, is a tendency to perceive linkages related to the tendency to make global attributions when goal pursuits go wrong? Global attributions also entail perceived linkages; they make the difference, for instance, between blaming a failed relationship on the specific way one dealt with it and blaming it on one's pervasive incompetence in maintaining relationships. There is evidence that people who attribute globally are also more likely to become depressed following failure (e.g, Robins, 1988), though the connection is not especially strong. (Its effects may also not be independent of other attributional effects [Hull & Mendolia, 1991]; that would mean that other attributional variables incorporate globality.) Are these two constructs functionally identical, merely associated, or unrelated? If they are related but not identical, is one the real contributor to depression and the other merely incidental (and in that case, which is which?), or do both contribute independently?

Other Original Ideas. Martin and Tesser (this volume) hypothesize that "frustration of a series of lower order goals. . .summates to make the nonattainment of a higher order goal salient" (p. 13) and at that point rumination is triggered. This is an interesting, testable hypothesis. It again raises the question of mechanism.

One could posit that closely spaced frustrations lead to progressively stronger emotional responses to cues of the frustrated goals. (Martin and

7. THEORIES OF THOUGHT FLOW 109

Tesser are silent on the necessary temporal spacing of these frustrations.) That condition leads current concerns theorists to predict rumination, whether or not a higher order goal has become salient. The cognitive realization that the stakes in failure are higher than those of the low-level goals would also increase intensity of emotional response and, according to current-concerns theory, make rumination more likely. It would be interesting to try disentangling the emotional and cognitive consequences of repeated frustration and relate them to rumination independently, in order to assess the mechanism responsible. Thus, Martin and Tesser's formulation suggests some intriguing parametric investigations, varying the spacing of frustrations and cognitions about their consequences, with significant theoretical implications.

The hypothesis that a perceived goal may not be the individual's real goal would not have surprised Freud, but it is cast here in an interesting and probably testable form. Similarly, the hypothesis that rate of movement toward or away from a goal influences the intensity of positive or negative affect associated with the rumination is an original, testable application to thought flow. Both hypotheses hold important theoretical possibilities.

Empirical Contributions

Martin and Tesser's theoretical framework has yielded a rich set of results. The series of experiments on linkage (McIntosh & Martin, 1992; McIntosh, Harlow, & Martin, in press) provide important findings; so do colleagues Beckmann (1995) and Isbell, Gohm, and Wyer (1994, as cited by Martin & Tesser, this volume). Finally, the series of investigations involving strategic distraction (Beckmann & Martin, 1994, as cited by Martin, Tesser, & McIntosh, 1993) provide provocative results. However, the conclusions regarding the strategic rather than passive use of distraction raise some questions.

The investigators let all subjects succeed at a business-game task, but some subjects received feedback that they had succeeded through luck whereas others were told that they had succeeded through skill. Only the latter group were able to meet the goal of demonstrating their intelligence. Later, while performing a word recognition task, some subjects were subjected to a distracting tape recording, and others were not. The recognition task contained some words relating to intelligence, others to business, and others to neither. When considering only the words related to intelligence, the subjects who had received both luck feedback in the business game and distraction during word recognition recognized the intelligence-related words significantly more slowly than all other groups, presumably because these words reminded subjects of their failure to reach the goal of demonstrating their intelligence. Because there was no apparent slowing for the luck-feedback subjects who received no distraction and also none for the skill-feedback group that did receive distraction, the authors concluded that the luck-feedback group was inclined to make active use of distraction to avoid recognizing the intelligence-related words.

The problem with this conclusion is apparent by inspection of Table 1.2. Considering only the intelligence-related words, the authors' description of the results is accurate. However, when one considers the other words as well, it is apparent that the luck-feedback group under distraction produced latencies approximately the same as those that the other groups produced for the other word classes. In this framework, it is less the case that the luck-feedback/distraction subjects were especially slow in recognizing intelligence-related words than that the other three groups were especially fast in recognizing those words. This looks less as if the luck-feedback/distraction subjects were actively seeking distraction than that they allowed distraction to offset the special sensitization to intelligence-related words that they shared with the other groups, thereby normalizing their recognition latencies.

THE REPRESENTATION OF CURRENT CONCERNS

Chapter 1 reflects some healthy cross-fertilization between Martin and Tesser's theory of rumination and current-concerns theory. However, the current-concerns construct and its theory are in a few instances represented in ways that could lead to erroneous conclusions. This section serves to set the record straight.

Confusion of Conscious Content With Underlying States

In their frequent references to current concerns, a central construct of a theory with which I am identified (Klinger, 1975, 1977a, 1987a), Martin and Tesser occasionally use the term in ways inconsistent with its properties in the theory. In these instances, perhaps they are using it in a lesser, popular-language sense. (Current-concerns theory has no copyright on the expression and should perhaps have adopted a more abstruse term.) Be that as it may, it is important to point out those occasions when the properties that Martin and Tesser ascribe to current concerns are quite different from those that current-concerns theory implies. For example, I have used the term *current concerns* to refer to a nonconscious directive (brain) process that persists from the time of commitment to a particular goal to the termination of the pursuit. However, Martin and Tesser write, "our definition includes the following as modes of rumination: anticipation, basking, counterfactual thinking, current concerns, regret, [etc.]" (p. 8). This usage suggests that current concerns are a class of mental content and hence confuses conscious content (i.e., concern-related mentation) with underlying states (i.e., current concerns). In Table 1.1 the authors also seriously misrepresent the current-concern concept by treating it as a "mode of ruminative thought" and placing it in a cell labeled NEGATIVE and *Present*. This placement violates three theoretical properties of current concerns: They are constructs that refer to underlying, nonconscious brain processes or states, not to modes of conscious content, each current concern maintains the process of striving for some goal, which is more often positive (i.e., appetitive) than negative (i.e., aversive), and although the concern state always takes place in the present, the temporal orientation of the thought may be present, past, or future.

There is also some misunderstanding regarding the effect of goal thwarting in current-concerns theory. On p. 4, we read: "nor did we [Martin and Tesser] assume that goal blockage causes people to disengage from goal pursuit." Neither do I, unless it becomes plain to the individual that goal attainment is impossible or too costly, and then only after a protracted process. In fact, a number of publications (Klinger, 1975, 1977a [ch. 5], 1987a, 1993a, 1993b, in press-a) are devoted in part or whole to the processes, including rumination, that are set in motion by goal blockage.

Finally, Martin and Tesser theorize, again in apparent distinction to current-concerns theory, "In fact, if a person is committed to a goal but is making nonproblematic progress, then the person will experience little or no conscious thoughts about the goal" (p. 4). This has been a long-standing prediction of current-concerns theory (Klinger, 1971), and we have provided some evidence to that effect (Klinger, Barta, & Maxeiner, 1980).

POINTS OF IDENTITY AND FERTILE CONTRASTS

There are now a considerable number of treatments that attempt to be more or less comprehensive with respect to some large aspect of thought flow. Some of these clearly incorporate all thought flow and extend to all consciousness (Baars, 1988; Farthing, 1992) or to all thinking (Gilhooly, 1988). Others are focused on the sequencing, timing, and other determinants of mental content (Klinger, 1971, 1977a, 1978, 1987a, 1990) or of specific aspects of thought flow: daydreaming (Singer, 1975) and now rumination (Martin & Tesser, this volume). The last three of these have also contributed to the empirical literature of thought flow.

Of these latter three, the two most closely related in style and substance are Martin and Tesser's rumination theory and the current-concerns theory. They are in important ways alike, as indicated in Chapter 1. They are also in other important ways at theoretical odds, which is a welcome development in a field that has suffered from a lack of head-to-head theoretical differences, especially differences that were also readily subject to empirical investigation.

Which Theory is the General One, and Which is the Special Case?

Martin and Tesser state that their model "suggests a way in which to integrate what are currently separate yet related literatures on ruminative phenomena (e.g., meaning analysis, daydreaming, problem solving, reminiscence, anticipation)" (p. 2). However, many instances of these phenomena do not satisfy the authors' criteria for rumination. In particular, daydreaming and reminiscence need not satisfy the requirement of recurrence as that is delineated in the example on pages 2–3. Martin and Tesser do not define what precisely is meant by "instrumental," as in "revolve around a common instrumental theme" (p. 7), but by many definitions there are instances of daydreams and reminiscences that also do not satisfy that criterion.

On the other hand, the current-concerns theory addresses rumination in all its forms as a subset of the mental activities that make up thought flow (Klinger, 1971, 1977a, 1990). It proposes emotional responsivity mechanisms for the general case that clearly accommodate the phenomenon of rumination (Klinger, 1990, in press-a). There is thus no need to specify special mechanisms. This is not to deny the value of considering the special case and its possibly emergent properties, which is precisely the contribution of Martin and Tesser's chapter, but that is a different matter from viewing this treatment of the special case as the broader integration.

There are other ways in which current-concerns theory of thought flow encompasses elements of the rumination theory, besides those acknowledged in chapter 1. For example, the "mental simulations" attributed to Taylor and Schneider (1989) are, except by that name, a long-standing part of the current-concerns theory, included in chapters and articles (Klinger, 1971, 1977b, 1990) that describe the response organization of thought segments and argue, in virtually these words (Klinger, 1987b, 1990), that "they help people prepare for future events, interpret past events, and alter their emotional states" (Martin & Tesser, this volume, p. 6).

The rumination theory holds that "the tendency to experience ruminative thoughts is a function of an automatic rather than a controlled process . . . people do not have ruminative thoughts on purpose" (p. 32). This has been from the beginning a tenet of the current-concerns theory as it applies to respondent (i.e., undirected) thought, which includes most rumination as well as most other daydreaming. Furthermore, current-concerns theory posits that even when concern-related cues do not initiate thought segments, they are processed automatically at nonconscious levels. A growing body of research results supports this supposition: During sleep, when volitional activity is presumably minimized, concern-related cues redirect dream content (Hoelscher, Klinger, & Barta, 1981); during waking, even ostensibly ignored cues place a load on cognitive processing when they are concern related (Young, 1987) or emotionally arousing (Schneider, 1987), especially in subjects who are high in affective intensity or state orientation; and concern-related and emotionally arousing cues retard reaction time in Stroop and quasi-Stroop tasks (Cox, Blount, & Cools, 1992; Johnsen, Laberg, Cox, Vaksdal, & Hugdahl, 1994; Riemann, 1993). Research within other theoretical frameworks (e.g., construct accessibility, attitude relatedness) has provided similar findings (e.g., Bargh, Chaiken, Govender, & Pratto, 1992; Bargh & Pratto, 1986; Fazio, Sanbonmatsu, Powell, & Kardes, 1986) regarding automaticity of response. This body of research is reviewed in greater detail, and the latest form of the theory is described more fully, elsewhere (Klinger, in press-b).

Martin and Tesser restrain themselves from extending their theory into areas of psychopathology. By contrast, current-concerns theory has attempted integrations with psychopathology from the beginning (Klinger, 1971, 1975, 1977a, 1977b, 1990, 1993a, 1993b, in press-a, in press-b), especially in regard to depression. Given the present interest among depression researchers in rumination (e.g., Lyubomirsky & Nolen-Hoeksema, 1993; Nolen-Hoeksema, Parker, & Larson, 1994), there is little doubt that both theories would find ready application there, and for similar reasons.

The Functionality of Rumination

Martin and Tesser (this volume) seem committed to finding a direct instrumental benefit from all rumination. For example, they write that "in every case, the recurrent thoughts have the same function: They are instrumental to reducing some form of discrepancy [between actual and desired states]" (p. 6). In another place, we read:

> But what about reminiscing and basking? ... Where is the initiating discrepancy? We suggest that in these cases, rumination is in the service of bolstering or maintaining, rather than attaining, the goal. ... When recurrent thoughts do not directly address a discrepancy, they aid in reaffirming the lack of one. (p. 10)

That seems a rather strained bit of theorizing to maintain the functionality of rumination.

Why need rumination be in the service of something? I have no doubt that the existence of rumination in general conveys important benefits, as pointed out previously, but to state that this must be so *in every case* seems unconvincing and very hard, if at all possible, to test.

This is one point of difference from current-concerns theory. There ruminative thoughts may or may not be instrumental, but they are determined by processes originally set in motion by the discrepancy—that is, via current concerns. Cognitive processing, including thought, is elicited automatically by emotional responses (or, more commonly, what I have dubbed *protoemotional* responses; Klinger, 1994, in press-b—incipient emotional, purely neural responses) to what are usually concern-related cues. The resulting thoughts consist of verbal ideation and mental imagery that are related in various ways to goal striving, but in spontaneous thought they usually remain unevaluated and only occasionally serve to advance the individual toward his or her goals. Thus, rumination can be functional stochastically and yet not constantly.

Just the elicitation of unextinguished emotional responses, originally potentiated by then-current concerns, carries with it imagery consisting of perceptual and motor components, which can account for reminiscence and basking. Putting the matter in these terms relieves the theorist of having to postulate improbable functions and also unifies these phenomena with those less pleasant but still common experiences of spontaneously reliving moments of embarrassment and horror.

Emotion Versus (?) Accessibility as Fundamental Mechanisms: A Difference Potentially Fertile for Future Research

The most central theoretical difference between Martin and Tesser's rumination theory and the current-concerns theory of thought flow lies in the role of emotional (and protoemotional) processes in the latter and in its replacement in the former by construct accessibility. Construct accessibility depends on the richness of the associative net in which the construct is embedded. Martin and Tesser (this volume) recognize affect as a correlate of rumination but deny it any direct role:

> [R]umination and affect covary primarily because the two are influenced by many of the same factors . . . Can affect cause rumination? Yes, indirectly. It does so by influencing people's perceptions of goal attainment. It appears that people often interpret their emotional states as information relevant to judging the status of their goals. (pp. 17–18)

I agree that affect in fact plays these roles (Klinger, 1971, 1977a; cf. Mowrer, 1960; Tomkins, 1962), but not that it plays only these. In contrast to this limited delineation of emotional effects, current-concerns theory of thought flow assigns to protoemotional responses the central role of triggering topical changes in mental content. In this conception, protoemotional responses mediate the effects of encountering current-concern-related stimuli. They do this by setting off the first postsensory stage of cognitive analysis, the results of which determine whether processing is terminated and at a conscious level the stimulus is ignored, or whether processing continues to higher stages where additional components of emotional responses are recruited. Thus, protoemotional responding, potentiated by current concerns or by respondent conditioning, is theoretically the direct trigger mechanism for cognitive processing, including rumination and other thought flow.

The Case for Emotion as Part of the Trigger Mechanism for Rumination. There is growing evidence to support the conception that protoemotional responses mediate the effects of current concerns. Stimuli that are concern related also tend to evoke emotion (Bock & Klinger, 1986; Klinger, et al., 1980) and skin conductance responses (Nikula, Klinger, & Larson-Gutman, 1993). In Young's (1987) results, in which ignored concern-related stimuli slowed subjects' lexical decisions, concern-relatedness was strongly correlated with variables that are conceptually closely related to emotion. Using a procedure somewhat similar to Young's, Schneider (1987) found that distractor stimuli rated as emotionally arousing had a similar slowing effect on lexical decision time. That emotional processes were responsible for this slowing is supported by the additional finding that the slowing effect was stronger for subjects high rather than low in affective intensity scores. In other investigations, both concern-related and emotionally arousing words are recalled better than those that are neither, but when one is partialed out of the other, emotional arousal is the better predictor of free recall (Bock & Klinger, 1986; Klinger, Bock, & Bowi, 1990).

Although these latter studies did not examine rumination as such, they shed light on determinants of cognitive processing, and they suggest a role for emotion. Because the time frame for effects on lexical decision making was so small—fractions of a second—it is reasonable to ascribe the emotional effect to the hypothetically incipient, emotion-related processes dubbed here protoemotional processes. This conclusion is strengthened by findings that information regarding the emotional valence of stimuli is extracted nearly completely at near-theshold exposure times, whereas cognitive processing benefits substantially from longer exposures (Bock, Klinger, & Schneider, 1992).

Under this conception (Klinger, 1977, 1990), rumination about something occurs when people are disposed to respond with intense emotion to its associated cues. Intense responding to the class of cues is likely to mean suprathreshold responses to more of them than would be the case if emotional intensity were weaker; the generalization gradient broadens out.

Because these cues may be internal as well as external, people in this situation will find more internal cues (i.e., in their own stream of verbal thoughts and images) eliciting protoemotional responses and hence initiating repeated processing of information related to the concern.

This produces the recurrence noted by Martin and Tesser, and, of course, the associated affect. As in their model, the affect need not be negative. People who are happily in love ruminate quite a bit about their relationship, just as they will less happily when it ends. (I suspect that lovers ruminate about their relationships even when it is going neither more nor less well than expected—a violation of one of Martin and Tesser's tenets. This does not contradict the current-concerns theory, as long as the relationship has not become routinized or highly predictable.)

The current-concerns model of rumination also accounts for other phenomena described by Martin and Tesser (this volume), some of which are noted in passing throughout the previous sections, though different mechanisms are hypothesized. Finally, it accommodates the prediction that "[t]he more extreme these consequences [of attaining or not attaining the goal], the higher will be the priority granted to constructs related to that goal" (p. 15) if we assume that the prospect of more extreme consequences potentiates stronger emotional response.

A Critique of Accessibility as a Mechanism. Potentially, the most important theoretical contrast between the two theories lies in the positing of an emotional mechanism in current-concerns theory versus Martin and Tesser's (this volume) reliance on "accessibility, the mechanism presumed to be underlying rumination" (p. 23). The extent to which this contrast is productive depends on what precisely Martin and Tesser intend by the term *accessibility*. Taken by itself, it refers to the ease with which a given response can be elicited by a stimulus in a given situation. By itself, then, accessibility is not a mechanism but a descriptive term. If it is to be labeled a mechanism, it is necessary to add something to it—some process that accounts for the accessibility. Conventionally, accessibility of a response (often couched as a concept) is conferred by the number, design, and activity levels of associative pathways, which respond to learning histories, frequency and recency of encounters with associated cues, priming, and sets (as, for instance, instructional sets).

Current-concerns theory explains the accessibility of protoemotional responses to concern-related stimuli in terms of sensitization to those stimuli by the concern state, following commitment to pursue the respective goal. This idea is somewhat similar to Lewin's (1928) concept of a "quasi-need." It may well rest on a specific process of long-term potentiation, whose role in, for example, acquired fears is becoming plainer.

It is not clear from chapter 1 how, precisely, Martin and Tesser explain differential accessibility, but there are a number of clues. We already know that they rule out affect as having a direct role. We also know that "the model begins with the assumption that most thoughts are goal-driven" (p. 17) and that the accessibility under discussion is to "goal-related concepts" (p. 24); but it remains unclear just how goals drive thoughts.

Martin and Tesser have assessed accessibility using a word recognition task on the assumption that "the more subjects were ruminating about the goal of demonstrating their intelligence, the more accessible words related to intelligence would be and the faster subjects would recognize these words" (p. 23). However, the assessment procedure is neutral with regard to mechanism, and the rationale likewise omits specifying the link beteen prior rumination and accessibility. In a discussion of channelization, Martin and Tesser link accessibility with having established a rich associative network related to this thought (p. 17). Is being embedded in a rich associative network *the* mechanism, or is it one of several?

For the sake of argument, let us focus on associative richness, along with frequency and recency effects, as determiners of accessibility. A direct comparison between these and the concepts of concern-relatedness and emotional arousal value of stimuli is problematic because they are so heavily confounded. People with a current goal, especially a troubled one, are likely to have dealt with its cues more frequently and recently than with cues of other goals and will most likely have developed a richer set of associative connections. Therefore, it is hard, though presumably not impossible, to distinguish between the two kinds of explanation operationally. In any event, the necessary research has not yet been carried out.

If one takes the accessibility of certain concepts to be a somewhat enduring property of an individual's cognitive system, reflecting that person's perceptual–cognitive dispositions, there are a number of reasons to suppose that accessibility cannot adequately replace formulations employing current concerns and emotional activity. These reasons are spelled out elsewhere (Klinger, in press-b); not all apply here, but a few may. In particular, Mogg, Mathews, and Eysenck (1992) reported that patients diagnosed with generalized anxiety disorder (GAD), as compared with former GAD patients who had recovered, showed a significant attentional sensitivity to threat-related words. The paradigm used by Mogg et al. is of special interest here, for the results obtained with their methods do not lend themselves readily to explanation through accessibility constructs: Faster reaction times to dot-probe stimuli were found when the dots were located in the previous positions of the threat-related words than when they appeared in the previous positions of the neutral words. It is hard to argue that the faster the common, supraliminal words can be understood, the longer the eye focuses on them, but that would be necessary to facilitate reaction time to a subsequent dot at that location. It is much easier to argue the contrary view. On the other hand, the result is easily accommodated by the current-concerns view that subjects attend to current-concern-related stimuli more closely than to others. Additionally, words may achieve comparable accessibility whether they are concern-related or emotionally arousing to a subject. Yet as discussed previously evidence is accumulating to indicate that emotional arousal value of a stimulus is the more direct predictor of recall. However hard or easy it may be to make this finding jibe with an associative accessibility mechanism, it is clearly incompatible with a theory that regards thoughts as goal-driven and yet emotions as having no direct effect on them. Finally, Young's (1987) data showed that the presence of disattended concern-related distractors slows lexical decisions about focal stimuli and that distractors related to important concerns slow lexical decisions more than those related to unimportant concerns. It is hard to imagine how associative accessibility could account for such a result without imbuing the construct of accessibility with motivational properties at least sufficient to create response competition that deflects cognitive resources. When a disattended stimulus sets off processing that conflicts with the response to an attended stimulus, it appears that something less passive is going on than is suggested by accessibility. It is necessary to formulate a mechanism that includes prioritizing processes such as emotional arousal.

Implications for Future Research. The contrast in mechanisms is nowhere more pointed than in explaining the perseveration of rumination beyond goal attainment (p. 17). Martin and Tesser attribute this "channelization" to richness of associative networks. Within the current-concerns framework, I attribute it to, among other factors, the persistence of as-yet unextinguished conditioned emotional responses. That should be a researchable difference.

This discussion clearly points to important future research directions. It points toward investigations that try to disentangle the various factors that contribute to accessibility in order to pinpoint the processes that in fact underlie it as it relates to rumination. The contrast between sensitization of protoemotional processes to concern-related cues in current-concerns theory on the one hand and the factors hinted at in Martin and Tesser's formulation provide indications of where one might begin looking.

REFERENCES

Baars, B. J. (1988). *A cognitive theory of consciousness.* Cambridge, England: Cambridge University Press.

Bargh, J. A., Chaiken, S., Govender, R., & Pratto, F. (1992). The generality of the automatic attitude activation effect. *Journal of Personality and Social Psychology, 62,* 893–912.

Bargh, J. A., & Pratto, F. (1986). Individual construct accessibility and perceptual selection. *Journal of Experimental Social Psychology, 22,* 293–311.

Beckmann, J. (1995). Self-presentation and the Zeigarnik effect. In R. Nygard, & T. Gjesme (Eds.), *Advances in motivation* (pp. 13–27). Oslo: Universitets for Laget.

Bock, M., & Klinger, E. (1986). Interaction of emotion and cognition in word recall. *Psychological Research, 48,* 99–106.

Bock, M., Klinger, E., & Schneider, K. (1992, July). *Are emotional effects of words mediated by lexical meaning?* Paper presented at the 25th International Congress of Psychology, Brussels, Belgium.

Cox, W. M., Blount, J. P., & Cools, J. (1992). [Effects of color-friction, concern-related, and emotional word content on reactions to quasi-Stroop stimuli]. Unpublished raw data.

Farthing, G. W. (1992). *The psychology of consciousness.* Englewood Cliffs, NJ: Prentice-Hall.

Fazio, R. H., Sanbonmatsu, D. M., Powell, M. C., & Kardes, F. R. (1986). On the automatic activation of attitudes. *Journal of Personality and Social Psychology, 50,* 229–238.

Gilhooly, K. J. (1988). *Thinking: Undirected and creative.* New York: Academic Press.

Hoelscher, T. J., Klinger, E., & Barta, S. G. (1981). Incorporation of concern- and nonconcern-related verbal stimuli into dream content. *Journal of Abnormal Psychology, 49,* 88–91.

Hull, J. G., & Mendolia, M. (1991). Modeling the relations of attributional style, expectancies, and depression. *Journal of Personality and Social Psychology, 61,* 85–97.

Johnsen, B. H., Laberg, J. C., Cox, W. M., Vaksdal, A., & Hugdahl, K. (1994). Alcoholics' attentional bias in the processing of alcohol-related words. *Psychology of Addictive Behaviors, 8,* 111–115.

Klinger, E. (1971). *Structure and functions of fantasy.* New York: Wiley.

Klinger, E. (1975). Consequences of commitment to and disengagement from incentives. *Psychological Review, 82,* 1–25.

Klinger, E. (1977a). *Meaning and void: Inner experience and the incentives in people's lives.* Minneapolis: University of Minnesota Press.

Klinger, E. (1977b). The nature of fantasy and its clinical uses. *Psychotherapy: Theory, research and practice, 14,* 223–231.

Klinger, E. (1978). Modes of normal conscious flow. In K. S. Pope & J. L. Singer (Eds.), *The stream of consciousness: Scientific investigations into the flow of human experience* (pp. 225–258). New York: Plenum.

Klinger, E. (1987a). Current concerns and disengagement from incentives. In F. Halisch & J. Kuhl (Eds.), *Motivation, intention and volition* (pp. 337–347). Berlin: Springer.

Klinger, E. (1987b). The power of daydreams. *Psychology Today, 21,* 36–39, 42, 44.

Klinger, E. (1990). *Daydreaming.* Los Angeles: Tarcher/Putnam.

Klinger, E. (1993a). Clinical approaches to mood control. In D. M. Wegner & J. W. Pennebaker (Eds.), *Handbook of mental control* (pp. 344–369). Englewood Cliffs, NJ: Prentice-Hall.

Klinger, E. (1993b). Loss of interest. In C. G. Costello (Ed.), *Symptoms of depression* (pp. 43–62). New York: Wiley.

Klinger, E. (1994). Motivation and imagination. *Psychologische Beiträge, 34,* 127–142.

Klinger, E. (in press-a). The contents of thoughts: Interference as the downside of adaptive normal mechanisms in thought flow. In I. G. Sarason, B. R. Sarason, & G. R. Pierce (Eds.), *Cognitive interference: Theories, methods, and findings.* Hillsdale, NJ: Lawrence Erlbaum Associates.

Klinger, E. (in press-b). Emotional influences on cognitive processing, with implications for theories of both. In P. M. Gollwitzer & J. A. Bargh (Eds.), *Action science: Linking cognition and motivation to behavior* (pp. 168–189). New York: Guilford.

Klinger, E., Barta, S. G., & Maxeiner, M. E. (1980). Motivational correlates of thought content frequency and commitment. *Journal of Personality and Social Psychology, 39,* 1222–1237.

Klinger, E., Bock, M., & Bowi, U. (1990). [Emotional mediation of motivational factors in word recall]. Unpublished raw data.

Lewin, K. (1928). Wille, Vorsatz und Bedürfnis. *Psychologische Forschung, 7,* 330–385.

Lyubomirsky, S., & Nolen-Hoeksema, S. (1993). Self-perpetuating properties of dysphoric rumination. *Journal of Personality and Social Psychology, 65,* 339–349.

Martin, L. L., Tesser, A., & McIntosh, W. D. (1993). Wanting but not having: The effects of unattained goals on thoughts and feelings. In D. M. Wegner & J. W. Pennebaker (Eds.), *Handbook of mental control* (pp. 552–572). Englewood Cliffs, NJ: Prentice-Hall.

McIntosh, W. D., Harlow, T. F., & Martin L. L. (in press). Linkers and nonlinkers: The relation between goals, beliefs, rumination, and depression. *Journal of Basic and Applied Psychology*.

McIntosh, W. D., & Martin, L. L. (1992). The cybernetics of happiness: The relation between goal attainment, rumination, and affect. In M. S. Clark (Ed.), *Review of personality and social psychology* (pp. 222–246). Newbury Park, CA: Sage.

Mogg, K., Mathews, A., & Eysenck, M. (1992). Attentional bias to threat in clinical anxiety states. *Cognition and Emotion, 6,* 149–159.

Mowrer, O. H. (1960). *Learning theory and behavior.* New York: Wiley.

Nikula, R., Klinger, E., & Larson-Gutman, M. K. (1993). Current concerns and electrodermal reactivity: Responses to words and thoughts. *Journal of Personality, 61,* 63–84.

Nolen-Hoeksema, S., Parker, L. E., & Larson, J. (1994). Ruminative coping with depressed mood following loss. *Journal of Personality and Social Psychology, 67,* 92–104.

Riemann, B. C., & McNally, R. J. (1995). Cognitive processing of personally-relevant information. *Cognition and Emotion, 9,* 325–340.

Robins, C. J. (1988). Attributions and depression: Why is the literature so inconsistent? *Journal of Personality and Social Psychology, 54,* 880–889.

Schneider, W. (1987). *Ablenkung und Handlungskontrolle: Eine «kognitiv-motivationale Perspektive»* [Distraction and action control: A "cognitive-motivational perspective"]. Unpublished diploma thesis, University of Bielefeld, Germany.

Singer, J. L. (1975). *The inner world of daydreaming.* New York: Harper & Row.

Taylor, S. E., & Schneider, S. K. (1989). Coping and the simulation of events. *Social Cognition, 7,* 174–194.

Tomkins, S. S. (1962). *Affect, imagery, consciousness* (Vol. 1). New York: Springer.

Young, J. (1987). *The role of selective attention in the attitude–behavior relationship.* Unpublished doctoral dissertation, University of Minnesota.

Chapter 8

Attention Inhibition: Does It Underlie Ruminative Thought?

Patricia Linville
Duke University

Rumination involves persistent, recurring thoughts that revolve around a common theme and unintentionally enter consciousness, thus shifting attention away from one's current task goals. Martin and Tesser have moved us toward an understanding of rumination within a general cognitive framework. Their most important contribution is an elaboration of goal-directed processes—ruminative thoughts arise from discrepancies in the progress toward meeting a higher order goal. They provide a number of useful insights while fleshing out this goal-directed nature of ruminations. First, rumination appears to depend not simply on unmet goals but rather on perceptions of lack of movement or progress toward a goal. Second, ruminations involve automatic as well as controlled processes. For example, the onset of ruminative thoughts occurs largely without intention; ruminations are goal directed, but people largely are not conscious of their goals; yet the product of ruminative processes is conscious thought. Third, the possible modes of rumination may be quite broad (e.g., counterfactual thinking, mental simulation, basking, worry, regret). And fourth, there are rich, process-oriented links between affect and rumination.

The main theme of this chapter is that an attentional mechanism—inhibition—may underlie rumination. Inhibitory attentional mechanisms need not supplant other mechanisms of rumination. In fact, I build on Martin and Tesser's theory in suggesting how two key players in rumination—goals and affect—also play key roles in inhibition. The argument I develop goes as follows: Attentional inhibition acts as an automatic cognitive gatekeeper, hindering access to consciousness of marginally relevant or irrelevant external information and internal thoughts, thus focusing attention on current task goals. With this cognitive architecture, how do ruminative thoughts unintentionally make it through the gateway to consciousness? I suggest two answers stimulated by the ideas of Martin and Tesser. To preview, first, ruminative thoughts may gain unintended access under normal inhibition functioning because they are goal directed, as Martin and Tesser propose. Because normal inhibition processes are also goal directed, sometimes information irrelevant to a current task goal will gain access to working memory because of its relevance to another high priority goal that has just been cued. These ruminative thoughts are goal relevant, just not relevant to the goal underlying the task at hand. Second, we know from the attention literature that weakened inhibitory mechanisms allow information and thoughts irrelevant to current goals to leak into working memory. Ruminative associations may be one source of this type of thought. What weakens inhibitory processes? We have recent evidence (Linville, 1994; Linville, Connelly, & Hasher, 1994) that stress and depression weaken inhibition and thus potentially increase ruminative thoughts. Thus, in these two ways, inhibition processes may foster rumination.

In this chapter, I first summarize current theory in the cognitive attention literature, which includes the dual mechanisms of excitation and inhibition in the selective attention of information. Then I speculate on several ways that inhibition processes may play a role in ruminative thoughts. These include how normal inhibitory processes allow rumination, drawing on the role of goals proposed by Martin and Tesser, and how weakened inhibitory ability may underlie ruminative thought. Finally, I suggest that stress and depression weaken one's ability to inhibit off-goal information and thoughts, and this weakened inhibitory mechanism may foster rumination. I present some new data linking stress and depression to weakened inhibitory ability.

SELECTIVE ATTENTION: THE ROLE OF INHIBITION

What Is Inhibition?

The environment is rich with an array of information, producing a constant flow of information. And mental associations are numerous. To maintain a coherent mental life, some information is selected for further processing while other information is ignored. Only a subset of available information is selected for further processing, so what happens to nonselected information? It was once thought that its activation passively decayed when it received no further processing. A current view is that selective attention involves two mechanisms—*excitation* of selected, relevant information plus active *inhibition* of nonselected, irrelevant information (e.g., Hasher & Zacks, 1988; Neill, 1977; Neumann, 1987; Tipper, 1985; Tipper & Cranston, 1985). There is an initial perceptual analysis of a broad range of stimuli, involving the identification of objects encoded by the perceptual system whether or not they are attended to, followed by the suppression of activation of the cognitive representation of irrelevant information not selected for further processing. By actively inhibiting the representation of off-goal, distracting information and thoughts, information that is less relevant to the task goal is kept from interfering with goal-relevant thought. Inhibition is thus essential for maintaining a coherent stream of thought. For example, how are you able to attend to this chapter while ignoring distractions such as the color of the room, anxious thoughts over the deadline of the chapter you are writing, a replay of a recent argument, or plans for dinner tonight? Inhibition enables people to engage in goal-relevant thought (e.g., comprehension of this chapter) by screening out irrelevant, marginally relevant, or off-goal information. Attention inhibition is basic to efficient cognitive processing, playing a key role in a variety of cognitive tasks including memory, language comprehension, speech production, and problem solving (e.g., Engle, in press; Gernsbacher, 1990; Gernsbacher, Varner, & Faust, 1990; Hasher & Zacks, 1988; MacDonald & MacWhinney, 1990).[1]

How Do Inhibitory Processes Work?

In general, inhibition operates by screening out irrelevant information and by dampening the activation of irrelevant or no longer relevant information. A commonality between inhibition and rumination is that both appear to be goal-directed processes. Let me elaborate on the operations of inhibition processes in this light. Hasher and Zacks (1988; Stoltzfus, Hasher, & Zacks, in press; Zacks & Hasher, 1994) proposed that efficient functioning of working memory depends on inhibitory attention processes that limit

---

[1] Inhibition processes have been proposed in language comprehension (Gernsbacher, 1990; MacDonald & MacWhinney, 1990). For example, as we first hear or read an ambiguous word, multiple possible meanings are often activated (e.g., *bug* can refer to insect or covert microphone). Then contextual cues lead us to one interpretation (e.g., "Bugs and spiders were in the house"). Research suggests that immediately after seeing an ambiguous word in its context, multiple meanings of the word are activated (both the context-appropriate and inappropriate meanings) even though one meaning is implied by the context. For example, subjects respond as quickly to the word *ant* as *spy*, even though the context implies *ant*. However, after a very short delay, the mechanism of inhibition dampens the activation of the less relevant meaning, leaving the relevant meaning activated.

the access of information into working memory and update the contents of working memory by removing no longer relevant information. Efficient processing, and thus cognitive performance, depend then on having the contents of working memory closely represent current task goals. Hasher and Zacks suggested several ways in which inhibitory control of working memory operates. First, inhibition prevents access to working memory of off-goal information that may be activated along with goal-relevant information. Sources of off-goal information may be environmental stimuli or internal thoughts and associations. Inhibition also quickly dampens the activation of goal-irrelevant information that leaks into working memory. Second, inhibition dampens the activation of information that once was relevant but now is irrelevant because of a change in goals. A goal (e.g., trying to figure out how to take care of an ailing parent) may have been satisfied (your parent goes to live with a sibling), supplanted by a more important one (your spouse wants a divorce), or supplanted by a more salient one (you feel hungry and start to plan dinner). Inhibition helps eliminate thoughts from working memory that are relevant to the previous goal, allowing one to switch attention in response to new goals. Third, inhibition suppresses the activation of rejected hypotheses or interpretations of information, preventing attention from returning to discarded ideas (e.g., a failed or considered yet rejected path toward meeting a goal). In sum, inhibition functions in the service of goals by focusing attention on current, goal-relevant information.

What Happens When Inhibitory Mechanisms Are Weak?

When inhibitory mechanisms are weak, negative consequences result (see Hasher & Zacks, 1988, for an extensive theoretical and empirical summary with older adults). First, too much irrelevant information gets into working memory along with goal-relevant information. As a consequence, links between relevant and irrelevant information are created in working memory and are then stored in long-term memory, setting the stage for slow and less accurate retrieval of relevant information. Second, irrelevant information that leaks into working memory is sustained longer. For these reasons, one is more easily distracted by irrelevant information and thoughts, more likely to experience cognitive deficits in performance, and more likely to lose a train of thought.

Several populations show weakened inhibition. There is evidence that deficient inhibitory attentional mechanisms may account for some of the cognitive memory problems with older adults (e.g., Hasher, Stoltzfus, Zacks, & Rypma, 1991; Kane, Hasher, Stoltzfus, Zacks, & Connelly, 1994; McDowd & Oseas-Kreger, 1991; Tipper, 1991) as well as some of the cognitive symptoms of children with Attention Deficit Disorder (e.g., Bjorklund & Harnishfeger, 1990; Pennington, Groisser, & Welsh, 1993), obsessive-compulsive patients (e.g., Enright & Beech, 1990), and schizophrenics (e.g., Beech, Powell, McWilliams, & Claridge, 1989; Frith, 1979). These groups on average show less ability to ignore irrelevant information.

INHIBITION UNDERLYING RUMINATION

I suggest that inhibition is one of the processes underlying ruminative thought. The selective attention literature has focused on fairly micro-cognitive processes and has not considered how inhibitory attention processes foster rumination. Here I suggest several ways in which this might occur.

Normal Inhibition Processes

Rumination can occur even when inhibition functions normally. First, because normal inhibition processes are goal directed, ruminative thoughts irrelevant to one's current task goal may gain unintended, repeated access to working memory because of their link to a high priority goal that has just been cued (e.g., comprehending why one's child had to die). This is consistent with Martin and Tesser's notion that ruminations are goal directed. These ruminative thoughts are goal relevant, simply not relevant to the goal underlying the task at hand. Second, inhibition processes are not perfect, so off-task thoughts (e.g., worries or regrets, personal associations, daydreams, or counterfactual thinking) will sometimes leak into working memory. The activation of these ruminations may be quickly dampened by efficient inhibitory mechanisms, allowing attention to return to current task goals.

Weakened Inhibition

There are individual differences in ability to inhibit, and there is evidence from the attention literature that certain normal (e.g., older adults) and clinical populations have weakened inhibitory attention mechanisms. Weakened inhibition may foster rumination. I speculate on several ways this might occur.

First, weakened inhibition could allow intrusive ruminative thoughts to enter working memory and disrupt one's current stream of thought. For example, recurrent thoughts of a recent robbery of one's home might intrude while reading a novel on vacation. In such cases, the contents of working memory might represent two trains of thought—thoughts associated with the current task goal plus thoughts about a recurrent, unmet goal (e.g., comprehension of reading material plus achieving security). This sets the stage for poor, inefficient processing of information toward meeting either the current or long-term, unmet goal.

Second, weakened inhibition could allow information related to a previous goal, once relevant but now irrelevant because the goal was satisfied or replaced, to maintain activation and grab attention away from one's current task goal. For example, a woman may not be able to shake persistent ruminations related to breast cancer even after hearing the good news that the lump is benign. Weakened inhibition thus may foster what Martin and Tesser call channelized ruminations—nonmotivated ruminations arising from the simple activation of the rich associative network of thoughts connected to a previous goal.

Third, weakened inhibition could allow the return of considered yet rejected ideas, such as an incorrect interpretation of behavior, a rejected scenario for meeting a goal, or the replay of a failed attempt to satisfy a goal. For example, a friend not returning your call might instigate several interpretations, such as "She has rejected me." Upon learning that your friend was out of town, you dismiss this interpretation. However, a weakened inhibition mechanism might maintain recurrent ruminations about her possible rejection of you. Weakened inhibition might also allow continued activation of unsuccessful paths to a goal, disrupting attempts to generate and follow alternative paths to the goal. For example, repeated mental replay of an unsuccessful romance might block thoughts and plans for new interpersonal opportunities.

Fourth, weakened inhibition could allow the intrusion of lower level, less central, or less urgent goals to grab one's attention. Martin and Tesser are probably correct in suggesting that higher order goals are the more frequent focus of rumination, yet weakened inhibition could disrupt this goal hierarchy and allow activation of ruminations relevant to less central goals. For example, while trying to finish the writing of an important article, your mind continually wanders to thoughts of whether you should have waited for the next generation of laptop computers rather than buying the current model.

Inhibition and Rumination: Complex Issues Regarding Goals

Thinking through the links between rumination and inhibition raises several complexities regarding the operation of goals. For instance, it may be too simple to say, as in the attention literature, that inhibition mechanisms suppress irrelevant information in favor of goal-relevant information. Surely inhibited information is often goal relevant, but relevant to goals not currently active. Likewise, it may be too simple to say that goal-discrepant thought intrudes on current thought. Current thought is also largely goal directed, related to unmet needs. We have multiple goals, occurring at multiple levels of salience and importance. Current thoughts, unintended intrusive thoughts, and successfully suppressed thoughts may all reflect goals.

This raises the issue of what is goal-irrelevant information. If a manager is deciding who to hire for a position, her goal is to comprehend the application material and decide who best fits the position. However, the manager simultaneously could be *worrying* about whether the new person might get her current office or outperform her, repeatedly *regretting* that she did not have her assistant do the initial screening of applicants, *mentally simulating* asking for an extra week of vacation, *basking* in thoughts of how successful she was when she started in that position, or *reminiscing* with pain about an old lover who looks like one of the applicants. Each may be considered rumination, and each is off-task or goal irrelevant in terms of the current task goal. In each case, however, the contents of working memory may reflect a goal of the manager, and in this light few thoughts are totally goal irrelevant.

STRESS AND DEPRESSION WEAKEN INHIBITION

One goal of this chapter is to explore for the first time the potential links between stress and affect, inhibitory selective attention mechanisms, and rumination. One potential theoretical story is that stress and negative affect weaken inhibitory attention mechanisms, which in turn foster rumination. Thus stress and negative affect may be associated with increased rumination via the mechanism of inhibition. Although there is no direct test of this model, there is support for connections among these concepts.

What evidence is there for these links? In the previous section, I suggested how a weakened inhibitory mechanism could result in rumination. In the next section, I note the substantial research showing that stress and negative affect are associated with rumination. I then summarize some new data suggesting that those stressed or depressed show weakened inhibition.

Stress and Affect Linked With Rumination

There is ample evidence that ruminative thoughts are linked with stress and negative affect (see Martin and Tesser, this volume, for a discussion of this research). For example, those experiencing stressful events tend to experience involuntary, intrusive, distressing ruminations in the form of associations, memories, and images related to the event (Horowitz, 1975; Silver, Wortman, & Klos, 1982; Wegner, 1988), and ruminations related to major life events often persist for years (Tait & Silver, 1989). The ongoing experience of these ruminations is associated with reported stress and negative affect, a lack of recovery from the event, lower life satisfaction, and longer depression (Horowitz, 1975; Nolen-Hoeksema, 1991; Tait & Silver, 1989). Other evidence comes from the nature of depressive thought. Depressed individuals appear plagued with intrusive, recurring, involuntary thoughts around the theme of negative self-evaluation and self-reproach (Beck, 1967; Beck, Rush, Shaw, & Emery, 1979; Wenzlaff, Wegner, & Roper, 1988). For example, thoughts such as "I'm boring" and "No one likes me" intrude during social interactions, even thought they are irrelevant to the context (e.g., Moretti & Shaw, 1989). Finally, Martin and Tesser suggest that negative affect may lead people to infer that they are making poor progress toward their goals, which in turn instigates rumination.

Stress and Depression Weaken Inhibition

I suggest that stress and depression can result in weakened inhibitory mechanisms. Although no previous research has directly looked at this, several lines of research are consistent with such a link. First, there is some cognitive disfunctioning with stress and depression. For example, people under stress are more distractible, engage in lower levels of thinking, make more errors on some cognitive tasks such as proofreading, and experience a narrowed focus of attention that improves memory for central details but impairs memory for peripheral details of emotional events (e.g., Christianson, 1992; Cohen, 1978; Cohen, Evans, Krantz, & Stokols, 1980; Easterbrook, 1959; Glass & Singer, 1972; Mandler, 1982; Pennebaker, 1989). Depressed individuals show deficits in recall and some recognition tasks, problem solving, general learning, motor speed, and intellectual functioning (e.g., Alloy, 1988; Ellis, 1990, 1991; Ellis & Ashbrook, 1988; Hartlage, Alloy, Vazquez, & Dykman, 1993; Hertel, 1994; Hertel & Hardin, 1990; Hertel & Rude, 1991; Ingram, 1990; Williams, Watts, MacLeod, & Mathews, 1988). Various models of attention allocation have been proposed for memory impairment in both stressed and depressed populations. Second, persistent, involuntary, distracting, intrusive off-goal thoughts increase with stress (e.g., ruminations associated with stressful life events) (Horowitz, 1976, 1982; Klinger, 1975; Silver, Boon, & Stones, 1983; Tait & Silver, 1989) and with depression (e.g., automatic cycles of negative self-relevant thoughts) (Beck, 1967; Beck, Rush, Shaw, & Emery, 1979; Moretti & Shaw, 1989; Wenzlaff, Wegner, & Roper, 1988).

One mechanism underlying these cognitive deficits and intrusions may be weak inhibition. To investigate this, I and my colleagues (Linville, 1994; Linville et al., 1994) have been conducting research on affective factors that influence inhibition. We used a standard cognitive paradigm measuring attention inhibition to address how stress affects inhibition and how depression affects inhibition.

Various tasks in the selective attention literature have been used to assess the momentary consequences of the inhibition of a stimulus. A negative priming task is one such task often used to tap inhibitory ability (e.g., Hasher, et al., 1991; Neill, 1977; Tipper, 1985). We have used this paradigm to access the inhibitory ability of those under stress or depression. On each of a series of trials, the subject sees two words displayed on a computer monitor, one in red and one in green. The subject's task is to say the word in red, ignoring the word in green (or vice versa). The words are presented very briefly (e.g., 100 ms in our study), and subjects usually cannot recall the distractor word. The attention literature suggests that the act of selecting relevant information (here, the target word in red) also automatically entails suppressing irrelevant information (here, the distractor word in green). How can we test this here? If "barn" is inhibited as the distractor word on one trial and then appears as the target on the next trial, subjects should be slower to say "barn" than they would if the word had not appeared as the distractor on the previous trial. In general, selection of the relevant word also entails inhibition of the unselected word on a trial, and this should impair the ability to respond to that word on the subsequent trial. This slowdown (called a *negative priming effect*) is taken as evidence of active inhibition. (If the process was one of simple decay of the unselected word, then the response time in the suppression and the control conditions would be the same, or one might even find facilitation.) This negative priming effect has been found in a large number of studies using a range of stimuli (words, letters, pictures, Stroop items), timing variants, and types of suppression tasks (e.g., suppression of identity or suppression of location of a target) (e.g., Hasher, et al., 1991; Kane, et al., 1994; Lowe, 1979, 1985; Neill, 1977; Tipper, 1985; Tipper & Cranston, 1985; Tipper & Driver, 1988).

Most subjects performing this task show a slowdown in response time to a target that was the previous distractor, presumably because they have successfully inhibited the word. Some populations (e.g., older adults; Hasher & Zacks, 1988) do not show this showdown in response time, presumably because they have not inhibited the distractor word, and this lack of slowdown is interpreted as diminished inhibitory attention ability. The current issue is how people under stress and depression perform on this task. In our studies with college students, high and low stress subjects, as well as depressed and nondepressed subjects, completed this word-naming task (Linville, 1994; Linville et al., 1994).

Are stressed subjects less able to inhibit? Low stress subjects showed a significant negative priming effect, indicating a strong ability to inhibit irrelevant information. High stress subjects, however, showed diminished inhibitory attention ability. Correlation data also support this finding.

Stress levels and negative priming effects were significantly negatively correlated ($r = -.66$). The more stressed, the less able subjects were able to suppress irrelevant information. Are depressed subjects less able to inhibit? Nondepressed subjects showed a significant negative priming effect, indicating a strong inhibitory ability. In contrast, depressed subjects showed diminished inhibitory ability. Thus, depression limits one's ability to inhibit or ignore distracting, irrelevant information.

In sum, people under high stress or depressed are less able to ignore stimuli irrelevant to the goal at hand, indicating a decline in inhibitory attention ability. These findings have several implications for the stress and depression areas. First, they help to explain why people undergoing a major stressful life event have cognitive deficits that make it harder to cope, problem-solve, and make decisions. Second, the findings also suggest why regular, daily situations that increase stress level, such as time pressure, work load, or interpersonal conflict, decrease one's effectiveness in problem solving and decision tasks in various contexts, including the work place. Third, the results have clinical implications, suggesting that the cycle of negative, self-relevant thoughts that characterize depression may be understood in terms of diminished inhibitory attention mechanisms. Fourth, these data suggest a mechanism for increased ruminations during stress and depression.

CONCLUSION

Martin and Tesser's theorizing has moved us toward an understanding of rumination in a framework of cognitive structures and processes. Particular advances include an elaboration of goal-directed processes (e.g., ruminations arise from problematic progress toward a goal), a distinction between automatic and controlled processes (e.g., ruminations are unintended, but their product gains conscious awareness), and rich process-oriented links between affect and rumination.

Building on some of their assumptions, I have suggested an additional mechanism that may underlie ruminative thought—attentional inhibition. I have considered the links between stress and affect, attention inhibition, and rumination. I have suggested that stress and depression weaken attention inhibition, which in turn fosters rumination. In this fashion, weakened inhibition may mediate the known effects of stress and depression on ruminative thought.

REFERENCES

Alloy, L. B. (1988). *Cognitive processes in depression*. New York: Guilford.
Beck, A. T. (1967). *Depression: Clinical, experimental and theoretical aspects*. New York: Harper & Row.

Beck, A. T., Rush, A. J., Shaw, B. F., & Emery, G. (1979). *Cognitive therapy of depression*. New York: Guilford.

Beech, A., Powell, T., McWilliams, J., & Claridge, G. (1989). Evidence of reduced "cognitive inhibition" in schizophrenia. *British Journal of Clinical Psychology, 28*, 109–116.

Bjorklund, D. F., & Harnishfeger, K. K. (1990). The resources construct in cognitive development: Diverse sources of evidence and a theory of inefficient inhibition. *Developmental Review, 10*, 48–71.

Christianson, S. -A. (1992). Emotional stress and eyewitness memory: A critical review. *Psychological Bulletin, 112*, 284–309.

Cohen, S. (1978). Environmental load and the allocation of attention. In A. Baum, J. E. Singer, & S. Valins (Eds.), *Advances in environmental psychology* (Vol. 1, pp. 253–268). Hillsdale, NJ: Lawrence Erlbaum Associates.

Cohen, S., Evans, G. W., Krantz, D. S., & Stokols, D. (1980). Physiological, motivational, and cognitive effects of aircraft noise on children: Moving from the laboratory to the field. *American Psychologist, 35*, 231–243.

Easterbrook, J. A. (1959). The effect of emotion on cue utilization and the organization of behavior. *Psychological Review, 66*, 183–201.

Ellis, H. C. (1990). Depressive deficits in memory: Processing initiative and resource allocation. *Journal of Experimental Psychology: General, 119*, 606–612.

Ellis, H. C. (1991). Focused attention and depressive deficits in memory. *Journal of Experimental Psychology: General, 120*, 310–312.

Ellis, H. C., & Ashbrook, P. W. (1988). Resource allocation model and the effects of depressed mood states on memory. In K. Fiedler & J. Forgas (Eds.), *Affect, cognition, and social behavior*. Toronto, Ontario, Canada: Hogreff.

Engle, R. W. (in press). Working memory and retrieval: An inhibition–resource approach. In J. T. E. Richardson (Ed.), *Working memory and human cognition*. Oxford University Press.

Enright, S. J., & Beech, A. R. (1990). Obsessional states: Anxiety disorders or Schizotypes? An information processing and personality assessment. *Psychological Medicine, 20*, 621–627.

Frith, C. D. (1979). Consciousness, information processing, and schizophrenia. *British Journal of Psychiatry, 134*, 225–235.

Gernsbacher, M. A. (1990). *Language comprehension as structure building*. Hillsdale, NJ: Lawrence Erlbaum Associates.

Gernsbacher, M. A., Varner, K. R., & Faust, M. E. (1990). Investigating differences in general comprehension skills. *Journal of Experimental Psychology: Learning, Memory, and Cognition, 16*, 430–445.

Glass, D. C., & Singer, J. E. (1972). *Urban stress*. New York: Academic Press.

Hartlage, S., Alloy, L. B., Vazquez, C., & Dykman, B. (1993). Automatic and effortful processing in depression. *Psychological Bulletin, 113*, 247–278.

Hasher, L., Stoltzfus, E. R., Zacks, R. T., & Rypma, B. (1991). Age and inhibition. *Journal of Experimental Psychology: Learning, Memory, and Cognition, 17*, 163–169.

Hasher, L., & Zacks, R. T. (1988). Working memory, comprehension, and aging: A review and a new view. In G. H. Bower (Ed.), *The psychology of learning and motivation* (Vol. 22, pp. 192–225). New York: Academic Press.

Hertel, P. T. (1994). Depression and memory: Are impairments remediable through attentional control? *Current Directions in Psychological Science, 6*, 190–193.

Hertel, P. T., & Hardin, T. S. (1990). Remembering with and without awareness in a depressed mood: Evidence of deficits in initiative. *Journal of Experimental Psychology: General, 119*, 45–59.

Hertel, P. T., & Rude, S. S. (1991). Depressive deficits in memory: Focusing attention improves subsequent recall. *Journal of Experimental Psychology: General, 120*, 301–309.

Horowitz, M. J. (1975). Intrusive and repetitive thoughts after experimental stress: A summary. *Archives of General Psychiatry, 32*, 1457–1463.

Horowitz, M. J. (1976). *Stress response syndromes*. New York: Aronson.

Horowitz, M. J. (1982). The responses to traumatic events scale. In L. Goldberger & S. Bareznitz (Eds.), *Handbook of stress: Theoretical and clinical aspects* (pp. 723–763). New York: The Free Press.

Ingram, R. E. (1990). Self-focused attention in clinical disorders: Review and a conceptual model. *Psychological Bulletin, 107,* 156–176.

Kane, M. J., Hasher, L., Stoltzfus, E. R., Zacks, R. T., & Connelly, S. L. (1994). Inhibitory attentional mechanisms and aging. *Psychology and Aging, 9,* 103–112.

Klinger, E. (1975). Consequences of commitment to and disengagement from incentives. *Psychological Review, 82,* 1–25.

Linville, P. W. (1994). *Inhibition gone awry: Negative priming effects with stress and depression.* Paper presented at the Society of Experimental Social Psychology, Reno, NV.

Linville, P. W., Connelly, L., & Hasher, L., (1994). *Inhibitory processes in stress and depression.* Unpublished paper, Duke University.

Lowe, D. G. (1979). Strategies, context and the mechanisms of response inhibition. *Memory & Cognition, 7,* 382–389.

Lowe, D. G. (1985). Further investigations of inhibitory mechanisms in attention. *Memory & Cognition, 13,* 74–80.

Mandler, G. (1982). Stress and thought processes. In L. Goldberger & S. Breznitz (Eds.), *Handbook of stress: Theoretical and clinical aspects* (pp. 88–104). New York: The Free Press.

MacDonald, J., & MacWhinney, B. (1991). Measuring inhibition and facilitation from pronouns. *Journal of Memory and Language, 29,* 469–494.

McDowd, J. M., & Oseas-Kreger, D. M. (1991). Aging, inhibitory processes, and negative priming. *Journal of Gerontology: Psychological Sciences, 46,* 340–345.

Moretti, M. M., & Shaw, B. F. (1989). Automatic and dysfunctional cognitive processes in depression. In J. S. Uleman & J. A. Bargh (Eds.), *Unintended thought* (pp. 383–421). New York: Guilford.

Neill, W. T. (1977). Inhibitory and facilitatory processes in selective attention. *Journal of Experimental Psychology: Human Perception and Performance, 3,* 444–450.

Neumann, O. (1987). Beyond capacity: A functional view of attention. In H. Heuer & A. F. Sanders (Eds.), *Perspectives on perception and action* (pp. 361–394). Hillsdale, NJ: Lawrence Erlbaum Associates.

Nolen-Hoeksema, S. (1991). Responses to responses and their effects on the duration of depressive episodes. *Journal of Abnormal Psychology, 100,* 259–282.

Pennebaker, J. W. (1989). Stream of consciousness and stress: Levels of thinking. In J. S. Uleman & J. A. Bargh (Eds.), *Unintended thought* (pp. 327–350). New York: Guilford.

Pennington, B, F., Groisser, D., & Welsh, M. C. (1993). Contrasting cognitive deficits in attention deficit hyperactivity disorder versus reading disability. *Developmental Psychology, 29,* 511–523.

Silver, R. L., Boon, C., & Stones, M. H. (1983). Searching for meaning in misfortune: Making sense of incest. *Journal of Social Issues, 39,* 31–102.

Silver, R. L., Wortman, C. B., & Klos, D. S. (1982). Cognition, affect, and behavior following uncontrollable outcomes: A response to current human helplessness research. *Journal of Personality, 50,* 480–514.

Stoltzfus, E. R., Hasher, L., & Zacks, R. T. (in press). Working memory and aging: Current status of the inhibitory view. In J. T. E. Richardson (Ed.), *Working memory and human cognition.* Oxford University Press.

Tait, R., & Silver, R. L. (1989). Coming to terms with major negative life events. In J. S. Uleman & J. A. Bargh (Eds.), *Unintended thought* (pp. 351–382). New York: Guilford.

Tipper, S. P. (1985). The negative priming effect: Inhibitory priming by ignored objects. *The Quarterly Journal of Experimental Psychology, 37A,* 571–590.

Tipper, S. P. (1991). Less attentional selectivity as a result of declining inhibition in older adults. *Bulletin of the Psychonomic Society, 29,* 45–47.

Tipper, S. P., & Cranston, M. (1985). Selective attention and priming: Inhibitory and facilitatory effects of ignored primes. *The Quarterly Journal of Experimental Psychology, 37A*, 591–611.

Tipper, S. P., & Driver, J. (1988). Negative priming between pictures and words in a selective attention task: Evidence for semantic processing of ignored stimuli. *Memory & Cognition, 16*, 64–70.

Wegner, D. M. (1988). Stress and mental control. In S. Fisher & J. Reason (Eds.), *Handbook of life stress, cognition, and health* (pp. 685–699). New York: Wiley.

Wenzlaff, R. M., Wegner, D. M., & Roper, D. W. (1988). Depression and mental control: The resurgence of unwanted negative thoughts. *Journal of Personality and Social Psychology, 55*, 882–892.

Williams, J. M. G., Watts, F. N., MacLeod, C., & Mathews, A. (1988). *Cognitive psychology and emotional disorders*. New York: Wiley.

Zacks, R. T., & Hasher, L. (1994). Directed ignoring: Inhibitory regulation of working memory. In D. Dagenbach & T. H. Carr (Eds.), *Inhibitory processes in attention, memory, and language* (pp. 241–264). New York: Academic Press.

Chapter **9**

Chewing the Cud and Other Ruminations

Susan Nolen-Hoeksema
University of Michigan

Martin and Tesser's insightful analysis focuses on the conditions under which rumination will or will not occur. Their primary assertion is that rumination occurs when people are not making expected progress toward a goal. For example, when a person is not meeting his or her personal goal for the number of publications to achieve each year, he or she will likely ruminate about attaining that goal. Martin and Tesser describe rumination as instrumental, meaning that its function is to reduce the discrepancy between the person's current position and the desired goal. For the person in this example, rumination might lead to the discovery of the obstacles that have impeded progress toward the goal and to the removal of those obstacles (e.g., the person is teaching so many classes that there isn't enough time to write; negotiations with the chair reduce the teaching load) or to giving up the goal, thereby eliminating the discrepancy (e.g., moving to another college where the publishing demands are not as great).

This characterization of rumination as instrumentally oriented suggests that it is adaptive, at least most of the time. Indeed, one might conclude from Martin and Tesser's analysis that rumination is necessary for reducing goal discrepancies; one must ruminate in order to determine the reason for the goal discrepancy and take action or give up the goal. In my comments on the chapter by Martin and Tesser, I take issue with the notion that rumination is instrumentally oriented and therefore adaptive. In particular, I highlight the difference between *problem solving* and forms of rumination that might not be so instrumental or adaptive. I also discuss the different effects of rumination when a person is in a neutral or positive mood and when the person is in a negative mood. Although Martin and Tesser's framework for defining rumination, as outlined in Table 1.1, is conceptually elegant and coherent, I think it leads to a characterization of rumination that is a bit too broad.

RUMINATION VERSUS PROBLEM SOLVING

At points in their chapter, Martin and Tesser note that rumination is not always adaptive. For example, they discuss Kuhl's (1984) work on state orientation and action orientation. State-oriented people have trouble giving up goals or generating alternative behaviors directed at a goal and instead focus on their goal discrepancy and the negative affective state associated with the goal discrepancy. This kind of rumination is not adaptive, according to Kuhl and to Martin and Tesser. In contrast, action-oriented people are able to give up an unattainable goal, divert their attention to another goal, or change their behaviors when a goal is thwarted. It is not clear from Martin and Tesser's discussion of action-oriented people what kind of rumination they think action-oriented people engage in. Martin and Tesser describe a study by Beckmann and Martin (1994), who found that action-oriented people are better able than state-oriented people to use distractors to turn their attention away from goal discrepancies. However, because distraction is a short-term and relatively ineffective strategy when one has a goal discrepancy to resolve, presumably the action-oriented people do not decide which action to take by engaging in distraction. Instead, they must engage in some sort of thought directed at choosing their next action. By Martin and Tesser's broad definition of rumination, any thought directed at reducing goal discrepancies is rumination; therefore, the action-oriented people must engage in rumination.

I suggest that it is useful to distinguish between problem solving and rumination. I define problem solving as thoughts directed at resolving some current or future problem (or reducing some goal discrepancy, if you wish). There is some progression in the thoughts over a reasonable period of time, such that early thoughts assess the problem, later thoughts evaluate possible solutions to the problem, and even later thoughts are decisions about which solution to choose (Baron, 1985; Janis & Mann, 1977). In contrast, the label *rumination* might be better left for thought processes that do not have the progression toward choice of a solution and instead are like the cow chewing the cud: The person keeps going over same general type of thought repeatedly. The specific thoughts the ruminating person considers might change over time as associative networks are activated and memories or ideas related to the person's current concern are brought to his or her attention. But the key feature of rumination is repetition of a theme in thoughts, without progression toward choice of a solution and a commitment to that solution.

When engaging in problem solving individuals may return to thoughts assessing the problem or evaluating possible solutions after they have chosen a solution if new information about the problem or the possible solutions arises. But if they continue to reassess the problem or reevaluate possible solutions without progressing toward choice of a solution, then they are engaging in rumination rather than problem solving.

I have suggested that progression toward choice of a solution to a problem should occur over a reasonable period of time in order for the thought process to be considered problem solving. What is a *reasonable* period of time for assessing a problem and considering a solution before choosing a solution? The answer to this question no doubt depends on the complexity and importance of the problem. It will typically take longer to evaluate complex and important problems (such as long-standing problems in one's marriage or career) than simpler and less important problems (such as what one should wear to work today). Evaluating problems and choosing solutions can also take longer when other people are involved and must be consulted in the choice of solutions than when other people are not involved. For example, when a person unhappy with his or her job is considering taking another job that would involve a significant drop in pay and moving to a new location, deciding is made more complex if he or she has a mate and children. However, having other people who will help assess the problem, evaluate possible solutions, and decide upon a solution can prevent a person from ruminating in isolation and instead push that person to engage in active problem solving (Nolen-Hoeksema, Parker, & Larson, 1994; Pennebaker, 1990).

At one point in their chapter, Martin and Tesser list problem solving as a mode of rumination, and their characterization of rumination as instrumentally oriented toward resolving goal discrepancies certainly makes it sound like problem solving. Later in the chapter, however, Martin and Tesser argue that "the tendency to experience ruminative thoughts is a function of an automatic rather than a controlled process. In other words, people do not have ruminative thoughts on purpose." (p. 32). This suggests that they consider active, conscious, problem solving to be distinct from rumination. I think the distinction they are actually concerned with is between automatic and purposeful thinking, and they view rumination as more automatic than purposeful. I suggest, however, that both rumination and problem solving (as I defined them) can occur both automatically and purposefully. When people who are facing a problem take out a piece of paper, write down the possible solutions to the problem and the pros and cons of each solution before deciding which solution to choose, they are engaging in conscious, purposeful problem solving. Some people, however, are probably able to go through much the same process in their heads, hardly noticing that they are engaging in problem solving. This may be particularly likely when a person is faced with a relatively simple problem that is similar to problems he or she has solved in the past. For example, an experienced cook who tastes the spaghetti sauce and judges that it is too sweet may automatically turn to the cabinet to get some red wine vinegar rather than deliberate at length on other possible solutions to the problem.

On the other hand, whereas repetitive, non-problem-solving ruminative thought probably goes on automatically much of the time, we have found that some people say they engage in ruminative thought quite purposefully. In questionnaire studies of dysphoric people, some say they think about their problems over and over, purposefully isolating themselves so that they are not interrupted in their thoughts (Nolen-Hoeksema & Morrow, 1991; Nolen-Hoeksema, et al., 1994). Many of these people *think* they are engaging in problem solving or at least in the kind of introspection that gives them insight into the themselves and the world (Lyubomirsky & Nolen-Hoeksema, 1993), but much of the time they are not progressing toward a choice of solutions to their problems and instead are like Kuhl's state-oriented people, focusing only on their negative affective state and their problems.

RUMINATION AND MOOD

Although they noted that mood and rumination can have reciprocal effects on each other, Martin and Tesser were careful to confine their model to normal ruminations occurring in mentally healthy people. The adaptiveness of rumination, when defined as unstructured self-focused thinking, may be heavily influenced by the mood the individual is in, however.

In a series of laboratory studies comparing dysphoric and nondysphoric people, we have found that inducing dysphoric people to ruminate leads to a worsening of their mood and a number of negative biases in their thinking. Inducing nondysphoric people to ruminate has no negative effects on their mood or thinking and may even enhance their problem-solving skills (Lyubomirsky & Nolen-Hoeksema, 1993, 1995; Morrow & Nolen-Hoeksema, 1990; Nolen-Hoeksema & Morrow, 1993) The basic paradigm for these studies is as follows. Subjects are first preselected for the dysphoric or nondysphoric group on the basis of a self-report questionnaire completed as part of a large packet of questionnaires. The preselected subjects are phoned and invited to participate in a study on "visualization and imagination" and are not told that they were selected because of their dysphoria scores. When they arrive at the lab, the subjects' moods are assessed. They then undergo either a rumination induction or a distraction induction. Both of these inductions are introduced as visualization and imagination tasks. Subjects are told that they will be presented with a series of ideas and that they should spend a few moments focusing silently on each idea, then move on to the next idea. In the rumination induction, the subjects focus on their current affective and physical state, their personality and goals in life, and how their life is going. They are not directed to think specifically of negative aspects of their lives. Rather, they are simply told to think about "the physical sensations you feel in your body," "the degree of clarity in your thinking right now," "your character and who you strive to be," and similar issues. In the distraction induction, the subjects focus on non-self-focused ideas or phrases such as "the shape of the Statue of Liberty," "the layout of the local mall," "raindrops sliding down a windowpane," and so on. Our items in rumination and distraction inductions have been rated as equally neutral by independent judges. After the rumination or distraction induction, subjects' moods are reassessed and they complete some measure of thinking or problem solving.

Our predictions with regard to the mood effects of the rumination and distraction inductions have been that the dysphoric subjects induced to ruminate would become more dysphoric, the dysphoric subjects induced to distract would become less dysphoric, and the nondysphoric subjects would show no effects of either the rumination or distraction inductions on their moods. These predictions have been supported in nine separate studies (Lyubomirsky & Nolen-Hoeksema, 1993, 1995; Morrow & Nolen-Hoeksema, 1990; Nolen-Hoeksema & Morrow, 1993). Martin and Tesser suggest that dysphoric people will have more goal discrepancies than nondysphoric people and so rumination will have more negative effects on the moods of dysphoric people than nondysphoric people. This indeed may be the reason that our rumination induction, although it does not explicitly focus subjects' attention on goal discrepancies, leads dysphoric people but not nondysphoric people to become more dysphoric. This suggests that the component of our rumination induction that causes dysphoric people to become more dysphoric is the self-evaluative component, the items in the induction that direct subjects' attention to how their lives are going and to evaluations of their personality. In contrast, the items in the induction that direct subjects' attention to their physical and emotional state but not to evaluations of their lives or personalities might have less of an effect on mood because these items are less likely to focus subjects on their goal discrepancies. Focusing on one's physical and emotional state when dysphoric may lead to thoughts about goal discrepancies as a way of trying to understand feelings of sadness, lethargy, and lack of motivation. However, encouraging dysphoric subjects to focus attention on evaluations of their lives and personalities should have a stronger effect on their moods than if they focus their attention on their physical and emotional state if it is a focus on goal discrepancies that is leading the dysphoric subjects in the rumination condition to become more dysphoric.

Morrow and Nolen-Hoeksema (1994) investigated the relative effects of these different components of rumination by inducing one group of dysphoric subjects to focus on evaluations of their lives and personalities (i.e., the self-evaluative group) and another group of dysphoric subjects to focus on their physical and emotional states (i.e., the emotion-focused group). A third group of dysphoric subjects focused on both self-evaluations and their physical and emotional states (i.e., the full rumination group). Contrary to what a goal-discrepancy model of mood suggests, the subjects in the emotion-focused group showed significantly greater increases in dysphoric mood than the subjects in the self-evaluative group. In addition, the effects of the emotion-focusing induction on dysphoric mood were as strong as the effects of the full rumination induction, whereas the subjects in the self-evaluative group remained significantly less dysphoric than the subjects in the full rumination group. This result suggests that focusing on one's negative emotions and physical state when in a dysphoric mood may enhance that mood even more than focusing on evaluations of one's life and personality.

This discussion of the effects of different components of rumination on mood is a diversion from the main focus of this section, however, which is the relation between mood, rumination, thinking, and problem solving. As noted, subjects in most of our studies have been presented with some measure of thinking or problem solving after undergoing the full rumination induction or the distraction induction. Our measures of thinking have included free recall of memories from the past, ratings of the likelihood of good and bad events happening in the future, and interpretations of hypothetical negative events. In each study, dysphoric subjects who had undergone the rumination induction subsequently recalled more negative past memories, expected less happy events to occur in the future, and interpreted hypothetical negative events in more self-defeating and pessimistic ways than dysphoric subjects who had undergone the distraction induction or nondysphoric subjects in either the rumination or distraction group (Lyubomirsky & Nolen-Hoeksema, 1993, 1995; see also Pyszczynski, Hamilton, Herring, & Greenberg, 1989; Pyszczynski, Holt, & Greenberg, 1987). Again, the negative, pessimistic thinking among the dysphoric subjects who had been induced to ruminate may have occurred because the rumination induction focused their attention on their goal discrepancies. Alternatively, their negative, pessimistic thinking may have occurred simply because the rumination induction drew their attention to the negative associative networks that had been activated by their dysphoric mood. That is, the dysphoric subjects walked into the laboratory in a dysphoric mood, with networks associated with that mood somewhat activated. The rumination induction drew their attention to those networks, enhancing their dysphoric mood. When they began the thinking task after the rumination induction, their responses were influenced by these activated associative networks. In contrast, the dysphoric subjects who engaged in the distraction task had their attention directed away from their negative associative networks. As a result, their mood subsided, and they were less likely to draw on those networks when they subsequently engaged in the thinking task. We do not yet have the data to determine whether the effects of the rumination and distraction inductions on dysphoric subjects' thinking were due to their effects on attention to goal discrepancies or on associative networks. What we do know, however, is that the effects of the rumination induction on the thinking of the subjects were determined by the mood they were in when they ruminated. Rumination led to pessimism among the dysphoric subjects but not among the nondysphoric subjects.

In another study, we had dysphoric or nondysphoric subjects engage in an interpersonal problem-solving task after undergoing the rumination or distraction induction (Lyubomirsky & Nolen-Hoeksema, 1995). In the problem-solving task, we presented subjects with common interpersonal problems that often cause dysphoria (e.g., the end of a relationship) and asked them to write down how they would solve that problem. Independent judges rated the quality of the solutions subjects generated. As predicted, dysphoric subjects who had gone through the rumination induction generated solutions that were significantly less effective than dysphoric subjects who had gone through the distraction induction and the nondysphoric subjects. In addition, the dysphoric subjects in the rumination condition were more self-defeating and pessimistic in their causal attributions for these interpersonal problems than subjects in the other three groups. Thus, even though dysphoric people may often engage in self-focused rumination because they want to understand and solve the interpersonal problems that led to their dysphoria, the data from this study suggest that unstructured rumination may actually interfere with the ability to solve these interpersonal problems. In contrast, the rumination induction had no negative effects on the problem-solving skills or attributions of the nondysphoric subjects. In fact, on one measure of problem solving, the nondysphoric subjects who went through the rumination induction generated *better* solutions to the problems than the nondysphoric subjects who went through the distraction induction or either of the dysphoric groups. It seemed that for the nondysphoric subjects, focusing on how their lives were going and how they felt before engaging in an interpersonal problem-solving task led them to generate a particularly large number of good solutions to these problems.

Thus, the adaptiveness of rumination in reducing goal discrepancies appears to be substantially influenced by the individual's mood at the time she or he engages in rumination. If a person is in a dysphoric mood, then unstructured ruminations are likely to lead him or her to think pessimistically about the past, current, and future concerns and to generate less optimal solutions to problems than if he or she is not in a dysphoric mood.

What's the dysphoric person to do then, to resolve goal discrepancies? Our studies suggest that if dysphoric people can lift their moods through benign distractions before engaging in analysis of their problems and making decisions about solutions to those problems, the decisions may be less biased and more wise. In addition, cognitive therapy techniques that teach dysphoric people to engage in structured problem solving, in which they weigh possible solutions to their goal discrepancies as objectively as possible, make a choice of solutions, then commit to that solution, may also help dysphoric people overcome their ruminations and resolve their goal discrepancies (cf. Beck, Rush, Shaw, & Emery, 1979). Again, however, there is an important distinction to be made between active problem solving and unstructured rumination.

RUMINATION AND CURRENT THEORIES

Finally, I comment on Martin and Tesser's argument that the content of ruminations is determined by people's current theories about the causes of their discontent. I agree that this is often the case. I want again to highlight the importance of mood, however, in influencing the adaptiveness of ruminations on current theories. Our studies on the effects of rumination on thinking and problem solving suggest that the current theories that dysphorics ruminate about are likely to be negatively biased. Thus, a ruminating dysphoric may see even more problems in marriage or career than exist. She or he may make decisions based on these negatively biased theories, decisions that may be unwise and may increase dysphoria.

Rumination may often arise, however, because people *do not* have a plausible theory for their discontent. In these cases, the rumination consists of asking questions: Why am I miserable? What's wrong with my life? What do I need to feel better? In the language of goal-discrepancy theory, people do not even know what goal they are not attaining. The rumination may continue until people have a theory of what is wrong, what goals they are not attaining. These questions must be answered, to some extent, before the person can move into active problem solving.

Therapy may often reduce rumination and relieve dysphoria primarily by providing the dysphoric with a theory of what is wrong in his or her life and a set of steps to take to overcome what is wrong (Frank, 1973). Therapy could have these effects even if the theory provided by the therapist is not objectively correct (e.g., it's not really true that you are depressed because your mother didn't provide you with enough nurturance when you were a small child; it's not really true that you are depressed because your serotonin levels are low). The important factor is whether or not the dysphoric person believes the theory (Burns & Nolen-Hoeksema, 1991; Fennell & Teasdale, 1987). If she or he believes the theory, she or he can stop the ruminative questions about what is wrong with life and follow the steps recommended by the theory or therapist for correcting the problems (e.g., confront one's mother, take antidepressant drugs). Of course, if the theory is wrong, then the problems that led to dysphoria will remain and may cause the dysphoria to persist or relapse. However, several different types of therapy based on quite different theories about the causes of dysphoria seem to work equally well in treating dysphoria, even when dysphorics are randomly assigned to therapies (Robinson, Berman, & Neimeyer, 1990). This suggests that providing dysphoric clients with any plausible rationale for their dysphoria and the hope that they can overcome that dysphoria by following the therapist's prescriptions goes a long way in interrupting the dysphoria–rumination–inaction cycle.

In sum, it is useful to distinguish between problem solving and the other forms of thought that Martin and Tesser characterize as rumination. Although people may often intend rumination to reduce goal discrepancies, I suggest that when people are engaging in simple cud-chewing rumination, they are unlikely to reduce goal discrepancies satisfactorily, especially if they are in a dysphoric mood. In contrast, if they engage in active problem solving in which their thoughts progress from evaluation of the problem to choice and implementation of a solution, they are more likely to reduce their goal discrepancies. For dysphoric people, this active problem solving may only be possible after their mood has been lifted, perhaps when they experience pleasant distractions, when they are explicitly taught problem-solving skills, or when their ruminative questions have been answered by a theory that their therapist provides for their dysphoria.

REFERENCES

Baron, J. (1985). *Rationality and intelligence.* Cambridge: Cambridge University Press.

Beck, A. T., Rush, A. J., Shaw, B. F., & Emery, G. (1979). *Cognitive therapy of depression.* New York: Guilford.

Beckmann, J., & Martin, L. L. (1994). *Distraction and disengagement: How people stop ruminating.* Manuscript in preparation.

Burns, D., & Nolen-Hoeksema, S. (1991). Coping styles, homework assignments and the effectiveness of cognitive-behavioral therapy. *Journal of Consulting and Clinical Psychology, 59,* 305–311.

Fennell, M. J. V., & Teasdale, J. D. (1987). Cognitive therapy for depression: Individual differences and the process of change. *Cognitive Therapy and Research, 11,* 253–271.

Frank, J. (1973). *Persuasion and healing: A comparative study of psychotherapy* (2nd ed.). Baltimore, MD: Johns Hopkins University Press.

Janis, I., & Mann, L. (1977). *Decision making.* New York: Free Press.

Kuhl, J. (1984). Volitional aspects of achievement toward motivation and learned helplessness: Toward a comprehensive theory of action control. In B. A. Maher (Ed.), *Progress in experimental personality research* (pp. 99–171). New York: Academic Press.

Lyubomirsky, S., & Nolen-Hoeksema, S. (1993). Self-perpetuating properties of depressive rumination. *Journal of Personality and Social Psychology, 65,* 339–349.

Lyubomirsky, S., & Nolen-Hoeksema, S. (1995). Effects of self-focused rumination on negative thinking and interpersonal problem solving. *Journal of Personality and Social Psycholog, 69,* 176–190.

Morrow, J., & Nolen-Hoeksema, S. (1990). Effects of responses to depression on the remediation of depressive affect. *Journal of Personality and Social Psychology, 58,* 519–527.

Morrow, J., & Nolen-Hoeksema, S. (1994). *Self-focus and the maintenance of depressed mood: Different viewpoints.* Unpublished manuscript.

Nolen-Hoeksema, S., & Morrow, J. (1991). A prospective study of depression and distress following a natural disaster: The 1989 Loma Prieta earthquake. *Journal of Personality and Social Psychology, 61,* 105–121.

Nolen-Hoeksema, S., & Morrow, J. (1993). The effects of rumination and distraction on naturally occurring depressed moods. *Cognition and Emotion, 7,* 561–570.

Nolen-Hoeksema, S., Parker, L., & Larson, J. (1994). Ruminative coping with depressed mood following loss. *Journal of Personality and Social Psychology, 67,* 92–104.

Pennebaker, J. W. (1990). *Opening up: The healing power of confiding in others.* New York: Morrow.

Pyszczynski, T., Hamilton, J., Herring, F., & Greenberg, J. (1989). Depression self-focused attention and the negative memory bias. *Journal of Personality and Social Psychology, 57,* 351–357.

Pyszczynski, T., Holt, K., & Greenberg, J. (1987). Depression, self-focused attention, and expectancies for positive and negative future life events for self and others. *Journal of Personality and Social Psychology, 52,* 994–1001.

Robinson, L. A., Berman, J. S., & Neimeyer, R. A. (1990). Psychotherapy for the treatment of depression: A comprehensive review of controlled outcome research. *Psychological Bulletin, 108,* 30–49.

Chapter **10**

Recurrent Thought: Implications for Attitudes and Persuasion

Richard E. Petty
W. Blair G. Jarvis
Lisa M. Evans
Ohio State University

Social psychologists who investigate attitudes and persuasion have long been interested in thought processes (e.g., Festinger, 1957; Hovland, Janis, & Kelley, 1953; Tesser, 1978; Wyer, 1974). For example, in the Elaboration Likelihood Model of persuasion (Petty & Cacioppo, 1981, 1986), as in much of the contemporary persuasion literature, two aspects of thinking have been emphasized because of their presumed importance for understanding attitude change. First, investigators have explored determinants of the *extent* of thinking. That is, what determines whether people think a lot or relatively little about some attitude object? Some variables have an impact on the extent of thinking by varying a person's motivation to think about the issue (e.g., increasing the personal relevance of the message enhances thinking; Petty & Cacioppo, 1979), whereas other variables have an impact on a person's ability to think about the issue (e.g., increasing distraction reduces message processing; Petty, Wells, & Brock, 1976).

The second aspect of thinking that has garnered considerable research attention concerns determinants of the *content* of thinking. Perhaps the most investigated content dimension is the overall valence of the thinking that occurs. That is, what determines whether one's thoughts are relatively positive or negative? For example, research indicates that when people are motivated and able to think, then their thoughts are more positive if strong rather than weak arguments are presented (e.g., Petty et al., 1976) or if they are in a positive rather than a neutral or negative mood (e.g., Petty, Schumann, Richman, & Strathman, 1993). Of course, content dimensions other than valence have been investigated. For example, research indicates that one can prime the extent to which people think about one aspect of an issue rather than another (e.g., Sherman, Mackie, & Driscoll, 1990).

Thus, considerable progress has been made in specifying and understanding the factors that can influence the extent of thinking and the content of thinking about persuasive messages (see Petty, Priester, & Wegener, 1994, for a review).[1] In addition, progress has been made in understanding the consequences of the extent of thinking and the content of thinking. Among the consequences of these dimensions that have received considerable attention are the *extremity* of judgments resulting from different thought content and the *strength* of the judgments that result from different amounts of thinking (e.g., see Petty, Haugtvedt, & Smith, 1995; Tesser, Martin, & Mendolia, 1995).

Importantly, each of these dimensions is typically viewed as a continuum. That is, the extent of thinking can vary from all to none, with many levels in between. Similarly, along any one content dimension, thoughts can range, for example, from very positive to very negative, or very much about oneself to very little about oneself, and so forth. The outcomes of extent and content of thinking can also be viewed as falling along a continuum. That is, one can examine the degree of extremity in judgments, or the degree of strength of a judgment, and so on.

We view the chapter by Martin and Tesser as highlighting additional dimensions of thinking that can also be viewed as falling along various continua. The most important of these dimensions is the recurrence of the thinking. That is, whatever the overall amount of thinking (i.e., high, medium, low) that occurs, or whatever its content (e.g., positive, neutral, negative), how frequently does it occur? Does it occur all at once, or is it spaced out over a day, or a year, or a decade? Martin and Tesser refer to recurrent thought as rumination. They argue that there is no qualitative

---

[1] In some studies, content variables are examined along with extent variables. For example, when a manipulation of argument quality is crossed with a manipulation of distraction, an interaction is obtained such that when the arguments are cogent, distraction reduces persuasion by interfering with the favorable thoughts that would have arisen, but when the arguments are specious, distraction enhances persuasion by interfering with the counterarguing that would have taken place (Petty et al., 1976).

difference between ruminative and nonruminative thought, that it is not possible to define how many thoughts are necessary to be considered rumination, and that it is not possible to define over what time period thought must occur to be considered ruminative. Of course, such decisions could be made but would be arbitrary. Given this state of affairs, our preference is to categorize thinking along at least three dimensions: extent, content, and recurrence. Our specific goals in this chapter are to comment on the Martin and Tesser chapter and to outline some of the implications of recurrent thinking for understanding attitudes and persuasion.

We have already described the extent and content dimensions, but what about the recurrence dimensions? Consider a person who is relatively low on the extent of thinking dimension—thinking only three thoughts about some issue. This person might have these three thoughts all at once, or these thoughts might be spread out over the course of a month. Similarly, a person who is high on the extent of thinking dimension—thinking 20 thoughts about some issue—might think these thoughts all at once without interruption (i.e., at one occurrence), or these thoughts might occur in two blocks of 10 thoughts each (2 occurrences), or 10 blocks of 2 thoughts each (10 occurrences). The more total thoughts a person thinks (e.g., 20 rather than 3), the higher the person is on the extent of thinking dimension. The more specific episodes of thought about an object or issue (e.g., 10 versus 1), the higher the person is on the recurrence dimension. This analysis avoids the term rumination and suggests instead that all thinking can vary in extent, content, and recurrence.

Just as the extent of thought and the content of thought have been of interest to investigators because specific outcomes have been tied to these thought dimensions, the recurrence dimension would be of special interest to the extent that it has unique outcomes. Stated simply, does it matter if a person's 20 thoughts occur all at once, or if they are spread over 2 or 10 occasions?[2] To the extent that the number of occurrences makes a difference over and above what can be predicted based on the extent of thinking alone (e.g., the total number of thoughts generated; or the total amount of time devoted to thinking), then recurrence of thought is of considerable interest. To the extent that meaningful consequences result from recurrence, then it is important to understand the determinants of recurrence. That is, why does thinking about some things occur all at once and only

---

[2]Various measurable aspects of recurrence in addition to the mere number of occurrences of thought are likely to be of interest in any research program. For example, one could calculate the average spacing of the thought occurrences (e.g., Does the person think about the issue on average of once per day or per year? Do 10 or 100 unrelated thoughts intervene between each relevant occurrence?).

once, versus twice over the course of a year, versus 100 times over the course of a month?[3]

INITIATION AND TERMINATION OF THINKING: AN INITIAL MODEL

Figure 10.1 presents a model outlining some ways in which thought can become recurrent. This model, like the Elaboration Likelihood Model of persuasion (ELM; Petty & Cacioppo, 1986), begins with variables that initiate thinking and determine its extent. Until a thought process is initiated, it makes little sense to ask how intense the thought is, what its content is, or whether the thinking will recur.

Initiation of Thinking

In the ELM, it is assumed that some thinking is initiated when a persuasive message is received. In laboratory settings, when people receive a message, they typically are told that they are being exposed to the message for some purpose (e.g., to analyze the personality of the writer; to assess the sound quality of a tape-recording, etc.), and thus some thinking is initiated by the participants' desires to accomplish their assigned task. However, extra thinking (not required by the experimenter-provided goal) can occur if the message is particularly relevant or interesting. If a persuasive message is encountered outside of the laboratory, however, a thought episode might or might not be initiated.

In general, a host of variables can initiate thinking. At the most simple level, the mere encountering of some object toward which one has an accessible attitude can lead to thinking about that object (e.g., seeing a

---

[3]Martin and Tesser's analysis also suggests other dimensions of thinking. For example, is the thought deliberate or spontaneous, intended or unintended? We view these as separate dimensions along which thought can be categorized. That is, recurrent thought (as well as nonrecurrent thought) can be extensive or minimal, deliberate or spontaneous, intended or unintended, positive or negative, and so on. Martin and Tesser highlight the spontaneous and unintended aspects of recurrent thought in their treatment of rumination, yet deliberate and intended recurrent thought may have many of the same consequences. Other dimensions that are likely to be consequential include whether the thoughts are wanted versus unwanted and unique versus duplicative. Martin and Tesser note that unwanted recurrent thoughts can be problematic, but so too can thoughts that occur only once—it's just that the more often undesired thoughts occur (i.e., the more they recur), the more problematic they are. In any case, we favor viewing each of these variables as continuous dimensions along which thinking can vary.

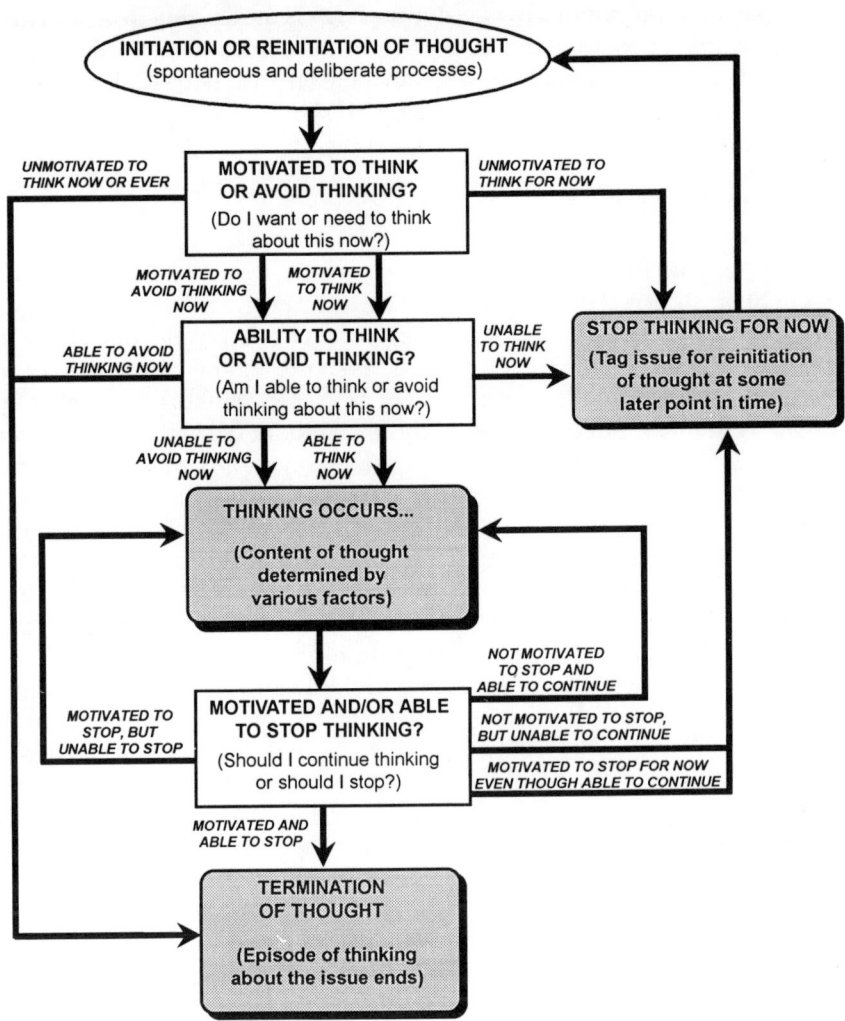

FIG. 10.1. Model of initiation and termination of a thought episode.

picture of one's boyfriend or girlfriend; cf. Fazio, 1995). Of course, specific tasks assigned by others can initiate thinking (e.g., being given a puzzle to solve or a survey question to answer). As highlighted by Martin and Tesser, failure to complete one's goal or making unexpected progress toward one's goal can initiate thinking in the absence of any external demand (e.g., Why have I failed? What can I do differently?). Noticing incongruities and being confused or surprised can initiate thinking in an attempt to resolve the incongruity and restore clarity (e.g., Pyszcynski & Greenberg, 1981). For example, thinking about a persuasive message is more likely to be initiated when people encounter the unexpected information that a majority of people disagrees rather than agrees with them on some issue (Baker & Petty, 1994; see also Maheswaran & Chaiken, 1991).

Extent of Thinking

Consistent with the ELM, Fig. 10.1 shows that the extent of thinking in any thought episode is determined in part by how motivated and able people are to consider the issue. For example, consider two people, one about to make a decision on which candy bar to purchase, another about to make a decision on which house to purchase. In each case, thinking is initiated by the need to make a decision. However, the amount of thinking will differ in each case. The house purchase is considerably more consequential and important and will motivate greater thought (Petty & Cacioppo, 1990). Similarly, as noted by Martin and Tesser, problematic progress toward some goal will initiate thinking. However, the extent of thinking will be determined by the importance of the goal toward which one is making unexpected progress (e.g., is the goal a higher or lower order goal?).[4]

If a person is particularly motivated to think, whether thinking will occur or not depends on the person's ability to think. Such practical considerations as whether the person has sufficient time to think can be important in determining whether thought occurs at that point in time. Also, a person who is highly motivated to think about some problem might have plenty of time but insufficient knowledge to generate thoughts on the issue. In such instances a person might simply tag this issue as worthy of further thought when circumstances permit (Klinger, 1975).

It is important to note that people are sometimes highly motivated to avoid thinking rather than neutral with respect to thinking (Schwarz, 1990). For example, when people are in a good mood, they particularly do not wish to think about things that are unpleasant (Wegener, Petty, & Smith,

---

[4]Our working assumption is that variables such as personal relevance or importance influence the extent of thinking. For example, high relevance subjects think a lot during a message presentation, and low relevance subjects exert less effort and rely on cues (e.g., Petty, Cacioppo, & Goldman, 1981). It is assumed that when it is time for a judgment to be expressed, subjects simply report the judgment formed based on much or little thinking. A second possibility, however, is that high involvement subjects engage in on-line thinking at the time of message presentation but that low involvement subjects do not think until the attitude question is posed (cf. Hastie & Park, 1986). That is, under high involvement, thought is initiated at message presentation, but under low involvement, thought is not initiated until the attitude question is posed (see Haugtvedt & Petty, 1992). Thus, involvement may induce differences in the timing of the thinking as well as the extent of thinking.

1995). Thus, a happy person might simply decide to put off thinking about an unpleasant problem now but tag it to return to later. Of course, just because a person is motivated to avoid thinking about some issue does not mean that thinking will be avoided (cf. Wegner, 1994). The person must also have the ability to stop the unwanted thoughts. Martin and Tesser note that in such circumstances, if some distraction is available, the person might be able to terminate thinking at least until some other stimulus reinitiates thought.

Content of Thinking

Whether a person is motivated and able to think or is motivated to avoid thinking but unable to suppress the thoughts, the content of thought can be determined by a number of factors. In their Table 1.1, Martin and Tesser categorize various modes of ruminative thought. Their categorization scheme is potentially quite valuable, especially because these categories of thought appear to apply to all thought, not just ruminative thought. For example, if a survey taker asks a person about his or her most recent clothing purchase, the respondent might reply that the purchase was a mistake because the shirt wrinkles so easily. This thought is clearly a negative reaction to past attainment—a "regret" thought. However, it presumably is not ruminative in that it does not recur and is elicited by situational demand. Similarly a person can have one "basking" thought or one "optimistic" thought.

Because the organizational scheme in Table 1.1 appears to apply to all thinking, it provides a useful starting point for uncovering the most important content dimensions along which people's thoughts can be categorized. Interestingly, two of the dimensions in Table 1.1 might be captured in part by individual difference variables. For example, the *optimism—pessimism scale* (Scheier & Carver, 1987) might be useful in assessing the likelihood of generating positive versus negative thoughts, and the *consideration of future consequences scale* (Strathman, Gleicher, Boninger, & Edwards, 1994) might tap into the extent to which people's thoughts focus on the future rather than the past or present. Other individual difference constructs suggest other content dimensions. For example, all the thoughts in Table 1.1 appear to be "evaluative" in nature, but recent research indicates that there are individual differences in the tendency to generate evaluative thoughts (i.e., the need to evaluate; Jarvis & Petty, in press; see also Petty & Jarvis, in press). This suggests that the authors might include a category for neutral or "factual thoughts" (e.g., a person who has recurrent thoughts about what the future will be like). The persuasion literature suggests that another dimension of potential utility is the extent to which the thoughts are self-relevant or not (e.g., one can "worry" about oneself or "worry" about the world economy; cf. Shavitt & Brock, 1986). Of course, the number of content dimensions can easily become overwhelming, and thus some criteria for inclusion should be specified.

According to Martin and Tesser, which of the specific types of thought in Table 1.1 will occur is determined by which goal the person believes has been thwarted. Although this is clearly an important variable, other factors can determine the content of thought whether or not this thought is ruminative. For example, as noted previously, a person's mood can influence the valence of thinking. The authors appear to agree in that they note that negative moods can lead people to think that they are falling short of their standards whereas positive moods provide a more optimistic bias. Our point is that the content of thinking in general, whether ruminative or not, is likely to be influenced by thwarted goals, moods, accessible constructs, and many other factors.

Although Table 1.1 provides an excellent start in categorizing the content of people's thoughts, it does not offer much guidance in understanding whether the various types of thought (e.g., regret, basking, etc.) recur in the absence of some external demand. Thus, our preference is simply to talk about thinking and to examine the dimensions of thinking that are important for the phenomena at hand. The aspect of thinking highlighted by Martin and Tesser is the likelihood of recurrence.

Recurrence of Thought

After an initial occurrence of thought about an object, what determines whether the thinking about the object or issue will occur again? Figure 10.1 depicts a number of ways in which thinking about an issue can recur. First, consider a situation in which thinking about some problem is initiated and the person is motivated to think diligently about the problem because it is important. However, before generating the first substantive thought, the phone rings, stifling thought about issue 1 and initiating thought about another issue. The phone call sends the person hurrying off to work at the hospital. The problem (or discrepancy or confusion) that initiated thought has not been resolved, and the person makes a mental note to think about the issue at some time in the future. Later that day (e.g., after dinner when it is quiet and ability to think is present), the person may begin to think about the issue until other demands require termination. The person may continue to think about the issue on and off until the problem is solved (or the discrepancy is resolved or the confusion is made clear; i.e., one's goal is reached).

In other instances, people might initially have the motivation and ability to think about the issue at the time thought is initiated, and many initial thoughts occur, but they are interrupted from reaching closure. There are many reasons why people might not be able to finish thinking after it is started. First, time could run out—it is time to prepare dinner, or go to work, and so on. Second, time might not be a problem, but the person might not be able to reach closure (e.g., the person cannot decide what to buy because there is insufficient information available in the store; the person runs out of solutions to the problem and is not happy with any of the solutions generated). Alternatively, the topic might be so pleasant to think about that the issue is tagged for thought whenever the person is feeling bad (e.g., retrieving a pleasant memory to alleviate a negative mood; see Smith & Petty, 1995). Thus, once thinking begins, there are a number of factors that can lead a person to tag the issue as worthy of further thought and return to it later. We are not suggesting that the people necessarily set aside time to think about the issue in a conscious or deliberate way. Rather, by making a mental note of wanting to think, this topic is more likely to come to mind than if the issue was tagged as resolved or closed. It is even possible that people are not consciously aware that they want to engage in additional thought about the issue, but at some level they are unsatisfied with the solution they have arrived at, and thus the issue keeps popping into mind.

Yet another possibility is that a person reaches closure (i.e., stops thinking) and is happy with the solution or judgment reached initially, but something later causes the person to doubt the initial solution (e.g., "I thought I would major in psychology, but this new class makes me wonder"). This instance is distinguished from the others in that in the earlier examples, thought was initiated by factor 1, and the thought reoccurred periodically over time until the initial provocation to think reached some resolution. In the current instance, the thinking initiated by factor 1 reaches closure, but some new provocation (factor 2) initiates thinking on the same topic.

Termination of Thinking

With rare exceptions (e.g., Lassiter, Pezzo, & Apple, 1993), research on the thought processes leading to attitude change has focused on the thought that occurs during an initial thought episode. Yet the consideration of rumination and thought recurrence raise the important need to understand not only what initiates thinking but also what gets it to recur and then finally stop. First, we know that some individuals are more eager to reach closure quickly than others (Webster & Kruglanski, 1994). Individuals high in their need for closure are expected to stop thinking (i.e., reach closure) more quickly than those who are low in need for closure, but if the individuals high in this need were prevented from reaching closure, it is likely that they would be more susceptible to recurrent thought. Also, some people like to think and problem solve. These individuals are considered high in the need for cognition (Cacioppo & Petty, 1982) and are expected to persevere in thinking about a problem or task longer than individuals who are low in need for cognition. Because high need for cognition individuals are task focused, they are not more likely to engage in non-task-relevant thoughts (e.g., irrelevant daydreams) than are low need for cognition individuals.

Importantly, however, just as there are *start rules* or heuristics that initiate thinking (e.g., "begin thinking when a problem is presented") and *shift rules* that move thinking into high gear (e.g., "process carefully when the issue is important"), there are also *stop rules* that allow a person to decide when to terminate thinking (Petty & Priester, 1994). Martin and Tesser emphasize that thinking about an issue is stopped when progress toward a goal is no longer problematic. For example, in a persuasion situation, if the overall goal is to form a veridical opinion (Petty & Cacioppo, 1986), then people are likely to stop thinking when they can be confident that the opinion they have formed is accurate (e.g., Priester & Petty, 1995). Chaiken, Liberman, and Eagly (1989) suggested that people will stop thinking about an issue (or resort to heuristic processing) when their level of confidence in their attitude reaches their desired level of confidence (i.e., the "sufficiency threshold").

Other stop rules for thinking are also possible, and these rules are typically tied to the goals that initiated thinking in the first place. For example, if people are motivated to maintain a positive mood, they may continue thinking about a message as long as thinking about the message is enjoyable and maintaining happiness is a current goal (Wegener & Petty, in press). Investigations of stop rules are just beginning, but it is already clear that different stop rules are likely to be used in different situations. Furthermore, the framing of a stop rule appears to be important. For example, Martin, Ward, Achee, and Wyer (1993) compared the cognitive performance of individuals in good or bad moods who were given different stop rules. Instructing people to work on a task for as long as they felt like continuing led to greater thought among happy than among sad individuals. If people ask themselves if they should continue thinking, people in a good mood may be more likely to continue because they interpret their good mood as a sign that the task is enjoyable. People in a bad mood may see the task as unpleasant and will be less likely to continue. However, when people were told to work on the task until they felt it was a good time to stop, sad people exerted more cognitive effort than happy people. If people ask themselves if they should stop, people in a good mood may be more likely to feel satisfied with the thoughts generated and feel that enough thinking has been done. People in a bad mood may feel dissatisfied and think that additional thought is necessary prior to stopping.

Outcome of Thinking

As noted earlier, the dimensions of thinking we have identified are of interest to the extent that there are specific consequences of each. Previous research has already documented consequences of the amount of thinking and the content of thinking. Fewer implications of recurrent thinking have been demonstrated. Of interest are such questions as whether recurrent thinking leads to overall evaluations that are different in any way (e.g., more polarized or stronger) than evaluations formed as a result of the same amount of thinking that occurs all at once.

POSSIBLE CONSEQUENCES OF RUMINATION IN THE ATTITUDE CHANGE LITERATURE

As noted previously, the vast majority of attitude change studies appear to assume that any thinking about a persuasive message (or issue) is done at one time. Little attention is paid to the recurrence of thought and its consequences or what might lead to recurrence. However, a number of attitudinal phenomena in addition to the work on attitude persistence mentioned by Martin and Tesser (e.g., Lassiter et al., 1993) lend themselves to a recurrence analysis.[5] Inspired by Chapter 1, we present ideas on the implications of recurrent thought for two theories of attitude change—the theory of cognitive dissonance (Festinger, 1957) and the elaboration likelihood model of persuasion (Petty & Cacioppo, 1986).

Recurrent Thought and Cognitive Dissonance

Although contemporary theorists disagree about the precise triggering event for cognitive dissonance to occur, each of the popular perspectives

---

[5] Interestingly, the cited work on attitude persistence may have less relevance to rumination than it initially appears. Lassiter et al. (1993) exposed subjects to a message that induced attitude change. Some subjects were then assigned the task of transmitting the message to another subject but were interrupted from doing so. Other subjects were allowed to complete their transmission. When attitudes were assessed 10 weeks later, interrupted subjects showed greater persistence of attitude change than individuals who were not interrupted from transmitting. One explanation for this finding is that task-incomplete subjects continued to think about the incomplete task over the 10 weeks and this rumination helped to maintain their newly changed attitudes. However, Downing (1994) showed that if subjects are interrupted but then allowed to complete their transmission just 10 minutes later, they show persistence comparable to subjects who don't complete their transmission until 8 weeks later (and both groups showed greater persistence than uninterrupted subjects). Thus, although task interruption may increase thought, it is possible that all the thought takes place shortly after the task interruption (e.g., "what would I have said if I got to transmit the message") and might not continue until the task (i.e., the transmission) is completed (see Petty et al., 1995, for further discussion).

suggests that dissonance occurs when people have done something they did not want to do. Some theorists focus on the fact that people have brought about an aversive or negative outcome (e.g., Cooper & Fazio, 1984). Others focus on the fact that people have engaged in behavior that is inconsistent with their own view of themselves (e.g., Aronson, 1968). Still others argue that dissonance occurs when people violate their self-integrity (e.g., Steele, 1988). In each case there is some type of discrepancy between the way things turned out and what was wanted. Such discrepancies are postulated by Martin and Tesser to bring about recurrent thought until the discrepancy is resolved. Thus, dissonance inductions are prime candidates for instigators of recurrent thought.

In the typical dissonance study, people are provided with an immediate chance to resolve the discrepancy by changing their attitudes. For example, if people see themselves as honest, then it is discrepant to tell a lie such as saying that a boring task is interesting (Festinger & Carlsmith, 1959). However, if people come to view the task as interesting, the self-discrepancy disappears (Aronson, 1968). It is often assumed that the motivation to resolve the discrepancy stems from the aversive feelings that such discrepancies induce. According to this view, reducing the unpleasant state by inducing a pleasant state may be sufficient to reduce dissonance. In fact, some research has shown that following a dissonance-inducing act with a comedy film is effective in reducing dissonance (Cooper, Fazio, & Rhodewalt, 1978). Yet a comedy film (or any other momentary distractor) does not eliminate the discrepancy.[6] Thus, if discrepancy reduction rather than negative state relief is behind dissonance effects (cf. Berkowitz & Devine, 1989), the comedy film will provide only temporary relief from dissonance. As long as the discrepancy remains unresolved, at some later point in time, thoughts about the discrepancy may arise. The more important the cognitions involved in the discrepancy, the more likely the person is to have recurrent thoughts about the unresolved discrepancy in the future. This raises the interesting possibility that in some studies where a treatment (e.g., comedy film) appeared to have eliminated dissonance, the treatment might in fact have only postponed dissonance reduction. In support of this view, Higgins, Rhodewalt, and Zanna (1979) found that dissonance processes could be reinitiated two weeks after dissonance was apparently attenuated by misattribution.

Dissonance theorists have also argued that any choice involving more than trivial consequences induces dissonance. People want to make perfect

---

[6]Cooper et al. (1978) argued that the comedy film reduced dissonance because subjects misattributed their dissonance arousal to the film, which caused them to see the film as more funny than in the no-dissonance condition. On the other hand, subjects might have seen the film as more funny in the dissonance conditions because of a judgmental contrast effect with their current aversive state serving as an anchor.

choices, but almost no choices are perfect. Thus, most choices are less than ideal in that people must accept the negative features of the chosen alternative and discard the positive features of the rejected alternative. For example, Brehm (1956) found that after people made a choice between two consumer products that they had originally rated as equally attractive, their ratings of the products diverged such that the chosen product was seen as more desirable and the rejected product was seen as less desirable.

Martin and Tesser suggested some factors that would likely influence the extent to which people engage in recurrent thought about their choices. Consider the following choice dilemma. Two individuals are standing in the supermarket and are trying to decide between purchasing the fat-free frozen yogurt or the sinfully rich double chocolate fudge ice cream. This decision might typically be framed as involving a lower order and rather immediate goal: "I need to choose a dessert for tonight." However, this same decision can be represented on a higher level (see McIntosh & Martin, 1992): A person may frame the choice as one of self-control versus freedom and autonomy. By choosing the fat-free yogurt, one maintains self-control but gives up free choice. By choosing the rich ice cream, one tosses self-control aside and declares freedom. This trade-off is clearly more central to the self-concept than the simple "What should I have for dessert" decision. Importantly, after consuming the evening's dessert, the lower order goal of selecting a dessert is completely resolved. However, even after consuming the dessert, the higher order battle between self-control and freedom remains, and thus the process of dissonance reduction may be more likely to continue over some period of time. Each instance of recurrent thought about the decision may reactivate the original dissonance arousal, resulting in a greater spreading of the alternatives. Interestingly, the alternatives spread apart may include the underlying values of freedom and control, which would in turn influence the desirability of the two dessert choices in the future.

Recurrent Thought and the Elaboration Likelihood Model

Elaboration and Attitude Strength. The Elaboration Likelihood Model of persuasion (ELM) has focused on variables that determine the extent and content of thinking. In addition, a key postulate of this model is that attitudes formed through extensive elaborative thought are more persistent over time, resistant to change, and more predictive of behavior than similar attitudes formed through less effortful means (Petty & Cacioppo, 1986). However, what has not been considered previously is whether two attitudes based on the *same extent* of object-based elaboration can vary in their persistence, resistance, and link to behavior as a function of the time course over which the elaboration occurred (i.e., the recurrence of thought).

An important step for future research is to examine the extent to which attitude formation and change processes are susceptible to thought recurrence. If we assume that people want to have correct attitudes about the many objects, issues, and people in their lives (Festinger, 1950) and that, to the extent that these targets are important, people engage in considerable target-relevant information processing activity in order to reach this goal (Petty & Cacioppo, 1986), then according to Martin and Tesser, any factor preventing the individual from completing this goal should encourage thought recurrence. For example, if initial thinking produced an ambivalent reaction (e.g., equivalent positive and negative thoughts), an overall evaluation might not be formed, and the individual might vacillate back and forth between positivity and negativity (Vallacher, Nowak, & Kaufman, 1994). This lack of evaluative closure could lead to recurrent thinking until the ambivalence was resolved. In addition, because a number of very common factors are known to disrupt motivated evaluative processing (e.g., lack of information or knowledge, distraction, competing goals, and so forth), it seems likely that thoughts recur during the development of attitudes, especially when objects of high personal relevance or importance are involved.

If thought recurrence is common in attitude formation and change settings, another question that should be addressed is whether recurrent thinking in such contexts involves unique thoughts or repetitive thoughts about the target. This is a potentially important question because the consequences of thought recurrence for attitudes vary depending on the nature of the recurrent thought. For example, if recurrence is limited to rethinking old thoughts (i.e., "mere" recurrence), the primary consequence will be maintaining one's attitude. In fact, getting people to memorize their cognitive responses to a persuasive message has been effective in producing enduring attitudes (see Petty et al., 1995). The rehearsal of previous thoughts should help to inhibit their normal decay over time, which should consequently encourage attitude persistence, discourage the attitude–behavior link from weakening, and prevent the attitude from becoming vulnerable to attack due to weakened accessibility of the attitude and bolstering thoughts. That is, the strength of mere recurrence lies in its capacity to maintain attitudes at or near the level of their initial activation.

However, if people tend to elaborate on their recurrent thoughts, generating unique ideas at each episode, then the extremity and strength of the attitude might increase over time. If new attitude-consistent thoughts are generated at each thought episode, attitudes could polarize (Tesser et al., 1995). Also, with additional elaboration, the attitude structure should become more extensive, better organized, and more differentiated from other structures in memory. Greater elaboration is thought to be associated with increased resistance because it provides the individual with a stronger basis for the attitude, preparing it to resist counterattacks more effectively (e.g., Haugtvedt, Schumann, Schneier, & Warren, 1994; Petty & Cacioppo, 1986).

Of course, the question of whether one's thoughts are unique or repetitive could be asked about the thinking that takes place on any one occasion. Thus, an essential question concerns whether the link between attitude elaboration and outcomes such as persistence, resistance, and attitude–behavior consistency becomes stronger when it occurs gradually over time (i.e., when holding the *extent* of elaborative processing constant). This finding would have important implications for attitude change strategies. For example, will the disruption of attitude formation processes prior to completion be a more effective means of persuasion (assuming strong arguments) than encouraging subjects to reach final closure during initial exposure to the attitude object? Although the effectiveness of gradual versus all-at-once elaboration remains an empirical question, some research suggests that information learned over a longer period of time is better retained and remains more accessible than the same information learned over a shorter period of time (e.g., see Underwood, Keppel, & Schulz, 1962; Smith & Rothkopf, 1984).

Multiple Roles for Recurrent Thought. According to the ELM, variables can serve multiple roles in determining attitude change (Petty, 1994), and thus recurrence of thought is likely to influence attitudes in multiple ways. Perhaps the most obvious implication of recurrence is that it provides individuals with an increased number of opportunities to engage in elaborative thought regarding the attitude object. In this regard it would be interesting to determine whether the effects of recurrent self-generated thought parallel effects obtained in research conducted on the effects of message repetition. Cacioppo and Petty (1979), for example, found that a moderate amount of repetition enhanced object-relevant elaborative thought, but a high amount of repetition led to tedium and negative reactions. Perhaps people react similarly when a issue repeatedly comes to mind. That is, moderate recurrence may lead to relatively objective elaboration of the topic, but a high degree of recurrence may lead to tedium and negative thoughts about the issue. Thus, recurrence can influence the amount and valence of thinking one does about an attitude object.

A second possibility is that when the likelihood of elaboration due to other factors is low (e.g., high distraction conditions), recurrence can influence attitudes by peripheral route processes. A number of lines of research make interesting predictions here. Wyer (1991) suggested that the likelihood of an event can be judged simply on the basis of the perceived familiarity of the event. Consistent with the familiarity idea, Arkes, Boehm, and Xu (1991) showed that mere repetition of a statement led to an increase in its perceived truthfulness. Thus, the more a person is exposed to an idea (i.e., the more it recurs), the more he or she is likely to believe that the idea is true. This effect is especially likely if critical thought about the idea is minimized (e.g., Gilbert, Krull, & Mallone, 1990). If recurrence of thought influences the perceived validity of the thought, this would be of central importance to subsequent processes involving deliberative evaluation. In expectancy-value models (e.g., Fishbein & Ajzen, 1975), for example, an evaluative response is in part determined by the likelihood of the consequences associated with the attitude object. If recurrence by itself facilitates the strengthening of belief, then recurrent thinking will lead to a corresponding polarization of the attitude. This is especially interesting given that this prediction requires no change in thought content over time!

The effects of mere recurrence may not be limited to strengthening beliefs. Zajonc's (e.g., 1968) research on mere exposure suggests that mere recurrence may also lead to an increase in the perceived desirability of the recurrent thoughts, especially when additional processing is limited (Bornstein, 1989). This suggests the possibility that people come to perceive the consequences associated with the object more favorably (or at least less negatively) as a function of recurrence, especially under restricted processing conditions. This also points to another useful distinction between elaborative and mere recurrence. The present analysis suggests that mere recurrence can make thoughts seem more likely and more desirable. It would be very interesting to find that more deliberative recurrence, in contrast, leads to polarization of the person's initial likelihood and desirability judgments (e.g., Judd & Brauer, 1995; Tesser et al., 1995).

Finally, it seems possible that under restricted processing conditions, people may simply infer their attitudes by the mere recurrence of thought, as might be expected by self-perception theory (Bem, 1972). For example, a man may infer his liking for a woman due to the frequency of his thoughts about her (e.g., "I must like her... I can't get her off my mind!").

SUMMARY

We have argued that there are various dimensions of thought that are relevant to understanding attitudes and other judgmental phenomena (e.g., extent, content, recurrence). We have further argued that numerous variables can influence each of these aspects of thought. The Martin and Tesser chapter is quite valuable in pointing to a dimension of thought that has been relatively ignored in the attitudes and persuasion literature—thought recurrence. In addition, Martin and Tesser have highlighted factors that produce recurrence, such as lack of goal attainment. One open question, however, is whether it is productive to separate ruminative thought as a special category of recurrent thinking or whether it will prove more useful to consider recurrence as just one of many dimensions along which thinking can be categorized. In any case, there is little question that many of us will be thinking (or ruminating) about the issues raised by Martin and Tesser for some time.

REFERENCES

Arkes, H. R., Boehm, L. E., & Xu, G. (1991). Determinants of judged validity. *Journal of Experimental Social Psychology, 27,* 576–605.

Aronson, E. (1968). Dissonance theory: Progress and problems. In R. Abelson, E. Aronson, W. McGuire, T. Newcomb, M. Rosenberg, & P. Tannenbaum (Eds.), *The cognitive consistency theories: A sourcebook* (pp. 5–27). Chicago: McNally.

Baker, S. M., & Petty, R. E. (1994). Majority and minority influence: Source–position imbalance as a determinant of message scrutiny. *Journal of Personality and Social Psychology, 67,* 5–19.

Bem, D. J. (1972). Self-perception theory. In L. Berkowitz (Ed.), *Advances in experimental social psychology* (Vol. 6, pp. 1–62). New York: Academic Press.

Berkowitz, L., & Devine, P. G. (1989). Research traditions, analysis, and synthesis in social psychological theories: The case of dissonance theory. *Personality and Social Psychology Bulletin, 15,* 493–507.

Bornstein, R. F. (1989). Exposure and affect: Overview and meta-analysis of research, 1968–1987. *Psychological Bulletin, 106,* 265–289.

Brehm, J. W. (1956). Post-decision changes in desirability of alternatives. *Journal of Abnormal and Social Psychology, 52,* 384–389.

Cacioppo, J. T., & Petty, R. E. (1979). Effects of message repetition and position on cognitive response, recall, and persuasion. *Journal of Personality and Social Psychology, 37,* 97–109.

Cacioppo, J. T., & Petty, R. E. (1982). The need for cognition. *Journal of Personality and Social Psychology, 42,* 116–131.

Chaiken, S., Liberman, A., & Eagly, A. H. (1989). Heuristic and systematic processing within and beyond the persuasion context. In J. S. Uleman & J. A. Bargh (Eds.), *Unintended thought* (pp. 212–252). New York: Guilford.

Cooper, J., & Fazio, R. H. (1984). A new look at dissonance theory. In L. Berkowitz (Ed.), *Advances in experimental social psychology* (Vol. 17, pp. 229–266). New York: Academic Press.

Cooper, J., Fazio, R. H., & Rhodewalt, F. (1978). Dissonance and humor: Evidence for the undifferentiated nature of dissonance arousal. *Journal of Personality and Social Psychology, 36,* 280–285.

Downing, J. D. (1994). *Transmitter tuning, self-relevant thinking, and persistence in attitude change.* Unpublished masters thesis, Ohio State University, Columbus, OH.

Fazio, R. H. (1995). Attitudes as object-evaluation associations: Determinants, consequences and correlates of attitude accessibility. In R. E. Petty & J. A. Krosnick (Eds.), *Attitude strength: Antecedents and consequences* (pp. 247–282). Hillsdale, NJ: Lawrence Erlbaum Associates.

Festinger, L. (1950). Informal social communication. *Psychological Review, 57,* 271–282.

Festinger, L. (1957). *A theory of cognitive dissonance.* Stanford, CA: Stanford University Press.

Festinger, L., & Carlsmith, J. M. (1959). Cognitive consequences of forced compliance. *Journal of Abnormal and Social Psychology, 58,* 203–211.

Fishbein, M., & Ajzen, I. (1975). *Belief, attitude, intention, and behavior: An introduction to theory and research.* Reading, MA: Addison-Wesley.

Gilbert, D. T., Krull, D. S., & Mallone, P. S. (1990). Unbelieving the unbelievable: Some problems in the rejection of false information. *Journal of Personality and Social Psychology, 59,* 601–613.

Hastie, R., & Park, B. (1986). The relationship between memory and judgment depends on whether the judgment task is memory-based or on-line. *Psychological Review, 93*, 258–268.

Haugtvedt, C. P., & Petty, R. E. (1992). Personality and persuasion: Need for cognition moderates the persistance and resistance of attitude changes. *Journal of Personality and Social Psychology, 63*, 308–319.

Haugtvedt, C. P., Schumann, D. W., Schneier, W., & Warren, W. (1994). Advertising repetition and variation strategies: Implications for understanding attitude strength. *Journal of Consumer Research, 21*, 176–189.

Higgins, E. T., Rhodewalt, F., & Zanna, M. P. (1979). Dissonance motivation: Its nature, persistence and reinstatement. *Journal of Experimental Social Psychology, 15*, 16–34.

Hovland, C. I., Janis, I. L., & Kelley, H. H. (1953). *Communication and persuasion: Psychological studies of opinion change.* New Haven, CT: Yale University Press.

Jarvis, W. B. G., & Petty, R. E. (in press). The need to evaluate. *Journal of Personality and Social Psychology.*

Judd, C. M., & Brauer, M. (1995). Repetition and evaluative extremity. In R. E. Petty & J. A. Krosnick (Eds.), *Attitude strength: Antecedents and consequences* (pp. 43–72). Hillsdale, NJ: Lawrence Erlbaum Associates.

Klinger, E. (1975). Consequences to commitment to and disengagement from incentives. *Psychological Review, 82*, 223–231.

Lassiter, G. D., Pezzo, M. V., & Apple, K. J. (1993). The transmitter-persistence effect: A confounded discovery? *Psychological Science, 4*, 208–210.

Maheswaran, D., & Chaiken, S. (1991). Promoting systematic processing in low-motivation settings: Effect of incongruent information on processing and judgment. *Journal of Personality and Social Psychology, 61*, 13–33.

Martin, L. L., Ward, D. W., Achee, J. W., & Wyer, R. S. (1993). Mood as input: People have to interpret the motivational implications of their moods. *Journal of Personality and Social Psychology, 64*, 317–326.

McIntosh, W. D., & Martin, L. L. (1992). The cybernetics of happiness: The relation between goal attainment, rumination, and affect. In M. S. Clark (Ed.), *Review of personality and social psychology* (Vol. 14, pp. 222–246). Newbury Park, CA: Sage.

Petty, R. E. (1994). Two routes to persuasion: State of the art. In G. d'Ydewalle, P. Eelen, & P. Bertelson (Eds.), *International perspectives on psychological science* (Vol. 2, pp. 229–247). Hillsdale, NJ: Lawrence Erlbaum Associates.

Petty, R. E., & Cacioppo, J. T. (1979). Issue-involvement can increase or decrease persuasion by enhancing message-relevant cognitive responses. *Journal of Personality and Social Psychology, 37*, 1915–1926.

Petty, R. E., & Cacioppo, J. T. (1981). *Attitudes and persuasion: Classic and contemporary approaches.* Dubuque, IA: Brown.

Petty, R. E., & Cacioppo, J. T. (1986). *Communication and persuasion: Central and peripheral routes to attitude change.* New York: Springer-Verlag.

Petty, R. E., & Cacioppo, J. T. (1990). Involvement and persuasion: Tradition versus integration. *Psychological Bulletin, 107*, 367–374,

Petty, R. E., Cacioppo, J. T., & Goldman, R. (1981). Personal involvement as a determinant of argument-based persuasion. *Journal of Personality and Social Psychology, 41*, 847–855.

Petty, R. E., Haugtvedt, C. P. & Smith, S. M. (1995). Elaboration as a determinant of attitude strength: Creating attitudes that are persistent, resistant, and predictive of behavior. In R. E. Petty & J. A. Krosnick (Eds.), *Attitude strength: Antecedents and consequences* (pp. 93–130). Hillsdale, NJ: Lawrence Erlbaum Associates.

Petty, R. E., & Jarvis, W. B. G. (in press). An individual differences perspective on assessing cognitive processes. In N. Schwarz & S. Sudman (Eds.), *Answering questions: Methodology for determining cognitive and communicative processes in survey research.* San Francisco: Jossey-Bass.

Petty, R. E., & Priester, J. R. (1994). Mass media attitude change: Implications of the Elaboration Likelihood Model of persuasion. In J. Bryant & D. Zillmann (Eds.), *Media effects: Advances in theory and research* (pp. 91–122). Hillsdale, NJ: Lawrence Erlbaum Associates.

Petty, R. E., Priester, J. R., & Wegener, D. T. (1994). Cognitive processes in attitude change. In R. S. Wyer & T. K. Srull (Eds.), *Handbook of social cognition* (2nd ed., Vol. 2, pp. 69–142). Hillsdale, NJ: Lawrence Erlbaum Associates.

Petty, R. E., Schumann, D. W., Richman, S. A., & Strathman, A. J. (1993). Positive mood and persuasion: Different roles for affect under high and low elaboration conditions. *Journal of Personality and Social Psychology, 64,* 5–20.

Petty, R. E., Wells, G. L., & Brock, T. C. (1976). Distraction can enhance or reduce yielding to propaganda: Thought disruption versus effort justification. *Journal of Personality and Social Psychology, 34,* 874–884.

Priester, J. R., & Petty, R. E. (1995). Source attributions and persuasion: Perceived honesty as a determinant of message scrutiny. *Personality and Social Psychology Bulletin, 21,* 637–654.

Pyszczynski, T. A., & Greenberg, J. (1981). Role of disconfirming expectancies in the instigation of attributional processing. *Journal of Personality and Social Psychology, 40,* 31–38.

Scheier, M. F., & Carver, C. S. (1987). Dispositional optimism and physical well-being: The influence of generalized outcome expectancies in health. *Journal of Personality, 55,* 169–210.

Schwarz, N. (1990). Feelings as information: Informational and motivational functions of affective states. In E. T. Higgins, & R. M. Sorrentino (Eds.), *Handbook of motivation and cognition: Foundations of social behavior* (Vol, 2, pp. 527–561). New York: Guilford.

Shavitt, S., & Brock, T. C. (1986). Self-relevant responses in commercial persuasion: Field and experimental tests. In J. Olson & K. Sentis (Eds.), *Advertising and consumer psychology* (Vol. 3, pp. 149–171). New York: Praeger.

Sherman, S. J., Mackie, D. M., & Driscoll, D. M. (1990). Priming and the differential use of dimensions in evaluation. *Personality and Social Psychology Bulletin, 16,* 405–418.

Smith, S. M., & Petty, R. E. (1995). Personality moderators of mood congruency effects on cognition: The role of self-esteem and negative mood regulation. *Journal of Personality and Social Psychology, 68,* 1092–1107.

Smith, S. M., & Rothkopf, E. Z. (1984). Contextual enrichment and distribution of practice in the classroom. *Cognition and Instruction, 1,* 341–358.

Steele, C. M. (1988). The psychology of self-affirmation: Sustaining the integrity of the self. In L. Berkowitz (Ed.), *Advances in experimental social psychology* (Vol. 21, pp. 261–302). New York: Academic Press.

Strathman, A. J., Gleicher, F., Boninger, D. S., & Edwards, C. S. (1994). The consideration of future consequences: Weighing immediate and distant outcomes of behavior. *Journal of Personality and Social Psychology, 66,* 742–752.

Tesser, A. (1978). Self-generated attitude change. In L. Berkowitz (Ed.), *Advances in experimental social psychology* (Vol. 11, pp. 289–338). New York: Academic Press.

Tesser, A., Martin, L., & Mendolia, M. (1995). The impact of thought on attitude extremity and attitude-behavior consistency. In R. E. Petty & J. A. Krosnick (Eds.), *Attitude strength: Antecedents and consequences.* Hillsdale, NJ: Lawrence Erlbaum Associates.

Underwood, B. J., Keppel, G., & Schulz, R. W. (1962). Studies of distributed practice: XXII. Some conditions which enhance retention. *Journal of Experimental Psychology, 64,* 112–129.

Vallacher, R. R., Nowak, A., & Kaufman, J. (1994). Intrinsic dynamics of social judgment. *Journal of Personality and Social Psychology, 67,* 20–34.

Webster, D. M., & Kruglanski, A. W. (1994). Individual differences in need for cognitive closure. *Journal of Personality and Social Psychology, 67,* 1049–1062.

Wegener, D. T., & Petty, R. E. (in press). Effects of mood on persuasion processes: Enhancing, reducing, and biasing scrutiny of attitude-relevant information. In L. L. Martin & A. Tesser (Eds.), *Striving and feeling: Interactions between goals and affect.* Hillsdale, NJ: Lawrence Erlbaum Associates.

Wegener, D. T., Petty, R. E., & Smith, S. M. (1995). Positive mood can increase or decrease message scrutiny: The hedonic contingency view of mood and message processing. *Journal of Personality and Social Psychology, 69,* 5–15.

Wegner, D. M. (1994). Ironic processes of mental control. *Psychological Review, 101,* 34–52.

Wyer, R. S. (1974). *Cognitive organization and change: An information processing approach.* Hillsdale, NJ: Lawrence Erlbaum Associates.

Wyer, R. S. (1991). The construction and use of thought systems: Some theoretical ambiguities. In R. S. Wyer & T. K. Srull (Eds.), *Advances in social cognition* (Vol. 4, pp. 203–214). Hillsdale, NJ: Lawrence Erlbaum Associates.

Zajonc, R. B. (1968). Attitudinal effects of mere exposure. *Journal of Personality and Social Psychology, 9,* (No. 2, Pt. 2).

Chapter 11

When Do Unconscious Goals Cloud Our Minds?

James S. Uleman
New York University

Lamont Cranston, the central character in a recent motion picture and a radio serial of the 1940s, had "the power to cloud men's [sic] minds" so that he was invisible, enabling him to apprehend criminals and do other good deeds as The Shadow. The idea of invisible, purposive agents that influence human affairs certainly has a long history in psychology and an even longer one in literature and religious thought. Such agents are appealing because they appear to explain much and, being invisible, are difficult to detect and effectively challenge. They fit our earliest ideas about how things happen, as long as we are willing to believe in the simple additional feature of personal invisibility.

Those who are skeptics about the existence of such agents (as villains always were of The Shadow) need independent evidence of their existence, apart from whatever focal events and outcomes they produce. The key to knowing that The Shadow was at work was always his voice, speaking at crucial moments in the drama from some invisible echo chamber. (Fans in the audience also had the additional evidence of his alternate life as Lamont Cranston and were privy to some of his goals, which he discussed with Margo, his companion. The audience could interpret subsequent events that fit these goals as his doing, even when they were unaccompanied by his telltale voice.)

Like The Shadow, goals influence subsequent events in Martin and Tesser's (this volume) model of rumination. They cause rumination. Rumination "is a manifestation of people's tendency to persist in goal-directed action until they have either attained their goal or given up the desire for it" (p. 11). Like The Shadow, these goals are sometimes invisible to those they affect. These "goals are not always conscious" (p. 11). In fact, even when people believe they understand the nature of these goals, they may be wrong because "the content of rumination revolves around a goal that, according to a person's implicit theories..., is the goal that has been thwarted. This may or may not be the actual goal" (p. 14). Furthermore, rumination can be "in the service of bolstering or maintaining, rather than attaining" a goal such as positive self-esteem (p. 10). A wide variety of unconscious goals can cause rumination, as long as they have been neither satisfied nor relinquished.

Like The Shadow, unconscious goals can also "cloud men's minds" because rumination can be unwanted and disruptive, although not every rumination is. "Whether a ruminative thought is unwanted or not depends on the context in which the thought occurs" (p. 7). Often when goals are frustrated, "the result is frequent and unintentional thought related to the unattained goal" and the thought may "recur even in the face of attempts to stop it" (p. 15). People may attempt to distract themselves, but distraction "can be very difficult to accomplish or maintain" (p. 16). So unconscious goals can cause rumination that disrupts other cognitive activity.

This is an exciting hypothesis, especially when advanced by such accomplished experimenters as Martin and Tesser, because detecting unconscious goals is harder than detecting The Shadow. We cannot rely on the omniscient viewpoint of the audience or on voices emerging from an invisible echo chamber. We cannot ask the participants in the experiments about them because the goals are unconscious. (Even when they are conscious, participants' self-reports cannot be taken at face value. Thus, "when subjects have control over their response output, they sometimes indicate that they are not thinking about unattained goals when in fact they are"; p. 21). The challenge is to find other evidence of these goals' existence, independent of the focal events (i.e., conscious rumination) that they are invoked to explain.

This commentary focuses on unconscious goals because they characterize the parts of Martin and Tesser's theory that interest me most. The theory states that (conscious) ruminations are caused by unattained and unrelinquished goals, usually associated with a discrepancy between the current state and a desired state. Ruminations are not necessarily unwanted or disruptive (see Table 1.1). When the goals are conscious, the theory seems simply to say that people think about their goals—not a particularly surprising or interesting hypothesis. The possibility that unconscious goals also cause rumination is more interesting and offers a potential explanation of the unwanted and disruptive ruminations that are of such interest to those of us who expect to control our own thoughts. Do unconscious goals cloud our minds, and if so, when?

I suspect that Martin and Tesser are also more interested in unconscious goals than conscious ones, although they never draw this contrast as sharply as I hope to. Conscious goals are easily manipulated and checked in experiments. One simply gives the participants instructions on the goal to adopt and then asks what their goal is. Martin and Tesser never do that in their own studies, and they seldom cite studies that do. Their manipulation of goals is usually indirect and often with an intervening activity between induction and measurement of effects. They are interested in experimental situations where they "can know what goals are influencing the subjects' thoughts, feelings, and behaviors even if the subjects cannot tell us what these goals are" (p. 20).

"When do unconscious goals cloud our minds?" actually has two meanings. The first meaning is more Martin and Tesser's question than mine: When do unconscious, unattained goals produce rumination that disrupts intentional cognitive efforts? As Table 1.1 suggests, not all rumination is disruptive, and some is constructive. The traditional emphasis on rumination that is negative in content and outcome and the uncontrollable nature of some rumination make this question important. When do unconscious goals disrupt cognitive performance?

The second meaning is more my question than theirs, although they acknowledge it briefly in discussing whether their model is falsifiable. When do theories that employ the construct "unconscious goals" make us too credulous in evaluating the theories and the evidence advanced to support them? My tentative answer is, "usually, but not always." I do not believe that the concept of unconscious goals is never useful or justified. However, I find the concept extremely dangerous because it often seems to provide an explanation that dissipates like fog on closer examination. My major goal in this chapter is to examine unconscious goals with this question in mind and to thereby clarify how to decide when the concept has explanatory utility and when it is merely an illusion masquerading as an explanation.

It is worth noting at the outset that goal explanations of complex systems are different from mechanistic (for want of a better term) explanations. Goal explanations describe *what* is being done: what conditions instigate the goal, what outcome is sought, what conditions terminate the activity. Mechanistic explanations explain *how* it is being done: how the system operates, how the behavior is carried out, and so on. (Dennett, 1987, refers to these as physical explanations in contrast to design and intentional explanations. These latter concern the goals for which the system was designed and the system's intentions or goals, if it has any.) The operation of any complex system can be usefully explained in either way. These explanatory stances are complementary rather than mutually exclusive. Objecting to a goal explanation because it does not provide a mechanistic explanation misses the point; it's not supposed to. (Mechanistic explanations are usually accompanied by goal explanations because otherwise they are incomprehensible. Imagine explaining how a car works or how to drive one to someone who doesn't know the purpose of cars.) I will not fault the goal explanation of rumination for underspecifying mechanisms.

Perhaps the place to begin is with conscious goals. As far as I can tell, the only way to identify people's conscious goals is to ask them what they are doing. A wide range of things seems to determine the answers to this question. One of the simplest is prior instructions about what they should be doing. We ask our participants to do X and later, as a comprehension or manipulation check, we ask them what they did. We tend to believe them if they tell us X rather than Y, especially if their intervening behavior is consistent with doing X rather than Y. Instructions can create or manipulate conscious goals, in that they systematically and reliably affect how people answer the question, "What are you doing?"

Of course, even when they are following instructions successfully and are completely candid and forthcoming in answering, people can't answer the question exhaustively. They cannot tell you everything else they are doing (besides what you've instructed) because they are either unaware of it or don't know how to express it. In these cases, other evidence may indicate that they were doing something else as well. For example, my students and I (summarized in Uleman, Newman & Moskowitz, 1996) and others (e.g., Carlston & Skowronski, 1994) have shown that when people read sentences that imply personality traits, they often infer these traits without either the intention (i.e., conscious goal) of making trait inferences or any awareness of having done so. We call these *spontaneous trait inferences* or STIs. They seem to occur whether people read the trait-implying sentences to memorize them (e.g., Winter & Uleman, 1984) or merely as distractors from their primary task (e.g., Lupfer, Clark, & Hutcherson, 1990; Winter, Uleman, & Cunniff, 1985).

Uleman and Moskowitz (1994) showed that (unconscious) STIs occur under a wide range of conscious (i.e., instructed) processing goals. Using the cued-recall method that has predominated in this research to date, we found evidence for STIs when participants tried to memorize the trait-implying sentences without attending to their meaning (Experiment 1) or simply examined them to detect particular phonemes (Experiment 2). Cued recall evidence indicated that STIs occurred just as often when participants' goal was to judge their own similarity to events or to characters in the sentences, as when they intentionally made trait judgments (Experiment 3). Across the three experiments, different goals produced very different frequencies of STIs, demonstrating that conscious goals can have unintended effects on unintended inferences, but none of these studies involved unconscious goals.

If you haven't given participants prior instructions on what to do, then action identification processes (Vallacher & Wegner, 1987) and Grician conversational maxims (Grice, 1975) are apt to influence their answers to "What are you doing?" Action identification theory describes the multilevel goal hierarchies that can be used to characterize actions and the variables that determine which level is actually chosen for identifying action. When participants answer with goals at one level (e.g., "I'm memorizing sentences") rather than another level (e.g., "I'm processing graphemes"), it is not appropriate to characterize goals at the other levels as unconscious. Rather, the other goals are simply alternative identifications that participants may or may not understand and endorse if asked. Participants are infallible with regard to their conscious goals, by definition, but they do not always describe them in our terms. It may be useful to ask whether they endorse other goal descriptions. If they do so without experiencing insight or being badgered, these other goals may also be counted as conscious. Clearly the mere failure to endorse our goal description of what they are doing is an insufficient basis for claiming that they have that goal unconsciously.

Participants may also bias or distort their answer to "What are you doing?" because of impression management or social desirability concerns. This formulation assumes that they know that they really have another goal but intentionally lie. Evidence for such a formulation consists in showing that when impression management is not a concern, the other goal is readily reported.

This leaves us with cases where we may reluctantly adopt unconscious goals as an appropriate explanation. There are at least three reasons for reluctance. The first is that more extensive evidence is required to demonstrate the existence of unconscious than conscious goals. One must demonstrate a convincing subset of the usual behavioral criteria: identifiable instigating conditions, response intensity, returning to the activity without any clear external prompts whenever the opportunity arises, persistence in the face of obstacles, and equifinality (where X and Y are not merely alternative identifications of the same action). The instigating conditions may be physiological deprivation (as in the classic studies of drive during the behavioral era), psychological and readily perceived (as in much of social psychology), or even subliminal (Bargh, Barndollar, & Gollwitzer, 1993, as cited in Bargh & Gollwitzer, 1994). Whatever these conditions, there should also be independent evidence that the conditions have created a goal state within their target that mediates the effects of the instigating condition on the final behavior of interest. Otherwise, the purported goal adds nothing to the instigating condition's explanatory value, and parsimony dictates dropping it from the theory. One must also show that participants are unaware of these goals. A much more complex pattern of evidence is required than simply participants' reports of their goals.

A second reason for reluctance in adopting unconscious goals as explanations is that without evidence of the goals' existence that is independent of both instigating conditions and presumed effects, such explanation are circular. The third reason is that because unconscious goals sound explanatory, they are more readily accepted without critical examination. They fit our well-practiced schemata and conversational conventions about what constitutes an adequate account of events. I suspect that this was true long before psychoanalysis entered the popular culture (Moscovici, 1976). Erdelyi (1985, p. 57) noted that the idea of unconscious processes is at least as old as Plato and is important in many Western and non-Western religious traditions. Indeed, far from being radical explanations that provoke skepticism, unconscious goals are the common currency of lay explanations and easily elicit uncritical credulity. They are therefore dangerous.

However, they may provide useful, partial explanations of behavior when participants cannot answer "What are you doing?" even when unconcerned about impression management. In such cases, participants may even be asking themselves, "What am I doing?" Unconscious goals may also explain behaviors when, even though participants say that their goal is to do X, they are clearly doing Y by all the usual goal-pursuit behavioral criteria noted previously. Participants may be unable to identify their goal because they are poor at self-perception (Bem, 1967) or have erroneous theories about their behavior (e.g., Nisbett & Wilson, 1977). Whatever the reason for participants' ignorance of their goals, establishing that an unconscious goal exists requires converging evidence that the goal is being pursued and that participants are ignorant of this.

I assume that this conception of unconscious goals is noncontroversial and largely a matter of widely shared definitions. However, it goes beyond the oft-cited control theory in giving a central role to consciousness because it requires a distinction between conscious and unconscious goals. The steady state that a thermostat "tries" to achieve is neither a conscious nor an unconscious goal. Calling it a goal uses a very different meaning of that term and begs the issues of consciousness and intention that I take to be central in any analysis of the control of human behavior (e.g., Dennett, 1984, 1991; Uleman, 1989).

THE EVIDENCE

Now that we agree on the kind of case that should be made, let's see how good the evidence is for unconscious goals as the cause of rumination. Studies are discussed in the order in which they appear in Martin and Tesser's chapter.

Millar, Tesser, and Millar (1988) examined relationships among college freshmen's reports of important goal activities that were interrupted by going away to college and leaving behind companions with whom they had done those activities, substitute people who were found at college to take the lost companions' places, and ruminations that occurred about the lost companions. The model predicts that Ruminations = β_1 * Frustrations -β_2 * Substitutes.

Results supported this prediction, in that the ß coefficients had the predicted signs. However, β_2 was only marginally significant ($\beta_2 = .25$, $n = 76$, $p = .07$; $\beta_1 = .43$).

In addition, the 10-item measure of ruminations included many thoughts that are not obviously negative, disruptive, or unwanted, especially considering that all the subjects were women, 61% of the lost companions were their mothers, and 18% were boyfriends (Millar et al., 1988, p. 447). Items included "Any reminder of him/her brought back feelings" "I thought about calling or writing him/her," "The faces of strangers at a distance reminded me of him/her," "I spent time thinking about when we could see each other," "I put up pictures and other things to make me feel that he/she was near," and "I talked about him/her to other people I met."

Finally, the rumination measure followed a lengthy questionnaire about activities they had done with their lost companion. There was no control for an alternative explanation of the results—that recalling more activities done previously with the lost companion activated other memories of that person, temporarily inflating estimates of the frequency of ruminating about the person. In short, there are several simpler explanations for these results that do not require unconscious goals, including priming within the experiment itself and classifying intentional problem solving and conversation topics as rumination.

The second study (McIntosh & Martin, 1992, Experiment 2) examined relations among participants' linking unattained goals with the higher order goal of attaining happiness, being in an active romantic relationship or not, and quickly completing word stems that were either related or not related to romance. This last measure was taken to indicate chronic concept accessibility, which should be higher (faster) for those who ruminate about romance.[1] It was separated from the romance questionnaire by a 5-minute distractor task, perhaps so that participants would not be consciously

---

[1] This is a relatively novel interpretation of this measure. Word stem completions are usually interpreted as an implicit or indirect measure of memory for prior exposure to the printed words. The measure is highly sensitive to the modality and form (e.g., type font) of prior presentations and is therefore thought to be more data driven than concept driven. Such an interpretation is therefore at odds with interpreting it as a good measure of construct accessibility. For recent reviews of word stem completion, see Richardson-Klavehn and Bjork (1988), especially pp. 508–512; Roediger, Weldon, and Challis (1989).

preoccupied with their romantic status (although this was neither explicit nor tested). Linking other goals to happiness is thought to make rumination about those goals more likely. As predicted, linkers had faster RTs to romance words if they were not in a relationship than if they were.

Nonlinkers' RTs were unaffected by relationship status, suggesting that goal frustration alone is insufficient for rumination. Apparently goals must be linked to higher order goals such as happiness to be important enough to prompt rumination. More important, alternative explanations for these effects were not considered. For example, the associative networks of participants may have differed depending on whether they were linkers or nonlinkers and were in a romance or not. Such differences may arise from rumination differences, but other experiences are also possible sources of associative differences. Thus, the romance questionnaire could have primed romance words most effectively for linkers without a current romance. Unfortunately, there was no group of participants who completed the romance questionnaire after the RT task rather than before.

In addition, no published evidence is presented or cited to show that the word stem completion measure is uniquely sensitive to rumination (see footnote 1). The only work after 1972 cited by Martin, Tesser, and McIntosh (1993) in support of this measure is Fuhrman and Shavitt (1990). So there is some ambiguity in how to interpret this study. It clearly does not require (temporarily) unconscious romantic goals as the causal explanation of rumination.

McIntosh and Martin's (1992) other study used a self-report measure of rumination (though a different one from that used by Millar et al., 1988). They found that rumination correlated significantly ($rs > .28$, $ps < .01$) with unhappiness and linking. Regression analyses supported a model in which unattained goals related to happiness (i.e., linked) cause rumination, which then causes unhappiness. However, it is just as plausible that unhappiness causes rumination, which strengthens beliefs about the links between unattained goals and happiness (i.e., linking), thus providing participants with an explanation for their unhappiness. Such an alternative model was not tested. In any case, this study involved only conscious goals, so it has little bearing on my central question.

Studies of the Zeigarnik effect also have little bearing on my question. There is no reason to regard the goals of completion or success as unconscious.

Besides increasing construct accessibility and goal-related ruminations, Martin and Tesser's model also states that unattained goals can decrease accessibility (at least in the short term) if thinking about the goal is aversive and self-distraction is easy. In Martin and Tesser's (1993) two studies, participants were given a potential opportunity to demonstrate their intelligence in a business game. Some participants were frustrated in this goal by news flashes that made the outcome depend on luck rather than skill and intelligence. The dependent variable was the same word stem completion measure used by McIntosh and Martin (1992). Consistent with predictions, Experiment 2 demonstrated that word stem completions of *intelligent* and *smart* were slower for the frustrated, luck-dependent participants who had a distraction available (25.78 s) than for those who did not (21.64 s) and for those who were not frustrated (19.66 s).

One of the most interesting features of these results is that, although the distractor's 4.14 s effect on goal-related words was significant, its effect on business-related words (3.07 s) and control words (0.32 s) was not.[2] It would be very interesting to know how this selective distraction took place, evidently before the to-be-distracted words were even recognized. Were the slower participants intentionally setting higher recognition (or reporting) thresholds because they were still interested in demonstrating their intelligence (or fearful of demonstrating their stupidity), with the distractor providing a good rationale for higher thresholds? Was this an impression management strategy, or would it have occurred if the task were completely private? Or was the process more preconscious and independent of conscious strategies? The choice of an accessibility rather than a rumination measure suggests more interest in nonstrategic processes, but the authors' thinking on these possibilities is not presented. Unfortunately, the study was not designed to answer these questions. Participants' goals, strategies, and estimates of their own intelligence and hopes of demonstrating it were not assessed. We cannot tell whether these effects were due to the (conscious or unconscious) goals that the experimenters' intended or to these alternatives that come readily to mind.

In their other experiment, without any distractor provided, word stem completion was slower for the frustrated participants immediately after the business game than after a 5-minute delay. This suggested to the authors that the participants were better at intentionally and selectively distracting themselves from goal-related words initially than after a delay, when ruminations apparently began to surface and facilitate stem completions. Unfortunately, there are no measures of these hypothesized processes, independent of the effects they are presumed to explain. Thus neither of these studies provides clear evidence that unconscious goals cause rumination.

Very few details are provided about the Beckmann and Martin (1994) study except that it took a combination of participants' action orientation and exposure to distractor to reduce the frustrated goal concepts' accessi-

---

[2]Frustratingly, the published report of these studies includes no statistical tests. Therefore, it impossible to estimate how close to significance the effect on the business-related words was and impossible to know whether the interaction between word type and distractor presence was significant.

bility and presumably the rumination that it indicates. Unlike Martin and Tesser's (1993) Experiment 2, the distractor alone was not enough to avoid rumination. The authors interpret this to mean that self-distraction is strategic rather than passive. Of course, it is also possible that action-oriented participants are less likely to ruminate in the first place; the content of the state- and action-orientation scale suggests as much. In that case, the important manipulation may not have been the presence of the distractor but the instruction "to sit quietly until the next part of the experiment." Action-oriented participants influenced by this instruction apparently ruminated as much as state-oriented participants did in both conditions. Again, however, there were no measures of these processes, independent of the effects they purport to explain.

This study shows another problem with studies of goals that do not include a no goal condition or with models that assume that a no goal condition is impossible or illogical. What is the baseline to which the effects of goals should be compared? If subjects in all conditions have some kind of goal or instruction—and this is almost inevitable if unconscious goals and self-instructions are seriously entertained—then every condition provides a potentially competing explanation of whatever effects are obtained.

An as-yet-unpublished study by Young (1987) is presented as evidence that concepts related to unattained goals attract attention and thereby automatically detract from performance on a focal task. What we cannot tell from this brief presentation is whether other chronically activated concepts, unrelated to unattained goals but frequently activated for other reasons, also attract unintended attention. Does this study tell us anything unique about goals? The Isbell, Gohm, and Wyer (1994) unpublished results that are presented in support of the importance of automatic processes may reflect nothing more than subjects' theories about the causes of their thoughts.

Martin, Tesser, & McIntosh (1993) Experiment 3 seems to provide a good demonstration that unattained conscious goals can increase the accessibility of related constructs, thus providing an alternative explanation of Wegner's white bear rebound effect. However, unconscious goals do not seem to be involved here. Similarly, the Lassiter, Pezzo, and Apple (1993) and Martin (1986) studies seem to provide good evidence that unattained (i.e., interrupted) goals lead to subsequent goal-related thought. This thought (which is called rumination if we assume that participants were aware of it) can affect the persistence of attitude change (Lassiter et al., 1993) or subsequent impressions (Martin, 1986), but unconscious goals do not seem to be involved.

Finally, McIntosh, Harlow, and Martin (in press) report that stressful daily hassles cause more depression among linkers (who link unattained goals to happiness) than nonlinkers, two weeks later. I was as impressed by two omissions from these analyses as I was by the results. First, depression at Time 1 was apparently not controlled for in the regression analyses, even though it is probably the strongest predictor of Time 2 depression. In other words, the analysis should have addressed whether hassles and linking predict Time 2 depression beyond what Time 1 depression predicts. Second, rumination was not tested as a mediator of this relation even though the appropriate data had been gathered. This is an odd omission, especially in the section entitled "The effects of rumination on negative affect." I am very interested to know what such an analysis shows. (In any case, this study does not seem to have any direct bearing on the role of unconscious goals in causing rumination.)

To summarize, no clear evidence that unconscious goals cause rumination seems to be presented here. This is due in part to the complexity of demonstrating the existence and operation of unconscious goals. In addition, not all aspects of a new theory (Martin & Tesser, 1989) can be investigated at once, and this has apparently not been one of the theorists' central concerns. However, goal-based theories also seem to have a way of clouding our critical facilities, making mere redescriptions of effects in goal terms appear to be true explanations. Without independent evidence for the goals' existence and operation, such accounts are little more than redescriptions. This is no reason to abandon goals—even unconscious goals—as theoretical constructs. After all, The Shadow is one of the good guys, even if he clouds people's minds on occasion. But getting good evidence for such constructs is quite demanding. I hope that this commentary has clarified the need for such research and the standards it should meet enough to stimulate future research on the role of unconscious goals in causing rumination.

REFERENCES

Bargh, J. A., & Gollwitzer, P. M. (1994). Environmental control of goal-directed action: Automatic and strategic contingencies between situations and behavior. In *Nebraska Symposium on Motivation, 1992,* (pp. 71–124). Lincoln, NE: University of Nebraska Press.

Beckmann, J., & Martin, L. L. (1994). Manuscript in preparation.

Bem, D. J. (1967). Self-perception: An alternative interpretation of cognitive dissonance phenomena. *Psychological Review, 74,* 183–200.

Carlston, D. E., & Skowronski, J. J. (1994). Savings in the relearning of trait information as evidence for spontaneous inference generation. *Journal of Personality and Social Psychology, 66,* 840–856.

Dennett, D. C. (1984). *Elbow room: The varieties of free will worth wanting.* Cambridge, MA: MIT Press.

Dennett, D. C. (1987). *The intentional stance.* Cambridge, MA: MIT Press.

Dennett, D. C. (1991). *Consciousness explained.* Boston: Little, Brown.

Erdelyi, M. H. (1985). *Psychoanalysis: Freud's cognitive psychology.* San Francisco: Freeman.

Fuhrman, R. W., & Shavitt, S. (1990, April). *The effects of goal priming on the speed and favorableness of attitude judgments.* Paper presented at the meetings of the Midwestern Psychological Association, Chicago, Illinois.

Grice, H. P. (1975). Logic and conversation. In P. Cole & J. L. Morgan (Eds.), *Syntax and semantics 3: Speech acts* (pp. 95–113). New York: Academic Press.

Isbell, L., Gohm, C., & Wyer, R. S. (1994). Unpublished raw data.

Lassiter, G. D., Pezzo, M. V., & Apple, K. J. (1993). The transmitter-persistence effect: A confounded discovery? *Psychological Science, 4*, 208–210.

Lupfer, M. B., Clark, L. F., & Hutcherson, H. W. (1990). Impact of context on spontaneous trait and situational attributions. *Journal of Personality and Social Psychology, 58*, 239–249.

Martin, L. L. (1986). Set/reset: Use and disuse of concepts in impression formation. *Journal of Personality and Social Psychology, 51*, 493–504.

Martin, L. L. & Tesser, A. (1989). Toward a motivational and structural theory of ruminative thought. In J. S. Uleman & J. A. Bargh (Eds.), *Unintended thought* (pp. 306–326). New York: Guilford.

Martin, L. L., Tesser, A., & McIntosh, W. D. (1993). Wanting but not having: The effects of unattained goals on thoughts and feelings. In D. M. Wegner & J. W. Pennebaker (Eds.), *The handbook of mental control* (pp. 552–572). New York: Prentice Hall.

McIntosh, W. D., Harlow, T. F., & Martin, L. L. (in press). Linkers and non-linkers: The relation between goals, rumination, and depression. *Journal of Basic and Applied Psychology*.

McIntosh, W. D., & Martin, L. L. (1992). The cybernetics of happiness: The relation of goal attainment, rumination, and affect. In M. S. Clark (Ed.), *Review of personality and social psychology* (Vol. 14, pp. 222–246). Newbury Park, CA: Sage.

Millar, K. U., Tesser, A., & Millar, M. G. (1988). The effects of a threatening life event on behavior sequences and intrusive thought: A self-disruption explanation. *Cognitive Therapy and Research, 12*, 441–457.

Moscovici, S. (1976). *La psychanalyse: Son image et son public* 2nd ed.). Paris: Presses Universitaires de France.

Nisbett, R. E., & Wilson, T. (1977). Telling more than we can know: Verbal reports on mental processes. *Psychological Review, 84*, 213–259.

Richardson-Klavehn, A., & Bjork, R. A. (1988). Measures of memory. *Annual Review of Psychology, 39*, 475–543.

Roediger, H. L., III, Weldon, M. S., & Challis, B. H. (1989). Explaining dissociations between implicit and explicit measures of retention: A processing account. In H. L. Roediger, III & F. I. M. Craik (Eds.), *Varieties of memory and consciousness* (pp. 3–41). Hillsdale, NJ: Lawrence Erlbaum Associates.

Uleman, J. S. (1989). The self-control of thoughts: A framework for thinking about unintended thought. In J. S. Uleman & J. A. Bargh (Eds.), *Unintended thought* (pp. 425–449). New York: Guilford.

Uleman, J. S., & Moskowitz, G. B. (1994). Unintended effects of goals on unintended inferences. *Journal of Personality and Social Psychology, 66*, 490–501.

Uleman, J. S., Newman, L. S., & Moskowitz, G. B. (1996). People as flexible interpreters: Evidence and issues from spontaneous trait inference. In M. P. Zanna (Ed.), *Advances in Experimental Social Psychology*. Vol. 29 San Diego, CA: Academic Press.

Vallacher, R. R., & Wegner, D. M. (1987). What do people think they're doing? Action identification and human behavior. *Psychological Review, 94*, 3–15.

Winter, L., & Uleman, J. S. (1984). When are social judgments made? Evidence for the spontaneous of trait inferences. *Journal of Personality and Social Psychology, 47*, 237–252. Also see correction in *Journal in Personality and Social Psychology* (1986), *50*, 355.

Winter, L., Uleman, J. S., & Cunniff, C. (1985). How automatic are social judgments? *Journal of Personality and Social Psychology, 49*, 904–917. Also see correction in *Journal of Personality and Social Psychology* (1986), *50*, 381.

Young, J. (1987). *The role of selective attention in the attitude–behavior relationship*. Unpublished doctoral dissertation, University of Minnesota.

Chapter **12**

Rumination: When All Else Fails

Michaela Wänke
Jeannette Schmid
Universität Heidelberg

Martin and Tesser present a highly pragmatic definition of rumination. By defining rumination as the recurrence and intrusiveness of thoughts that involve a common theme, they circumvent fruitless discussions as to which modes of thinking qualify as rumination and which do not. This approach seems superior to mode or content-oriented definitions because it simplifies a construct that is already widely used and has been endorsed with a different meaning by several authors. The structural approach provides a common denominator to investigate the mechanisms of rumination. At the same time, the model integrates a variety of existing research areas and builds a bridge between more clinically oriented research and findings in social cognition. Both perspectives should benefit.

Their parsimonious definition in mind, we note that the model offered by Martin and Tesser does not address the recurrent nature of rumination to the extent one would expect. Particularly, the causes for the recurrence of thoughts can be analyzed in more detail. That goal blockage instigates thoughts does not sufficiently explain why these thoughts become recurrent and intrusive. In this chapter, we elaborate where we think some clarifications and modifications of the model are needed. The four points we discuss concern instigation by goal blockage, the suitability of the goal concept, the question of functionality, and finally the reported data. Consecutively, we outline some variables that may play a role in moderating the recurrence of similar thoughts. Foremost, we argue that sense of control is a prime moderator of recurrent thoughts. We hasten to add that our criticism is meant as a constructive suggestion to modify the model where it seems unnecessarily restricted and to clarify statements that may be misleading. By and large, we see our suggestions as compatible with the Martin and Tesser model presented in chapter 1.

POINTS OF DISAGREEMENT

The Role of Goal Blockage and the Content of Rumination

According to Martin and Tesser, rumination is instigated by goal blockage when a task is interrupted. Here, in our opinion, the model needs to distinguish between interruption as causing rumination versus interruption as enabling rumination. If interruption of a goal-directed activity were the cause for rumination, people would only ruminate when interrupted, and the target for rumination would be the goal that is blocked at that moment or a higher goal in the relevant goal hierarchy.

Two phenomena seem inconsistent with this view. First, sometimes intrusive thoughts may be so strong that they interfere with goal-directed activities by themselves. In other words, rumination may cause the interruption and not vice versa. Second, it seems hardly the case that rumination is restricted to contents relevant at the moment it occurs. Indeed, that possibility is noted by Martin and Tesser at various places throughout the chapter (e.g., thinking of the baby one expects while driving to work). Consider, for example, passengers in the gate area waiting for the departure of their flight. One of them may read, another may engage in people-watching, and a third may keep thinking about his unhappy marriage, how it happened, whether he should leave or stay. Given that this person has had similar thoughts for a long time we may well call his behavior rumination. But what task was interrupted? Even if we consider the waiting period as an interruption in traveling, the ruminative thoughts do not concern the interrupted task. In this respect, a task interruption constitutes an opportunity to ruminate but not necessarily its cause. Whether certain thoughts come to mind depends on their accessibility. Some may be so highly accessible that they interfere with other thoughts, for example concentrating on work or a book. Other thoughts may automatically come to mind when nothing else binds one's attention, and some may only emerge when situational cues trigger them. We agree that an interruption in goal-directed behavior may induce a discrepancy between an aspired state and the present reality and that the awareness of such a discrepancy is likely to instigate related thoughts. However, the activation of this discrepancy is not restricted to an actual task interruption. The discrepancy may come to mind any time and elicit related thoughts. Whether these thoughts become ruminative, however, is subject to other conditions outlined in the next sections.

The Goal Concept

A second and related problem refers to the goal concept. It is not sufficiently clear whether it is the goal itself that determines the rumination or a kind of metagoal, the normalization of rate of progress toward the goal. By the same token, it is not clear whether the maintenance of the goal is a goal itself.

Another more relevant issue concerns the content of goals. Consider, for example, victims of a traumatic event such as rape. Obviously, the crime impeded the achievement or maintenance of happiness. Taken in this broad sense, however, the goal concept does not seem to add much to our understanding. If we assume that the highest goal in human life is to achieve happiness, then of course every single event can bring us closer or threaten our achievement. What specific goals are thwarted in this example? In some cases the goal may come into play only retrospectively, to undo what has happened. The victim may brood for years on "what ifs" and "if onlys" and may fervently wish the event had never happened (Silver, Boon, & Stones, 1983). Still, we hesitate to call the wish to undo what has been done a goal rather than a wish. That all human behavior is goal directed or that human thinking is predominated by the achievement of goals seems arguable. Of course, in principle one can construct goals for every behavior, and, as Martin and Tesser state, these goals do not have to be conscious. In this respect, however, the goal concept risks becoming too general and consequently less explanatory.

We argue that it is not the unexpected rate of progress toward some goal that instigates rumination but rather is the awareness of an alternative state. This constitutes a discrepancy between what is and what might be, between what was and what might have been, or between various future states. It is exactly this discrepancy that can give impetus to rumination. Individuals may daydream about the child they never had, think of the answers they should have given in the exam, or wonder how they would have done had they chosen a different career. In all these examples one may find it hard to derive goals. Goals only constitute one type of alternative state and therefore the focus on goals as an explanation for the ruminating process seems more restricted than is necessary.

The Functionality of Rumination

We question the functionality of rumination. Martin and Tesser (this volume) argue that rumination serves the function of discrepancy reduction:

"The recurrent thoughts ... are instrumental to reducing some form of discrepancy" (p. 6) and "When recurrent thoughts do not directly address a discrepancy, they aid in reaffirming the lack of one" (p. 6). From the empirical data given, there is no evidence that rumination does indeed serve this function. This is not to say that, in principle, rumination never reduces a discrepancy. For example, as Martin and Tesser point out, successfully working through is helpful to put one's plaguing problems behind, but there is evidence that rumination intensifies emotion and lengthens the duration of the process (Lyubomirsky & Nolen-Hoeksema, 1993; Morrow & Nolen-Hoeksema, 1990; Nolen-Hoeksema & Morrow, 1991, 1993; Nolen-Hoeksema, Morrow, & Fredrickson, 1993; Wood, Saltzberg, Neale, Stone, & Rachmiel, 1990).

Again, we need to distinguish between initial thoughts that may help to solve a problem and the recurrence of thoughts, which, at least for some time, prolongs the problem. The former may be functional in overcoming whatever discrepancy is activated. However, sometimes people fail to resolve their discrepancies at the first attempts. These people may be forced to think the same or related thoughts over and over; in other words, these thoughts become ruminative in nature.[1] Thus, we argue that rumination is a symptom of a specific mental constellation; it does not serve a useful purpose by itself. In this sense, rumination is the dysfunctional residual of a failed discrepancy reduction. Later we elaborate on this assumption.

Empirical Evidence

Martin and Tesser report an impressive array of data, including their own as well as other authors' research. By and large, the reported research supports many of the conclusions. Nevertheless, some questions remain. The prime dependent variable in the reported experiments is the time it takes subjects to recognize words related to the goal that has been blocked. For some experiments the authors interpret shorter recognition latencies as indicators for rumination. However, exactly the opposite interpretation is offered for findings in other studies (e.g., Hong & Dweck, 1992; as cited in Martin & Tesser, this volume; Martin & Tesser, 1993, as cited in Martin & Tesser, this volume) because ruminating individuals should attempt to distract themselves and thus would be slower to recognize related words. This interpretation makes sense when a distractor was offered, as in the study by Martin and Tesser (1993, Exp. 2). However, in the condition where

---

[1] Of course, ruminators may eventually find a solution and stop ruminating. Ruminative thoughts may also disappear because the discrepancy may be resolved in other ways because, for example, the situation changes, or as Martin and Tesser state, the relevance of the discrepancy may be reduced.

no distractor was presented, subjects who according to the experimental manipulation should ruminate did not show shorter latencies (see Table 1.2). Of course, one might argue that ruminators tried to distract themselves regardless of whether or not a distractor was given. Despite its plausibility, this argument produces severe empirical problems if both longer and shorter latencies can imply rumination. More refined measures are needed to disentangle rumination, the distraction from rumination, and nonruminative thinking.

ALTERNATIVE SUGGESTIONS

What Constitutes Rumination?

We assume that people are constantly engaged in mental activity. Sometimes this mental activity is concerned with a certain task (e.g., flow, problem solving, decision making); at other times, when nothing binds their attention, people engage in free-floating thoughts. When one becomes aware of an alternative outcome to one's present situation, some mental activity begins, provided it is relevant enough and one has the mental capacity to engage in such activity. At this point, the mental activity may be helpful to reduce the perceived discrepancy between the present situation and the alternative. For example, the researcher whose paper was rejected may decide that the journal was the wrong outlet, may plan the additional study that will convince the reviewers, may draft an angry letter to the editor, may engage in daydreams of success, or may doubt his or her ability and wonder whether academia was the right career choice. Some of those thoughts may reduce the discrepancy or at least induce a feeling of control. Other thoughts, however, are ill suited to an eventual reduction. For example, the mother whose baby died may engage in daydreaming about the baby. At the moment when she is happily absorbed in her fantasy, the painful discrepancy between enjoying the baby and the loss is absent. However, the cruel reality may be easily brought to mind. Fantasizing in this case brings only temporary relief but does nothing to overcome the loss. In fact, it may even intensify the pain because it causes constant reliving. Even thoughts that are, in principle, directed at problem solving may fail because the discrepancy cannot be resolved easily.

Thus, a mental activity may contribute to an individual's perception of controlling the reduction of discrepancy. If it does not, the discrepancy will remain at a high level of accessibility. This accessibility in turn will repetitively elicit similar thoughts. It is precisely that repetitive quality that we, in agreement with Martin and Tesser, consider ruminative. It is not the content or any quality of the involved mental activity but rather the circularity of the process that is central to our understanding of what rumination is. The ruminative content can be negative as well as positive. Although in this perspective the modes of thinking are irrelevant different modes are differently prone to turning ruminative. For example, thoughts like "What can I do to improve the paper?" may enable the author in the previous example to move onward, find solutions and begin (mental) activities, whereas thoughts such as "Nothing ever works for me" or "One day I will be recognized" are less likely to develop new paths. Nevertheless, it is not the kind of thought but its recurrence that defines rumination.[2]

The vicious cycle is self-reinforcing in two ways. First, every activation of the discrepancy increases its accessibility (Higgins, 1989; Higgins, Bargh, & Lombardi, 1985; Srull & Wyer, 1989). Second, from the intrusiveness and recurrence of a certain theme people may conclude that this theme is highly relevant to them, which in turn heightens its relevance. In summary, rumination is dysfunctional in overcoming a bothering discrepancy because it keeps the discrepancy in memory. At the same time, repeatedly thinking the same thoughts that failed to help before may interfere with actually generating new strategies to resolve the discrepancy or with engaging in new activities, so the discrepancy may eventually become less relevant.

What Can Break the Cycle?

First, instead of engaging in a mental activity dedicated to some discrepancy, people may divert their capacity to some other task. In other words, they may distract themselves. Whether this strategy is successful depends on the accessibility of the discrepancy once the distractor terminates and how easily the discrepancy can be activated again. For example, the mother whose baby died may seek escape from her thoughts by plunging into work or going to a movie. She may immediately return to her thoughts when she is not otherwise preoccupied, but even if she manages to think of something else the sight of the empty cradle may trigger the tormenting thoughts once again.

Second, once a discrepancy is not considered as relevant any more, its accessibility should decrease. This aspect is discussed in detail by Martin and Tesser. Third and foremost, when people perceive control over the discrepancy, their thoughts should not become ruminative, and existing rumination should be broken.

Who Ruminates?

The aforementioned considerations imply that some people are more prone to experience ruminative thoughts than others—a thought also expressed

---

[2]By postulating rumination as a circular process we borrow from various models in control theory (for a review, see Hyland, 1988).

by Martin and Tesser. People who have no other tasks at hand to distract themselves should ruminate more than busy people. Likewise, people who are in a situation in which they are constantly reminded of an existing discrepancy may experience more rumination than those who experience a change in environment. Moreover, we assume individual differences in whether one focuses on the present situation and its challenges or whether one tends to let one's mind wander into the past or future. For the latter individuals more discrepancies should be accessible, and rumination may occur more, maintaining the discrepancies' accessibility. A related personality difference is described by Kuhl (1984) as the difference between state orientation and action orientation. Action versus state orientation can also apply to the (mental) behavior people may show in response to activated discrepancies. In addition, people may differ in their ability to use distractors (Borkovec & Lyonfields, 1993).

Furthermore, as Martin and Tesser propose, people differ in their flexibility regarding the relevance of discrepancies. Nonlinkers, for example, are more flexible and are thus less likely to ruminate.

Finally, whether mental activity leads to a feeling of control also depends on one's general level of control perception. People differ in their generalized beliefs about the degree of influence or control they have over the events encountered in their lives (Lefcourt, 1976). People with a high sense of control should be less likely to experience ruminative thoughts. They may be more likely to engage in problem solving in the first place, thus increasing the chances to find a solution. Independent of their mode of mental activity, they may be more likely to derive a perception of control from their thoughts. In our example of the researcher whose paper was rejected, the thought to plan the second study may instill a feeling of control, but it could also cue additional responses, such as, "What if the reviewers don't like that study either," "What if it won't work," "How in the world can I come up with a convincing design." For people who generally have a low sense of control, their thoughts should be less likely to instill a perception of control regarding a specific discrepancy. Thus, for these individuals, their thoughts are more likely to recur.

Empirical Data: The Link Between Control and Rumination

We tested the relation between rumination and locus of control. We assumed that people with a low sense of internal control would ruminate more than those with a high sense of internal control. In addition, we assumed that this relation explains the gender difference that women are more likely to ruminate than men (Butler & Nolen-Hoeksema, in press; Isbell, Gohm, & Wyer, 1994; Nolen-Hoeksema, 1987; Nolen-Hoeksema et al., 1993; Nolen-Hoeksema, Parker, & Larson, 1994). Although gender per se has no explanatory power, it can be used to detect the mediating variables in which men and women differ. One likely candidate is locus of control. Women have often been found to have a lower sense of internal control than men (DeWolfe, Jackson, & Winterberger, 1988; Maccoby & Jacklin, 1974; Roback, Rabin, & Chapman, 1988; Singh & Verma, 1990).

With a sample of 60 University of Heidelberg students we assessed internal control, control by powerful others and chance control, using a short form of the FKK (Krampen, 1991), a German adaptation and continuation of the IPC-Scale (Levensohn, 1981). In addition, we assessed self-reported rumination using a translated and shortened version of the scale developed by Isbell et al. (1994). As expected, we found a significant negative correlation between self-reported rumination and internal control ($r = -.45$) and a significant positive correlation between rumination and control by powerful others ($r = .25$). The data suggest that the less internal control people perceive in their lives the more they tend to ruminate.

In accordance with the literature (Butler & Nolen-Hoeksema, in press; Nolen-Hoeksema, 1987; Nolen-Hoeksema et al., 1993; Nolen-Hoeksema et al., 1994; Isbell et al., 1994) we found huge gender differences in the self-reported rumination in the expected direction: Women reported significantly more rumination. However, when internal control was used as a covariate, the gender effect was reduced to nonsignificance ($F < 1$).

These data support our notion that perceived control is a highly relevant moderator of whether or not people tend to ruminate. Although we would not call the perception of control as the cause of rumination, it seems an important influence on whether normal problem-oriented thinking becomes ruminative or not. The less control people perceive the more they ruminate. We would suggest that individuals with a high internal control perception exit the ruminative cycle earlier simply because they experience control in overcoming the discrepancy. Those individuals who do not perceive control initially have to go through the cycle several times until either they achieve control or the discrepancy is otherwise reduced. In this respect, we find it noteworthy that in two experiments cited by Martin and Tesser rumination was induced by giving subjects feedback on ability versus luck. An ability attribution is likely to elicit a sense of internal control, whereas an attribution to luck is likely to elicit a low sense of internal control (e.g., Rotter, 1966).

Of course, it is unclear what is cause and what is effect in the relation between control and rumination. Do people who believe to have no control ruminate because they cannot solve their problems otherwise? Or does rumination result in a perceived lack of control because people who ruminate do little else to solve their problems? Although this is an important question that correlational data cannot answer, the answer is less central where habitual rumination is concerned. People have no control in one situation and thus ruminate. Because they ruminate rather than taking action, they do not have an experience that results in a general sense of control. In the long run, both processes feed into each other.

Interestingly, the locus of control variable accounted for the gender differences in rumination in our study. We believe that women ruminate more because they perceive themselves to have little control. Lack of control has often been linked to depression (e.g., Abramson, Seligman, & Teasdale, 1978; Peterson & Seligman, 1984) and it is well established that women are more likely to suffer from depression than men (Chino & Funabiki, 1984; Radloff, 1975; Seiden, 1976; Silverman, 1968; Weissman & Klerman, 1977). Likewise, rumination has been linked with depression (Carver & Scheier, 1990; Fenigstein, Scheier, & Buss, 1975; Nolen-Hoeksema, 1991; Pyszczynski & Greenberg, 1987). From the present data it seems worthwhile to investigate how all three variables interrelate.

SUMMARY

In general, we find a definition focusing on the intrusive and repetitive features of rumination very useful. For many purposes, such a definition seems easier to handle than a definition that includes content as well. The suggestions we have made are not necessarily incompatible with the Martin and Tesser model. We suggested extensions and modifications which seem less restrictive and allow one to focus more on the repetitive nature of ruminative thoughts. Whereas Martin and Tesser assume a goal blockage, we suggest that the awareness of alternative states is a crucial variable. We question whether interruption is the cause of rumination or simply an opportunity to ruminate. Finally, we question the functionality of rumination and suggest that rumination occurs when people have nothing left to do to overcome the discrepancies between what is and what might be—between various alternative states or between reality and alternative states. People ruminate because they cannot do anything else. In their perception they lack control to tackle their problems. Unless they successfully distract themselves or the problem goes away either by itself or because its relevance is reduced, these people are bound to ruminate.

We would like to point out that some of the suggested concepts may not be independent. For example, it may well be that nonlinkers (McIntosh & Martin, 1992) who are more flexible in finding alternative paths to reach happiness, also perceive more control in their lives. Thus, it seems important to look at various personality concepts in more detail. Moreover, it is of crucial importance to develop a measure tailored to the circularity of the process. Accessibility measures are problematic insofar as they may not distinguish between a single mental activity that successfully reduces a felt discrepancy and the repeated thought. Because only the latter qualifies as rumination, we may not have tapped into a ruminative circle. Accessibility measures are only useful if some delay between the activation of an alternative state is involved, if they are administered more than once, or if we can otherwise assume a prolonged and repeated mental activity.

ACKNOWLEDGMENT

Preparation of this chapter was supported by grant B1 28615 from the Deutsche Forschungsgemeinschaft to H. Bless, N. Schwarz, and M. W nke and grant F: 294/10 from Deutsche Forschungsgemeinschaft to K. Fiedler. We thank Tilmann Betsch, Herbert Bless, Gerd Bohner, Norbert Schwarz, and Bob Wyer for stimulating discussions and comments on an earlier draft.

REFERENCES

Abramson, L., Seligman, M., & Teasdale, J. (1978). Learned helplessness in humans: Critique and reformulation. *Journal of Abnormal Psychology, 87*, 49–74.

Borkovec, T. D., & Lyonfields, J. D. (1993). Worry—thought suppression of emotional processing. In H. W. Krohne (Ed.), *Attention and avoidance: Strategies in coping with aversiveness*, (pp. 101–118). Göttingen, Germany: Hogrefe & Huber Publishers.

Butler, L. D., & Nolen-Hoeksema, S. (in press). Gender differences in depressed mood in a college sample. *Sex Roles*.

Carver, C., & Scheier, M. (1990). Origins and functions of positive and negative affect: A control-process view. *Psychological Review, 97*, 19–35.

Chino, A., & Funabiki, D. (1984). A cross-validation of sex differences in the expression of depression. *Sex Roles, 11*, 175–187.

DeWolfe, T. E., Jackson, L. A., & Winterberger, P. (1988). A comparison of moral reasoning and moral character in male and female incarcerated felons. *Sex Roles, 18*, 583–593.

Fenigstein, A., Scheier, M., & Buss, A. (1975). Public and private self-consciousness: Assessment and theory. *Journal of Consulting and Clinical Psychology, 43*, 522–527.

Higgins, E. (1989). Knowledge accessibility and activation: Subjectivity and suffering from unconscious sources. In J. Uleman & J. Bargh (Eds.), *Unintended thought* (pp. 75–123). New York: Guilford.

Higgins, E., Bargh, J., & Lombardi, W. (1985). The nature of priming effects on categorization. *Journal of Experimental Psychology: Learning, Memory, and Cognition, 11*, 59–69.

Hyland, M. (1988). Motivational control theory: An integrative framework. *Journal of Personality and Social Psychology, 55*, 642–651.

Isbell, L., Gohm, C., & Wyer, R. S. (1994). *On habitual rumination.* Unpublished raw data, University of Illinois, Champaign, IL.

Krampen, G. (1991). *Fragebogen zu Kompetenz- und Kontrollüberzeugungen (FKK)* (Locus of control for reinforcement questionnaire). Göttingen: Hogrefe.

Kuhl, J. (1984). Motivational aspects of achievement motivation and learned helplessness: Toward a comprehensive theory of action control. In B. A. Maher & W. B. Maher (Eds.), *Progression in experimental personality research.* (Vol 13. pp. 99–171). New York: Academic Press.

Lefcourt, H. (1976). *Locus of control.* Hillsdale, NJ: Lawrence Erlbaum Associates.

Levensohn, H. (1981) Differentiating among internality, powerful others, and chance. In H. M. Lefcourt (Ed.), *Research within the locus of control construct* (Vol. 1, pp. 15–63). New York: Academic Press.

Lyubomirsky, S., & Nolen-Hoeksema, S. (1993). Self-perpetuating properties of depressive rumination. *Journal of Personality and Social Psychology, 65,* 339–349.

Maccoby, E., & Jacklin, C. (1974). *The psychology of sex differences.* Stanford: Stanford University Press.

McIntosh, W. D., & Martin, L. L. (1992). The cybernetics of happyness: The relation of goal attainment, rumination, and affect. In M. Clark (Ed.), *Emotion and Social Behavior: Review of Personality and Social Psychology.* (Vol 14, p. 222–246). New York: Sage.

Morrow, J., & Nolen-Hoeksema, S. (1990). Effects of responses to depression on the remediation of depressive affect. *Journal of Personality and Social Psychology, 58,* 519–527.

Nolen-Hoeksema, S. (1987). Sex differences in unipolar depression: Evidence and theory. *Psychological Bulletin, 101,* 259–282.

Nolen-Hoeksema, S. (1991). Responses to depression and their effects on the duration of depressive episodes. *Journal of Abnormal Psychology, 100,* 569–582.

Nolen-Hoeksema, S., & Morrow, J. (1991). A prospective study of depression and distress following a natural disaster: The 1989 Loma Prieta earthquake. *Journal of Personality and Social Psychology, 61,* 105–121.

Nolen-Hoeksema, S., & Morrow, J. (1993). The effects of rumination and distraction on naturally occurring depressed moods. *Cognition and Emotion, 7,* 561–570.

Nolen-Hoeksema, S., Morrow, J., & Fredrickson, B. L. (1993). Response styles and the duration of episodes of depressed mood. *Journal of Abnormal Psychology, 102,* 20–28.

Nolen-Hoeksema, S., Parker, L., & Larson, J. (1994). Ruminative coping with depressed mood following loss. *Journal of Personality and Social Psychology, 67,* 92–104.

Pyszczynski, T., & Greenberg, J. (1987). Self-regulatory perseveration and the depressive self-focusing style: A self-awareness theory of reactive depression. *Psychological Bulletin, 110,* 538–543.

Radloff, L. (1975). Sex differences in depression: The effects of occupation and marital status. *Sex Roles, 1,* 249–265.

Roback, H. B.; Rabin, P. L. & Chapman, J. E. (1988). Gender differences in first year medical students' attitudes towards a discussion-oriented behavioral science course. *Social Behavior and Personality, 16,* 65–69.

Rotter, J. (1966). Generalized expectancies for internal versus external control reinforcement. *Psychological Monographs, 80* (Whole No. 609).

Peterson, C., & Seligman, M. (1984). Causal explanations as a risk factor for depression: Theory and evidence. *Psychological Review, 91,* 347–374.

Seiden, A. (1976). Overview: Research on the psychology of women: II. Women in families, work and psychotherapy. *The American Journal of Psychiatry, 133,* 1111–1123.

Silver, R. L., Boon, C., & Stones, M. H. (1983). Searching for meaning in misfortune: Making sense of incest. *Journal of Social Issues, 39,* 81–102.

Silverman, C. (1968). *The epidemiology of depression.* Baltimore: Johns Hopkins University Press.

Singh, B. G., & Verma, O. P. (1990). Cultural differences in locus of control beliefs in two Indian societies. *Journal of Social Psychology, 130,* 725–729

Srull, T., & Wyer, R. (1989). Person memory and judgment. *Psychological Review, 96,* 58–83.

Weissman, M., & Klerman, G. (1977). Sex differences in the epidemiology of depression. *Archives of General Psychiatry, 34,* 854–862.

Wood, J., Saltzberg, J., Neale, J., Stone, A., & Rachmiel, T. (1990). Self-focused attention, coping responses, and distressed mood in everyday life. *Journal of Personality and Social Psychology, 58,* 1027–1036.

Chapter 13

Clarifying Our Thoughts

Leonard L. Martin
Abraham Tesser
University of Georgia

Being asked to write the target chapter for a volume in this series was exciting. We had been trying to update and formalize some of our ideas on rumination (Martin & Tesser, 1989; Martin, Tesser & McIntosh, 1993) when we were asked to do it. The invitation provided a good opportunity to push a little faster on this project. However, even as the ink dried on the paper, we knew the work could benefit from the comments of knowledgeable, creative colleagues. On the basis of the judgment, tenacity, and track record of the editor, Bob Wyer, we were optimistic about getting the kind of commentary we needed.

If you have read the comments already you know that the commentators were, indeed, drawn from among the foremost researchers in this area. All of them have made or are making important contributions to the field of rumination or related phenomena. Moreover, each of the commentators appears to have read chapter 1 carefully and responded thoughtfully.

In order to discuss the commentaries efficiently, we extracted the issues raised in each chapter and grouped them into broad themes. In this way, we were able to address many (though not all) of the issues and to do so in a way that maintained the big picture. The broad themes we extracted include concerns over the definition of rumination, the mechanism underlying rumination, the role of emotion, the function of rumination, the lack of clarity in some key terms, our organization of the modes of ruminative thought, our treatment of individual differences, and the degree to which our definition and mechanism generalize to "real world" rumination.

Before turning to these themes, however, we provide a short sketch of how we came to develop the model described in chapter 1. Providing this short intellectual history serves two purposes. It helps to distinguish our model from similar models by pointing to differences in intellectual forbearers, and it demonstrates the robustness of a goal-based view of rumination, given that several researchers came to similar points of view while traveling very different theoretical routes.

A SHORT HISTORY

Our thinking about rumination began at an outdoor cafe in downtown Athens, over two bowls of gelato and a blank sheet of paper. We had recently been invited to the conference described by Leslie Clark in the opening of her chapter. Neither of us was particularly well versed in the literature on rumination (although one had been involved in research on the polarizing effect of thought; Tesser, 1978; Tesser, Martin, & Mendolia, 1995). We had a vague understanding that one of the defining characteristics of rumination was that it persisted beyond the occurrence of the initiating event. Our first task, therefore, was to find a mechanism that could account for such persistence.

Fortunately, Kurt Lewin had already addressed a similar problem. A laboratory prototype of rumination was first reported by and named for one of Lewin's student's, Bluma Zeigarnik (see Zeigarnik, 1938). She found that people had better recall for tasks they had not completed than for tasks they had completed. The initial parameters of this so-called Zeigarnik effect were laid out by Lewin (1951) and researched by his students. This early work demonstrated, among other things, that the Zeigarnik effect was a function of goal importance, distance from the goal, clarity of the goal, and substitutability. The general phenomenon reflected in the Zeigarnik effect was subsequently recast in cybernetic terms by Miller, Galanter, and Pribram (1960), who noted the importance of placing the effect into a richer cognitive structure.

These early ideas and experiments were the basis for the theoretical model we developed. We subsequently elaborated upon these ideas with concepts from Csikzentmihyli (1975) and Wicklund (1986) regarding a person's fit with environmental demands, Carver and Scheier (1990) regarding the role of velocity, acceleration, and affect in a control systems model, and Nisbett and Wilson (1977), who suggested that people supplement their sometimes weak introspective abilities with naive theories. It was only after we had these assumptions organized into a more or less coherent framework that we turned to the research directly involving rumination.

As we became better acquainted with this research, we realized two things. First, there was a lot of research going on, and for the most part, different investigators were using different labels for similar phenomena.

Indeed, many of the phenonema, although different in surface characteristics, appeared to be highly related and perhaps even functionally equivalent. Our model was, in part, an attempt to call attention to the fragmentary state of the field and an attempt to foster a more integrative approach. We have more to say about these issues when we discuss some definitional and taxonomic issues later in this chapter.

The second realization we had while reviewing the literature was that researchers coming from very different theoretical points of view came to similar conclusions regarding some of the model's most important parameters. Central to our thinking was the notion that rumination has its motivational origin in goal blockage and that the motivational base disappears when the goal is attained or abandoned. We arrived at this conclusion from a gestaltist, Lewinian point of view. The fact that researchers approaching the question from a learning theory point of view (e.g., Klinger, 1975) or a systems theory point of view (e.g., Carver & Scheier, 1981) converge on this central aspect of the model provides a kind of theoretical triangulation. Although this triangulation is not conducive to "crucial" tests (i.e., evidence that goals influence rumination does not distinguish among the models), it is nevertheless encouraging. When different theories point to the same conclusion, we tend to have greater confidence in the likelihood of that conclusion than if the theories arrived at different conclusions. Thus, this kind of triangulation makes us more confident that goals play an important role in rumination.

Before moving onto a discussion of some of the themes that emerged in the commentaries, it is worth noting in broad terms some of the features of our model that distinguish it from related models. First, we suggest that rumination not only has a motivational (i.e., goal-based) origin but also can result from amotivational associative processes (e.g., the channelization process). Few theorists in this area have concerned themselves with this cooler component of rumination. Second, we suggest that the content of rumination may be more reflective of an individual's implicit theories of his or her life circumstances than of the actual goal being blocked. Although a number of theorists have recognized the importance of belief in a just world, very few have recognized the relatively general importance of implicit theories in determining the content of rumination (but see Nolen-Hoeksema, this volume).

THE DEFINITION OF RUMINATION

A number of commentators disagreed with our definition of rumination. Three thought our definition was too broad. Specifically, Clark felt that the term *rumination* should be restricted to reactions people have following traumatic events, whereas Nolen-Hoeksema felt that it should be restricted to recurrent thinking that does not progress toward a solution. Gohm, Isbell, and Wyer did not wish to restrict usage of the term but did feel that placing various types of recurrent thought under a single heading could obscure the possibility that these thoughts have different antecedents, consequences, and mediating processes. Carver as well as Petty, Jarvis, and Evans came to the conclusion that we considered rumination to be a class of thinking distinct from nonruminative thought, and they cautioned against such a distinction. Finally, King and Pennebaker considered our examples of rumination to be too verbally oriented, and they pointed out that rumination often involves images, emotions, and the replaying of events in an almost movie-like fashion.

To appreciate our definition of rumination it is important to keep in mind that we are using the term *rumination* in a way that is different from the way it has typically been used in the literature. Typically, it has been used to refer to a specific kind of recurrent thought that can be contrasted with other kinds (e.g., problem-solving; Nolen-Hoeksema this volume; making sense, Silver, Boon, & Stones, 1983). We suggest using the term in its more generic sense (e.g., re-chewing) to refer to the entire class of thoughts that have a tendency to recur. Given this usage, the concept rumination has a semantic status similar to that of the concept fruit. It refers to a large class among which there are subclasses and specific species. Just as it makes little sense to suggest that the term *fruit* should refer only to apples or oranges, for us it makes little sense to say that the term *rumination* should refer only to meaning analysis or only to recurrent thinking that does not progress toward the goal. For us, rumination is a generic, organizational term that refers to several varieties of recurrent thinking, including making sense, problem solving, reminiscence, and anticipation. Although these varieties can be compared and contrasted with one another, they cannot be compared and contrasted with rumination because rumination is the larger class of which each of these are instances.

There were two reasons we chose this broad approach over the more traditional approach. First, we really do believe that many forms of recurrent thought are a function of the same general, goal-based mechanism. By placing these thoughts in a common class, we hoped to highlight this (assumed) similarity. Second, we feel that the investigation of recurrent thoughts is in need of integration. Our review of the literature suggested to us that researchers have generally been pursuing separate topics in relatively independent programs of research and that the distinctions and commonalities among various types of recurrent thought have rarely been directly addressed. By drawing the various phenomena into a single domain, we hoped to stimulate more research exploring the connections among different types of thought. Thus, one might ask, "How does daydreaming differ from anticipation?" "Is problem solving really more of a controlled process than is making sense?" "Do worry and event simulation have different antecedents?"

Another criticism of our definition was that it created a false distinction between ruminative and nonruminative thought. It is true that we crafted a definition that allowed us to distinguish between the two, but we also noted several times in our chapter that this distinction was arbitrary. We said that one cannot draw a line and say that this is rumination; this is not. For example, we wrote that "ruminative and nonruminative thoughts are a function of the same mechanism (i.e., goal attainment) and that there is no qualitative demarcation between the two" (Martin & Tesser, this volume, p. 8). We elaborated upon this idea by suggesting that rumination "differs from nonruminative thought primarily in that it takes longer for people to find what they are looking for" (p. 11). Finally, we made an analogy between the automatic/controlled distinction and the ruminative/nonruminative distinction by noting that ruminative and nonruminative thought "differ in terms of their recurrence and their relevance to a person's current processing objectives, but there is no precise dividing line between the two" (p. 8).

It should be clear from these statements that we are in total agreement with Carver when he writes that goal-directed action is:

> often aimed at the very same discrepancies to which rumination is directed. . . . Recurrence of the thoughts is necessary only when your efforts aren't moving you forward. Surely at the descriptive level a distinction between recurrence and nonrecurrence of the thoughts is useful. But emphasis on this distinction tends to obscure the fact that both kinds of thought have the same underlying purpose, moving the person toward the goal. (p. 51)

The last definitional criticism was that the subjective experience of rumination is much richer than was captured in our examples (Clark; King & Pennebaker). We agree. It may have been a mistake on our part, but we intentionally restricted our examples to relatively simple, verbal content. The point was to keep our examples clear and to highlight the commonalities among what we considered to be the various modes of rumination. It should be noted, however, that we indicated that rumination can entail images and feelings, but we did this only in a footnote. In future discussions, we will need to emphasize further the richness of the ruminative experience.

THE MECHANISM BEHIND RUMINATION

There was a variety of dissatisfactions with our goal-attainment mechanism. Erber and Wegner were unable to see a causal mechanism at all,

Klinger considered our accessibility mechanism to be more descriptive than explanatory, and Waenke and Schmid suggested that goal blockage was not sufficient to explain the recurrent, intrusive nature of rumination. These commentators then went on to suggest mechanisms of their own that they preferred to our goal-based mechanism. Erber and Wegner argued in favor of the ironic processes they believe to be involved in thought suppression, Klinger suggested that we consider emotion-induced shifts in attention, and Waenke and Schmid proposed that awareness of an alternative state was sufficient to engender rumination. A fourth alternative was suggested by Clark and by King and Pennebaker. They proposed that rumination is goal-directed but that it is in the service of making sense of the kinds of major life changes that follow traumatic events.

Of course, not all the commentators were dissatisfied with our mechanism, but even those that did not indicate disagreement suggested other mechanisms that might be operative. Carver recommended that we highlight the kind of emotion-based prioritization mechanism proposed by Simon (1967), King and Pennebaker suggested that we consider disequilibrium in a broader social context, and Linville raised the possibility that at least some intrusive thoughts result from a breakdown in inhibition.

Do we have a mechanism that is sufficiently specified that it can get us from some initiating event to the experience of rumination? Of course. Despite opinions to the contrary, there is no need for another squirrel in our treadmill (cf. Erber & Wegner). The cybernetic mechanisms we describe are sufficient, in and of themselves, to account for rumination (cf. Carver). It is certainly possible that other process, such as a breakdown in inhibition (cf. Linville), could lead to rumination, but these processes are not necessary. The cybernetic mechanism is sufficient.

To reiterate, here's how our model works. People are constantly in pursuit of a variety of goals, but they cannot pursue every goal at every moment. Because of this, people need a way to cease pursuit of some goals temporarily and a way to remember to resume pursuit of these goals when the time is right. When is the time right? When the temporarily abandoned goal has been tagged with a higher priority than the task in which people are currently engaged. Under these conditions, people are drawn back to pursue the more important goal. If they are able to resume actual pursuit, they do so. Otherwise, they pursue it only in thought (with the accompanying images and feelings). This is rumination.

The mechanism we use to "remind" the person to return to an as-yet-attained goal is concept accessibility. Concept accessibility is a hypothetical construct relating to the ease with which information is retrieved from memory. Its operational markers are relative automaticity of processing information related to the concept (e.g., Bargh & Thein, 1985), the tendency to interpret ambiguous information in terms of the concept (Higgins,

Rholes, & Jones, 1977), the tendency to select from the environment information related to the concept (Bruner, 1957), the tendency to perceptually enhance stimuli related to the construct (Bruner, 1957), an engendering of motives and behavior related to the concept (Bargh, in press; Carver, Ganellen, Froming, & Chambers, 1983; Herr, 1986), and an engendering of feelings associated with the concept (Fiske & Pavelchak, 1986; Higgins, 1987). Accessibility is determined by frequent or recent use of a concept, the relation of the concept to other already accessible concepts, and the relation of the concept to currently active goals (Higgins & King, 1981).

By placing accessibility within a control system mechanism, we get a complete bridge from the initiating event to the onset of rumination. People are reminded to return to pursuit of important goals by the accessibility of the concepts related to these goals. This accessibility makes it likely that people will detect goal-relevant information in the environment, interpret ambiguous information in terms related to the goal, and experience the motives and emotions associated with pursuit of that goal. The increased accessibility of goal-related concepts also makes it relatively easy for people to process information related to the goal. One implication of this last feature is that people can experience frequent intrusive thoughts even while involved in other activities. In short, the mechanisms specified in our model easily get us from the initiating event to the ruminative experience.

How do we deal with the possibility that mechanisms in addition to (or instead of) goal attainment can engender rumination? We wrote in chapter 1 that rumination was likely to be multicausal. In other words, there is likely to be more than one way to get thoughts to recur. In fact, our conclusion after our discussion of our white bear study was that our "results do not suggest, however, that all instances of the rebound effect are due to goal-based rumination" (p. 37). We made this point even stronger in earlier writings (Martin et al., 1993) when we noted that one should not conclude "that *all* instances of rumination are the result of a Zeigarnik effect, or even that all instances of rumination following thought suppression are the result of a Zeigarnik effect. Rather, we argue that both a Zeigarnik effect and an associative mechanism could cause rumination, and that it may be important to establish in any given situation the extent to which each mechanism is operative" (p. 561).

The bottom line is that we have no problem with the possibility that other mechanisms may also lead to rumination. In fact, this seems likely to us. We do not feel, however, that these other mechanisms should supplant a goal-directed mechanism. We see them as complementary. Our only reservation with regard to the alternative mechanisms depicted in the commentaries is that some of them do not seem sufficiently specified to account for rumination.

Consider, for example, Waenke and Schmid's suggestion that awareness of an alternative is sufficient to produce rumination. Taken at face value, this proposition suggests that a person who drinks tomato juice and then realizes he could have had a V-8 juice will ruminate about V-8 juice. Our model allows for this possibility but only if the person actually wanted the V-8 (i.e., there was a goal) and having the V-8 was either important in and of itself or was linked to the attainment of an important goal. In short, we believe that awareness of alternative states can engender rumination but only when it implicates an important goal. Mere awareness of an alternative is not sufficient to induce rumination.

Klinger suggested emotion-based shifts in attention as an alternative to our goal-accessibility mechanism. We noted in chapter 1 that emotion can play an important role in rumination. We do not believe, however, that emotion is necessary for rumination, nor do we believe that emotion has its effects by way of an automatic spread of activation through a network, as Klinger suggested. We return to these points later, in the discussion of emotion.

We agree with Linville that a breakdown in inhibition could be a factor in producing rumination. In fact, such inhibition seems useful in the context of a goal-based model. We elaborate upon this mechanism, however, in two ways (neither inconsistent with Linville's proposal). First, we suggest that the thoughts most likely to break through the inhibition are the ones with a high goal priority. Second, we assume that anxiety and other emotions are associated with a breakdown in inhibition, in part because these feelings inform people that their goals are being threatened (Cervone, Kopp, Schaumann, & Scott, 1994).

King and Pennebaker suggested that we consider disequilibrium in the broader sense (e.g., social interactions, talking about a traumatic event, emotion–cognition asynchronies). This seems reasonable to us and, as noted by King and Pennebaker, is consistent with a broader view of control systems (von Bertalanffy, 1968), a view with which we agree.

THE ROLE OF EMOTION

In chapter 1, we spent a considerable amount of time discussing the reciprocal relations between emotion and rumination. Not all of the commentators were satisfied with this discussion, however. Some argued that emotion plays a role different than the one we had assigned it (Klinger; Nolen-Hoeksema), and others argued that our description of the role of emotion did not do justice to the phenomenological experience of the ruminating person (King & Pennebaker).

According to Klinger and Nolen-Hoeksema, emotions influence rumination by means of a passive, automatic spread of activation through a semantic network. We suggested instead that emotions influence rumination because of the information the emotions provide about the status of one's goal progress. Evidence consistent with the assumption that emotions influence perceived goal progress has recently been obtained by Cervone, et al. (1994). These investigators placed subjects in either happy or sad moods and asked them to assess their performance during a task. Cervone et al. found that subjects in sad moods were more likely than those in happy moods to say that they were far from attaining their goals and that they were less likely to attain these, even though the sad and happy subjects were objectively equidistant from their goals. In other words, the emotions influenced the subjects' subjective sense of goal progress.

It should be noted that there is no necessary relation between any given mood and one's sense of progress. Martin and Stoner (1995) found that under some conditions, subjects in positive moods feel that they are progressing faster than do subjects in negative moods but that in other conditions the reverse is true. Such results are difficult to reconcile with the assumption that emotions have their effect passively and automatically through the spread of activation through a semantic network.

From our perspective, emotions and perceived discrepancies need not be perfectly correlated. In fact, they could vary orthogonally. Moreover, when this occurs, it is the discrepancy, not the emotion per se, that influences rumination. We know of no study that has tested this hypothesis using rumination as the dependent variable. However, there is some indirect evidence for this proposition in the dissonance literature. Higgins, Rhodewalt, and Zanna (1979) provided subjects with insufficient justification for engaging in behavior that was contrary to their attitudes. According to dissonance theory, this kind of inconsistency causes subjects to experience a negative affective state that in turn motivates them to change their attitude. So, the affective state is the immediate precursor of the attitude change, right? Not exactly. It is the information that the affective state conveys. How do we know this? When the subjects were informed that their affective state was due to a pill (thus making the affect uninformative with regard to their attitude-inconsistent behavior), the subjects did not change their attitudes.

Interestingly, when subjects do not change their attitudes, they should still possess a discrepancy because they have not resolved their attitude-behavior inconsistency. From a goal discrepancy perspective, these subjects should remain motivated to address the discrepancy until it has been reconciled. As we noted in chapter 1, "if there is a real discrepancy that has not been addressed by the reduction in affect, then the cessation of rumination is likely to be temporary" (p. 16). Consistent with this interpretation, when Higgins et al. (1979) reminded the subjects one week later of their attitude-inconsistent behavior, the subjects changed their attitudes to be consistent with their prior behavior. In short, the affective state motivated the subjects to address their discrepancy only when this state was not attributed to an irrelevant source, and one week later, the discrepancy itself was sufficient to motivate attempts to reduce the discrepancy. This is precisely the picture we have in mind when considering the role of discrepancies and emotion in rumination. Emotion motivates rumination when it informs people of a goal discrepancy, but it is the perceived discrepancy, not the emotion per se, that is the immediate precursor of the rumination.

Given our phenomenology regarding emotions, this account of the role of emotion may seem rather cold and mechanistic. Anyone who has experienced a serious loss or other tragedy has felt the power of emotions. They "know" how important these feelings are in driving their ruminations and behavior. It seems difficult to reconcile such phenomenal reality with our seemingly cold and mechanistic account. However, our view does not deny the existence of powerful emotions. Indeed, we recognize this power, and our explanation of the emotion–rumination connection relies on just those feelings. We suggest, however, that these feelings do not influence rumination directly, but rather through the information they convey. This view may be inconsistent with intuition or introspection, but it does not deny the subjective experience of emotion.

THE FUNCTION OF RUMINATION

We described rumination as instrumental to the attainment of a higher order goal. By this, we meant that rumination was engendered by problematic pursuit of a higher order goal. Klinger, Nolen-Hoeksema, and Waenke and Schmid took our use of the term *instrumental* as an indication that we believe that rumination is always beneficial, that it always aids in the attainment of a goal. Interestingly, King and Pennebaker came to a conclusion that was in some ways the mirror image of this one. They felt that our characterization of rumination portrayed conscious thought as necessarily at odds with productive goal pursuit. They wondered whether someone could be in flow and still be thinking. Clark had no problem with the instrumental nature of rumination but suggested that rumination was in the service of a very specific goal, namely, making sense of life disruptions (see also King & Pennebaker). And some commentators felt that at least some forms of rumination were not goal directed at all. Erber and Wegner suggested that recurrent thoughts are an unintended by-product of attempted thought suppression, whereas Linville suggested that at least some intrusive thoughts result from a breakdown in the inhibition process. And finally, two sets of commentators asked whether interrupted goal pursuit initiates rumination or whether rumination interrupts goal pursuit (King & Pennebaker, Waenke & Schmid).

We do not believe that rumination is always useful. We used the word *instrumental* to mean "in the service of, a tool, an agent." We did not suggest that rumination always involves efficient or effective goal attainment. In fact, we noted in our discussion of content that people often focus on the wrong content. Under these conditions, rumination may very well lead the ruminator away from goal attainment. We noted that when the content of rumination does not reflect the goal that is driving the rumination, if people attain the goal at all, they do so only fortuitously. Far from being helpful, rumination in these instances is actually misleading.

This point may become clearer with an example. Imagine a woman who has recently been divorced. Which of the woman's goals is threatened by the divorce? Is it friendship? Intimacy? Self-esteem? Social opportunities? Chances at parenthood? Disappointment to her parents? Violation of religious beliefs? Any or all of these could be affected by the divorce. The woman herself may not know. She may only sense a vague discontent and may ruminate about what (according to her implicit theories) is the most plausible cause for that discontent. She may begin to ruminate about being lonely and may take up with the first person available when the circus comes to town. Suppose this relationship brings her friendship, intimacy, and chances at parenthood, but the woman still feels discontent. She may then begin to ruminate about her self-esteem or about letting her parents down. And it may very well be that the dominant goal driving the rumination was resolving religious concerns. Thus, the woman's ruminations about intimacy, self-esteem, and so on were actually taking her away from her goal. In short, rumination can only be helpful when the content of that rumination is relevant to attaining the threatened goal. This will not always be the case.

As can be seen, we are in perfect agreement with Carver (this volume) when he writes that we:

> see rumination as an attempt at discrepancy reduction. It is an attempt at problem solving—even when it isn't resolving the problem. That fact that it doesn't always have its desired effect should not be surprising, nor should this distract from rumination's purpose. Not every attempt at goal attainment is successful, nor is all problem solving successful. Not every instance of rumination lights a path to the goal. Yet the assumption that rumination is aimed at discrepancy reduction points to a functional similarity between rumination and goal-directed action. (p. 50)

How do we deal with the possibility that some forms of recurrent thought are not goal directed? First, we have suggested that rumination is multicausal and that other mechanisms may operate to produce ruminative thought. Some of these may very well be the mechanisms suggested by the commentators. Second, we proposed a form of nonmotivated rumination within our own model. This was the channelization mechanism that produces recurrent thought through the cueing of an association network.

What about the possibility that rumination is goal-directed but is directed very specifically toward the goal of making sense of traumatic life disruptions? We see no justification for restricting the possible goals that drive rumination. This is particularly true given that making sense is neither necessary nor sufficient to produce rumination (Silver et al., 1983).

Does rumination interrupt goal-directed action or does the interruption of goal-directed action initiate rumination? Both. What has to be made clear, however, is which goals are doing what. Imagine a person pursuing three goals, A, B, and C. Imagine further that these goals are listed in descending order of importance. When the person is pursuing goal A, he or she will not be ruminating about goals B and C. This is because the person is currently pursuing the highest goal in his or her hierarchy. When the person attains goal A or temporarily puts it aside, thoughts about the next most important goal will rise into consciousness. In this way, interruption of task A sets the stage for rumination about goals B and C (as suggested by King & Pennebaker and Waenke & Schmid). Suppose, however, the person was pursuing goal C, the least important of the three goals. Thoughts about goals A and B may intrude as the person performs a task related to goal C because A and B are more pressing than what the person is currently doing. In short, rumination can interrupt ongoing action or can be initiated by interruptions of ongoing action, but which occurs depends on the relative priorities of the goals involved.

CLARITY OF EXPLANATORY TERMS

Uleman suggested that we need better criteria (both conceptually and operationally) for categorizing a process as unconscious, and Waenke and Schmid asked us to clarify certain aspects of our usage of the term *goal* (e.g., does a goal have to be in existence prior to the onset of rumination?).

We agree with Uleman's observation that the data we presented did not provide evidence for the operation of unconscious goals. They were not meant to. Although unconscious goals constitute an important part of the model, the studies we reported were designed to test other aspects of the model. Nevertheless, Uleman's point is well taken, and in future research we hope to address the role of unconscious goals in rumination. It is important to note in this context that research by Bargh and his colleagues (Bargh, 1990; in press) has begun to provide some interesting demonstrations of the existence of unconscious goals.

The second thrust of Uleman's commentary was semantic, rather than empirical. He asked us to clarify what we mean when we say that a goal is unconscious. For us, unconscious refers primarily to a lack of accuracy in covariation detection. People may be aware of their goals, aware of some situational event, and aware of ruminating but may not be aware of the connections among these. The end result? People may not ascertain the real reason for the onset of their rumination. Although we suspect that rumination can be engendered by goals of which a person is completely unaware, our model is not dependent on the existence of such goals. We are primarily concerned with people's abilities to ascertain the causes of their rumination. This view of unconscious goals was spelled out in more detail in our earlier writings (Martin & Tesser, 1989; Martin et al., 1992).

Waenke and Schmid asked whether a goal has to exist prior to the occurrence of any given instance of rumination. The answer, in brief, is no. For us, goals do not necessarily correspond to conscious representations of desired end states. They are hypothetical entities that are inferred on the basis of converging operations. A person is said to be operating toward the attainment of a goal when the person's behavior exhibits a certain constellation of features, including persistence, equifinality, and docility (cf. McDougal, 1923; Tolman, 1932). Persistence refers to the tendency of behavior to continue not only beyond the initiating stimulus (e.g., a traumatic event) but also until specific kinds of changes have been brought about (e.g., the person makes sense of the event). Equifinality means that any number of different actions may serve the same purpose (e.g., I can make sense of the event by saying it was God's will, it was my fault, or it was the doctor's fault). Docility refers to the tendency of behavior to eventually settle into the most efficient means of bringing about the end state (e.g., Does it make more sense to conclude that it was God's will or it was my fault?).

To the extent that a person's behaviors exhibit persistence, equifinality, and docility, the person can be said to have a goal. The person may or may not have a conscious representation of some endpoint, and he or she may or may not have a conscious desire to reach that endpoint. Neither of these is necessary for a person to be goal directed. The behavior just needs to exhibit persistence, equifinality, and docility. In our view, many of the phenomena discussed in the preceding chapters possess those features. Our assumption that various modes of rumination are goal directed is based on the features of the thinking, not on the phenomenology of the people experiencing those thoughts.

Do we need to assume that all goals exist prior to the ruminative period? No. As we noted in chapter 1, an action may be in the service of maintaining an existing state rather than reducing a discrepancy (see also Roney & Sorrentino, 1995). Under these conditions, a goal would be evidenced only when there was some change in the status quo. For example, people may not have a conscious goal to have their spleens functioning well, but if their spleens begin to dysfunction and they experience the painful consequences, their behavior is likely to exhibit many of the hallmarks of goal-directed behavior. They will attempt to find a way to relieve their suffering, and these attempts will continue until the suffering is relieved (i.e., persistence). There is usually more than one way to end the suffering, such as surgery, acupuncture, or pills (i.e., equifinality), and once people have found a way that works better than the others, they gravitate toward that solution as their first course of action in the future (i.e., docility). In short, behavior can show all of the characteristics that lead one to infer the existence of a goal, even when there is no conscious representation of the goal prior to the occurrence of the behavior.

ORGANIZATION OF THE MODES

A number of commentators raised questions about the particular distinctions we made (or distinctions we should have made) among the modes of ruminative thought. Carver as well as Gohm, Isbell, and Wyer suggested alternatives to the organization we depicted in Table 1.1. Petty, Jarvis, and Evans felt that our organization did not lead to an increased understanding of the phenomena.

Perhaps the first task in the systematic study of something is to lay out the domain so that objects or phenomena that are functionally equivalent are grouped together and those that are not are put into different categories. By functionally equivalent we mean that they are the same with respect to features that are theoretically important to the taxonomist. Objects that are functionally equivalent, given a particular theory, will not necessarily be equivalent across all their features. For example, an aggression theorist might argue that behaviors that result in intentional harm to another are equivalent. Such behaviors might be very different from one another in their surface features (e.g., hitting, insulting, plotting against, turning in). By putting these various behaviors into the same equivalence class, the theorist is not saying these other features are unimportant but rather that they are not part of the explanatory system.

As we read the literature pertaining to rumination, we encountered a variety of thoughts (e.g., working through, reminiscing) that, from our perspective, were functionally equivalent. These modes of thought are depicted in Table 1.1. These modes are functionally equivalent to one another because they satisfy our definition of rumination and, we argue, they have goal-related antecedents. On the other hand, the various modes of thought are similar to and different from one another in ways unrelated to their functional equivalence. Table 1.1 is our attempt to communicate parsimoniously some of these surface similarities and differences. The organization in Table 1.1 was not driven by the present model of rumination, it was not generated as an explanation, and it was not meant to guide research. The intention was to organize the many phenomena now being addressed only in relatively independent research programs.

Our reason for including the table was to suggest how phenomena with very different surface characteristics might profitably be brought together. The organizational dimensions of Table 1.1 are superficial from the perspective of the present model, and other organizations are clearly possible (see Carver; Gohm, Isbell, & Wyer; Petty, Jarvis, & Evans). Perhaps these or some other dimensions may ultimately turn out to be productive.

INDIVIDUAL DIFFERENCES

Several commentators expressed a concern that our model was not sufficiently attentive to individual differences (Gohm, Isbell, & Wyer) or that individual difference dimensions that we did not consider might be useful (Gohm, Isbell, & Wyer; Petty Jarvis & Evans; Waenke & Schmid).

We certainly recognize the importance of individual differences but our model of rumination is not an individual difference model. We attempted to specify what we believe are relatively general processes across individuals. Does that mean we expect no variance among individuals when they find themselves in the same circumstance? Of course not. Indeed, we believe that the addition of individual difference research is useful for testing or enriching the model, but only under some circumstances.

Suppose an investigator successfully predicts rumination from a variable, X, that has nothing to do with the model (e.g., need for cognition). Does that correlation cast doubt on the model? We think not. Rumination is assumed to be multiply determined; the model processes are only one route to rumination. Demonstrating a different set of antecedents or correlates is not inconsistent with the notion that the model is valid. By the same token, the failure of variable X to predict rumination cannot be read as support for the model.

From our point of view, individual difference research becomes consequential for evaluating or expanding the model only if it involves valid measures of model variables or if it demonstrates an interaction between a new variable and one or more of the model variables. In chapter 1, we reviewed some evidence of the use of an individual difference measure developed from the model. The model suggests that not attaining a higher order goal will generate more rumination than not attaining a lower order goal. The linking scale (McIntosh & Martin, 1992) is assumed to measure an individual's tendency to see specific outcomes in terms of higher order goals. Thus, the finding that linkers ruminate more than nonlinkers adds validity to the model's assumption.

Of course, an individual difference variable does not have to be directly related to any of the model variables or even directly related to rumination to be of theoretical interest. It is possible to imagine, for example, that for some identifiable individuals one of the model variable has different effects on rumination than it does for other people (i.e., the individual difference variable interacts with or moderates the effects of the model variable). We have not yet encountered such an individual difference variable. However, if one should turn up, it would be important to incorporate it into the model because the effects of the model variable (which interacts with the new variable) could not be specified without knowing the level of the new variable.

Having set the stage, we now briefly turn to the individual difference dimensions suggested by the commentators. Gohm, Isbell and Wyer presented a particularly thought-provoking case for the inclusion of individual differences in positive and negative thinking. They report on a factor analysis of a variety of items concerned with respondents' tendencies and motivations to think. This analysis yielded a positive thinking factor, a negative thinking factor, and a distractibility factor. Regrettably, Gohm et al. do not indicate how these dimensions are related to any of the model's variables. On the other hand, they argue that negativity of thinking may be correlated with perception of goal discrepancy and positivity of thinking may be correlated with ruminative control. The positivity–negativity distinction is emerging as an important one in affective experience (Watson & Tellegen, 1985) and in goal models as well (Carver & Scheier, 1990; Higgins, 1987). It may ultimately prove to be important in the study of rumination. Its potential linkages with goal discrepancy perception and control make it a particularly interesting variable to explore in the context of the model.

Waenke and Schmid suggested that feelings of control should be negatively associated with rumination. Indeed, they report a study in which they found a significant negative correlation between self-reported rumination and beliefs in internal control and a significant positive correlation between rumination and beliefs in control by powerful others. Moreover, when internal control was used as a covariate, an initially large gender difference in rumination (i.e., women ruminate more than men; cf. Nolen-Hoeksema, Parker, & Larson, 1994) was reduced to nonsignificance. Although we did not measure feelings of control in our research, Waenke and Schmid's interpretation of their data is not inconsistent with a goal-based view of rumination. This view suggests that rumination is less if the individual believes that he or she can overcome a goal discrepancy than if he or she does not. Waenke and Schmid (this volume) write " . . . individuals with a high internal control perception exit the ruminative cycle earlier simply because they experience control in overcoming the [goal] discrepancy" (p. 184).

Petty, Jarvis, and Evans referred to a number of individual difference dimensions that might relate to various modes of thought. More specifically, they suggested that optimism or pessimism (Scheier & Carver, 1987) might relate to positivity–negativity of thought, the consideration of future consequences scale (Strathman, Gleicher, Boninger, & Edwards, 1994) might predict one's tendency to think about the past versus the future, and the need to evaluate scale (Jarvis & Petty, 1995) might predict the tendency to be evaluative in one's thoughts. Petty et al. also point to individual difference variables that might be associated with the extent to which people ruminate (e.g., the need for cognition scale; Cacioppo & Petty, 1982, and the need for closure scale; Webster & Kruglanski, 1994).

It could be argued that the need for closure relates to an individual's tolerance for goal discrepancies. To the extent that such an argument is valid it is useful to consider this scale in working with the model. On the other hand, although the other individual differences may have some relation to modes of thinking or perhaps even to rumination itself, we do not see an obvious relation to the variables specified in our model.

CONNECTION TO REAL-WORLD RUMINATION

According to Clark (this volume), the model "pays too little attention to the literature examining ruminations in real-world contexts" (p. 65). Our use of relatively low-level and mundane examples in illustrating the model in chapter 1 made King and Pennebaker wonder if "the processes exemplified by these relatively low-level ends generalize to more magnificent obsessions" (p. 100).

As long as new contexts exist, the question of generalization will never be fully addressed. However, we believe that the bases for concern regarding this real-world issue are either weak or already anticipated in the model. Clark (this volume) provided a list of experiences that she assumed are associated with stressful life events but are less likely to be found in lower level, more mundane goal discrepancies. These include "suddenness of the threat, unknown future implications, [and] the individual's inability to mount immediate coping responses" (p. 65). Regrettably, Clark failed to show how these variables operate to affect the influence of goal discrepancies, naive theories, or accessibility on rumination. She also did not show how these variable fit into her own life narrative approach to rumination nor how they relate to what she termed "the usual gang of suspects" (i.e., problem solving, reminiscing). The variables she offered for consideration have a veneer of being consequential. However, under the surface there is (as yet) little empirical or theoretical reason to think that they will end up resulting in a major modification or enrichment of the model or that they will end up accounting for a large portion of the variance in rumination (cf. Kendall-Thackett, Williams, & Finkelhor, 1993).

King and Pennebaker (this volume) are concerned about generalization to the real world because of powerful emotional responses that accompany major life changes compared to more mundane events. Emotions may cue ruminations because those emotions are "gloriously out of sync" (p. 101) with ongoing, conscious cognitive processes. Actually, such a process is quite consistent with the model (see our discussion of emotion in this chapter and in chapter 1). King and Pennebaker also suggested that the model might not generalize to the real world because major trauma leads to rumination that "may serve to provide closure and, perhaps, lead to personal growth" (p. 102). Again, the model can accommodate this assertion. In chapter 1 we suggested that meaning analysis is one of several modes of rumination.

SUMMARY

We learned much from the commentaries. There were a number of helpful suggestions regarding alternative mechanisms and a number of recommendations that, if adopted, would make the model more complete. Although we did not agree with everything that was said, we have a better idea now of what are the unifying and dividing issues in the field, and we have a better idea of what we believe—and why we believe it. In light of the commentaries, we found some things we would like to change in the model. And, in spite of the commentaries, there are things we would not change.

The single most recurrent criticism was that our characterization of rumination was too broad—too broad to be useful in helping us to understand rumination in the real world, too broad to detect phenomena with different antecedents and consequences, or too broad to reflect the features of "real" rumination (e.g., meaning analysis). According to the Talmud, if one person calls you an ass, you should shrug it off. If two people call you an ass, you should listen carefully. If three people call you an ass, you should run out and buy a saddle. So why are we not going out to buy a saddle?

When we began our work, we felt that the field was ready for an integration in which the common features of various modes of ruminative thought would be abstracted such that work could proceed in a more concerted, additive, and productive way. Our definition and mechanism were left broad, in part to allow for such integration. Clearly, there are other approaches. Many of the authors in this volume argue that their approach is the more integrative or useful one, or that their approach is more representative of "real" rumination. But that's the way science proceeds. Regardless of what happens to the Martin and Tesser model, the kind of dialogue represented in this volume can't help but move us all closer to the kind of synthesis we hope will emerge.

REFERENCES

Bargh, J. A. (1990). Goal intent: Goal-directed thought and behavior are often unintentional. *Psychological Inquiry, 1,* 248–251.

Bargh, J. A. (in press). Automatic action: Priming of social behavior by environmental features. In P. M. Gollwitzer & J. A. Bargh (Eds.), *The psychology of action: Linking motivation and cognition to behavior.* New York: Guilford.

Bargh, J. A., & Thein, R. D. (1985). Individual construct accessibility, person memory, and the recall judgment link: The case of information overload. *Journal of Personality and Social Psychology, 49,* 1129–1146.

Bruner, J. S. (1957). On perceptual readiness. *Psychological Review, 64,* 123–152.

Cacioppo, J. T., & Petty, R. E. (1982). The need for cognition. *Journal of Personality and Social Psychology, 42,* 116–131.

Carver, C. S., Ganellen, R. S., Froming, W. J., & Chambers, W. (1983). Modeling: An analysis in terms of category accessibility. *Journal of Experimental Social Psychology, 19,* 403–421.

Carver, C. S., & Scheier, M. F. (1981). *Attention and self-regulation: A control-theory approach to human behavior.* New York: Springer-Verlag.

Carver, C. S., & Scheier, M. F. (1990). Origins and functions of positive and negative affect: A control-process view. *Psychological Review, 97,* 19–35.

Cervone, D., Kopp, D. A., Schaumann, L., & Scott, W. D. (1994). Mood, self-efficacy, and performance standards: Lower moods induce higher standards for performance. *Journal of Personality and Social Psychology, 67,* 499–512.

Csikzentmihalyi, M. (1975). *Beyond boredom and anxiety.* San Francisco: Jossey-Bass.

Fiske, S. T., & Pavelchak, M. A. (1986). Category-based vs. piecemeal-based affective response: Developments in schema-triggered affect. In R. M. Sorrentino & E. T. Higgins (Eds.), *Handbook of motivation and cognition* (pp. 167–203). New York: Guilford.

Herr, P. M. (1986). Consequences of priming: Judgment and behavior. *Journal of Personality and Social Psychology, 51,* 1106–1115.

Higgins, E. T. (1987). Self-discrepancy: A theory relating self and affect. *Psychological Review, 94,* 319–340.

Higgins, E. T., & King, G. (1981). Accessibility of social constructs: Information processing consequences of individual and contextual variability. In N. Cantor & J. J. Kihlstrom (Eds.), *Personality, congition, and social interaction* (pp. 69–121). Hillsdale, NJ: Lawrence Erlbaum Associates.

Higgins, E. T., Rhodewalt, F., & Zanna, M. P. (1979). Dissonance motivation: Its nature, persistence and reinstatement. *Journal of Experimental Social Psychology, 15,* 16–34.

Higgins, E. T., Rholes, W. S., & Jones, C. R. (1977). Category accessibility and impression formation. *Journal of Experimental Social Psychology, 13,* 141–154.

Jarvis, W. B. G., & Petty, R. E. (1995). *The need to evaluate.* Unpublished manuscript, Ohio State University.

Kendall-Thackett, K. A., Williams, L. M., & Finkelhor, D. (1993). Impact of sexual abuse on children: A review and synthesis of recent empirical findings. *Psychological Bulletin, 113,* 164–180.

Klinger, E. (1975). Consequences of commitment to and disengagement from incentives. *Psychological Review, 82,* 1–25.

Lewin, K. (1951). *Field theory in social science*. New York: Harper & Row.
Martin, L. L., & Stoner, P. (1995). Mood as input: What we think about how we feel determines how we think. In L. L. Martin & A. Tesser (Eds.), *Striving and feeling: Interactions among goals, affect, and self-regulation*. Hillsdale, NJ: Lawrence Erlbaum Associates.
Martin, L. L., & Tesser, A. (1989). Toward a motivational and structural theory of ruminative thought. In J. S. Uleman & J. A. Bargh (Eds.), *Unintended thought* (pp. 306–326). New York: Guilford.
Martin, L. L., Tesser, A., & McIntosh, W. D. (1993). Wanting but not having: The effects of unattained goals on thoughts and feelings. In D. M. Wegner & J. W. Pennebaker (Eds.), *The handbook of mental control* (pp. 552–572). Englewood Cliffs, NJ: Prentice Hall.
McDougal, W. (1923). *Outline of psychology*. New York: Scribner's.
McIntosh, W. D., Martin, L. L. (1992). The cybernetics of happiness: The relation between goal attainment, rumination, and affect. In M. S. Clark (Ed.), *Review of Personality and Social Psychology* (Vol. 14, pp. 222–246). Newbury Park, CA: Sage.
Miller, G. A., Galanter, E., & Pribram, K. H. (1960). *Plans and the structure of behavior*. New York: Holt, Rhinehart & Winston.
Nisbett, R. E., & Wilson, T. D. (1977). Telling more than we can know: Verbal reports on mental processes. *Psychological Review, 84*, 213–259.
Nolen-Hoeksema, S., Parker, L., & Larson, J. (1994). Ruminative coping with depressed mood following loss. *Journal of Personality and Social Psychology, 67*, 92–104.
Roney, C. J. R., & Sorrentino, R. M. (1995). Reducing self-discrepancies or maintaining self-congruence? Uncertainty orientation, self-regulation, and performance. *Journal of Personality and Social Psychology, 68*, 485–497.
Scheier, M. F., & Carver, C. S. (1987). Dispositional optimism and physical well-being: The influence of generalized outcome expectancies in health. *Journal of Personality, 55*, 169–210.
Silver, R. L., Boon, C., & Stones, M. H. (1983). Searching for meaning in misfortune: Making sense of incest. *Journal of Social Issues, 39*, 81–102.
Simon, H. A. (1967). Motivational and emotional controls of cognition. *Psychological Review, 74*, 29–39.
Strathman, A. J., Gleicher, F., Boninger, D. S., & Edwards, C. S. (1994). The consideration of future consequences: Weighing immediate and distant outcomes of behavior. *Journal of Personality and Social Psychology, 66*, 742–752.
Tesser, A. (1978). Self-generated attitude change. In L. Berkowitz (Ed.), *Advances in experimental social psychology*, (Vol. 11, pp. 289–338). New York: Academic Press.
Tesser, A., Martin, L. L., & Mendolia, M. (1995). The impact of thought on attitude extremity and attitude–behavior consistency. In R. E. Petty & J. A. Krosnick (Eds.), *Attitude strength: Antecedents and consequences*. Hillsdale, NJ: Lawrence Erlbaum Associates
Tolman, E. C. (1932). *Purposive behavior in animals and men*. New York: Century.
von Bertalanffy, L. (1968). *General systems theory*. New York: Braziller.
Watson, D., & Tellegen, A. (1985). Toward a consensual structure of mood. *Psychological Bulletin, 98*, 219–235.
Webster, D., & Kruglanski, A. W. (1994). Individual differences in need for cognitive closure. *Journal of Personality and Social Psychology, 67*, 1049–1062.
Wicklund, R. A. (1986). Orientations to the environment versus preoccupation with human potential. In R. M. Sorrentino & E. T. Higgins (Eds.), *Handbook of motivation and cognition* (pp. 64–95). New York: Guilford.
Zeigarnik, B. (1938). On finished and unfinished tasks. In W. D. Ellis (Ed.), *A source book of gestalt psychology* (pp. 300–314). New York: Harcourt, Brace, & World. (Reprinted, translated, and condensed from *Psychologische Forshung*, 1927, *9*, 1–85).

Author Index

A

Abelson, R. P., 15–16, 19, 44, 65, 71, 81, 95
Abramson, L., 185, 186
Achee, J. W., 18, 44–45, 101, 106, 154, 162
Ackerman, A. M., 68, 71
Ajzen, I., 160, 161
Alloy, L. B., 128, 130–131
Alverez, W., 19, 22, 44
Anderson, 22
Apple, K. J., 2, 38–39, 44, 153, 155, 162, 174, 176
Arkes, H. R., 160, 161
Aronoff, J., 98, 105
Aronson, E., 156, 161
Ashbrook, P. W., 128, 131
Asher, S. J., 68, 70
Atkinson, J. W., 22, 25, 42–43

B

Baars, B. J., 111, 118
Baker, S. M., 150, 161
Bargh, J. A., 8, 43, 63, 72, 81, 95, 113, 118, 169, 175, 182, 186, 194–195, 200, 207
Baron, J., 136, 143
Baron, R. A., 24, 43
Barta, S. G., 99, 106, 111, 113, 115, 119
Baumann, 30, 44
Beall, S. K., 69, 71, 103, 106
Beck, A. T., 1, 13, 39, 43, 128, 130–131, 142, 143
Beckmann, J., 26, 30, 43, 109, 119, 136, 143, 173, 175
Beech, A., 125, 131
Bem, D. J., 14, 43, 160, 161, 170, 175
Berkowitz, L., 156, 161
Berman, J. S., 143, 144
Bjork, R. A., 171, 176
Bjorklund, D. F., 125, 131
Blake, A. W., 74, 79
Bless, H., 18, 46
Block, J., 102, 105
Bloom, B. L., 68, 70
Blount, J. P., 113, 119
Bock, M., 115, 119
Bodenhausen, G. V., 76, 78
Boehm, L. E., 160, 161
Boninger, D. S., 38, 43, 151, 163, 205, 208
Boon, C., 1, 3–4, 6–7, 39, 46, 67, 71, 128, 132, 179, 187, 192, 200, 208
Borkovec, T. D., 2, 9, 35, 45, 183, 186
Bornstein, R. F., 160, 161
Bowi, U., 115, 119
Brauer, M., 160, 162
Brehm, J. W., 157, 161
Brock, T. C., 38, 43, 145–146, 152, 163
Bruner, J. S., 15, 43, 195, 207
Buhrfeind, E., 103, 106
Burns, D., 143, 143
Buss, A., 185, 186
Butler, L. D., 183, 184, 186

C

Cacioppo, J. T., 81, 90, 95, 145, 148, 150, 154–155, 157–159, 161–162, 205, 207
Carlsmith, J. M., 156, 161
Carlston, D. E., 168, 175
Carter, S. R., III, 16, 26, 35–36, 46, 74, 76, 78, 79, 81, 95
Cartwright, D., 24, 43

Carver, C. S., 2, 11, 15–16, 19, 26, 37, 42, *43*, 49–50, 53–54, 56–57, 60, 98, *105*, 151, *163*, 185, *186*, 190–191, 195, 204–205, *207–208*
Cervone, D., 12, 18, *43*, 196–197, *207*
Chaiken, S., 113, *118*, 150, 154, *161–162*
Challis, B. H., 171, *176*
Chambers, W., 195, *207*
Chapman, J. E., 184, *187*
Chino, A., 185, *186*
Christianson, S.-A., 128, *131*
Claridge, G., 125, *131*
Clark, L. F., 3, 7, *43*, 65–70, *70–71*, 168, *176*
Clark, M., 2, 9, 29, *44*
Clore, G. L., 81, *95*
Cohen, S., 128, *131*
Colder, M., 103, *106*
Coleman, P. G., 68–69, *71*
Collins, J. E., 3, *43*, 68, 70, *71*
Collins, R., 66, *71*
Connelly, S. L., 122, 124, 128–129, *132*
Conway, M., 81, *95*
Cook, T. D., 38, *43*
Cools, J., 113, *119*
Cooper, J., 156, *161*
Cox, W. M., 113, *119*
Coyne, J. C., 11, *43*
Cranston, M., 123, 129, *133*
Csikzentmihalyi, M., 3–4,12, 16, *43*, 100, *105*, 190, *207*
Cunniff, C., 168, *176*

D

Dennett, D. C., 167, 170, *175*
DeSilva, P., 5, *45*
Devine, P. G., 156, *161*
DeWolfe, T. E., 184, *186*
Downing, J. D., 155, *161*
Driscoll, D. M., 146, *163*
Driver, J., 129, *133*
Dweck, C. S., 34, *44*, 81, *95*
Dykman, B., 128, *131*

E

Eagly, A. H., 154, *161*
Easterbrook, J. A., 128, *131*
Edwards, C. S., 151, *163*, 205, *208*
Ellis, A., 1, 39, *43*
Ellis, H. C., 128, *131*
Emery, G., 128, *131*, 142, *143*
Emmons, R. A., 16, 19, *43*, 98–99, *106*

Engle, R. W., 123, *131*
Enright, S. J., 125, *131*
Erber, R., 74, 76, *79*
Erdelyi, M. H., 170, *175*
Eriksen, C. W., 25, *43*
Evans, G. W., 128, *131*
Eysenck, H. J., 91, *95*
Eysenck, M., 117, *120*

F

Falot, R. D., 69, *71*
Farthing, G. W., 111, *119*
Faust, M. E., 123, *131*
Fazio, R. H., 113, *119*, 149, 156, *161*
Fenigstein, A., 185, *186*
Fennell, M. J. V., 143, *143*
Festinger, L., 145, 155–156, 158, *161*
Finkelhor, D., 206, *207*
Fishbein, M., 160, *161*
Fiske, S. T., 64, *71*, 195, *207*
Flanary, R., 67, *71*
Fletcher, G., 68, *71*
Folkman, S., 3, 17, *44*, 54, *61*
Francis, M. E., 105, *106*
Frank, J., 142, *143*
Fredrickson, B. L., 180, 184, *187*
Frijda, N., 18, *43*
Frith, C. D., 125, *131*
Froming, W. J., 195, *207*
Fuhrman, R. W., 172, *175*
Funabiki, D., 185, *186*

G

Galanter, E., 11, 42, *45*, 190, *208*
Ganellen, R. S., 195, *207*
Garnick, N. N., 68, *71*
Garvin, K. S., 68, *71*
Gernsbacher, M. A., 123, *131*
Gilbert, D. T., 160, *161*
Gilhooly, K. J., 111, *119*
Glaser, R., 68, *71*, 103, *106*
Glass, D. C., 128, *131*
Gleicher, F., 151, *163*, 205, *208*
Glixman, A. F., 25, *43*, *44*
Gohm, C. L., 19, 32, *44*, 86–88, 90, 92, *95*, 174, 176, 183–184, *186*
Gold, D. B., 74, *79*
Goldberg, L. R., 90, *95*
Goldman, R., 150, *162*
Gollwitzer, P. M., 24, *47*, 169, *175*
Gordon, S. E., 11, *47*

AUTHOR INDEX

Govender, R., 113, *118*
Graesser, A. C., 65, *71*
Gray, J. A., 89, 91, *95*
Greenberg, J., 1, 10, 13, 40, *45*, 140, *144*, 149, *163*, 185, *187*
Greenwald, A. G., 25–26, *44*
Grice, H. P., 169, *176*
Groisser, D., 125, *132*
Gruder, G. L., 38, *43*

H

Hamilton, J., 140, *144*
Harber, K. D., 102, 105, *106*
Hardin, T. S., 128, *131*
Harlow, T. F., 18, 40–41, *44–45*, 109, *120*, 174, *176*
Harnishfeger, K. K., 125, *131*
Hartlage, S., 128, *131*
Harvey, J. H., 67–68, *71*
Hasher, L., 122–124, 128–129, *131–133*
Hastie, R., 150, *162*
Haugtvedt, C. P., 146, 150, 155, 158–159, *162*
Havighurst, R. J., 68, *71*
Helle, P., 101, *106*
Henry, S. M., 3, 7, *43*, 66–67, *71*
Herr, P. M., 195, *207*
Herring, F., 140, *144*
Hertel, P. T., 128, *131*
Higgins, E. T., 33, 39, *44*, 76, *78*, 156, *162*, 182, *186*, 194–195, 197, 204, *207*
Hirt, E. R., 18, *44*
Hodgson, R. J., 1–2, 5, *45*
Hoelscher, T. J., 113, *119*
Holahan, C. J., 54, *60*
Holt, K., 140, *144*
Hong, Y., 34, *44*
Horowitz, M. J., 1, 3–7, 16–17, 19, 22, 26, *44*, 65, 67, *71*, 127–128, *131–132*
Hovland, C. I., 145, *162*
Hsee, C. K., 15, 16, 19, *44*
Hugdahl, K., 113, *119*
Hull, J. G., 108, *119*
Huszti, H. C., 68, *71*
Hutcherson, H. W., 168, *176*
Hyland, D. T., 68, *71*
Hyland, M., 182, *186*

I

Ingram, R. E., 128, *132*
Isbell, L. M., 19, 32, *44*, 86–88, 90, 92, *95*, 174, *176*, 183–184, *186*
Isen, A. M., 2, 9, 29, *44*

J

Jacklin, C., 184, *187*
Jackson, L. A., 184, *186*
Janigan, A., 66, *72*
Janis, I. L., 136, *143*, 145, *162*
Janoff-Bulman, R., 3–4, 6–7, *44*, 66–67, *71*
Jarvis, W. B. G., 151, *162*, 205, *207*
Jetten, J., 76, *78*
Johnsen, B. H., 113, *119*
Jones, C. R., 39, *44*, 195, *207*
Judd, C. M., 160, *162*

K

Kaiser, H., 16, 19, *43*
Kane, M. J., 124, 129, *132*
Kardes, F. R., 113, *119*
Kaufman, J., 158, *163*
Kelley, H. H., 145, *162*
Kendall-Thackett, K. A., 206, *207*
Kenny, D. A., 24, *43*
Keppel, G., 159, *163*
Kiecolt-Glaser, J. K., 103, *106*
King, G. A., 33, *44*, 195, *207*
King, L. A., 98–99, *106*
Klein, S. B., 76, 78, *79*
Klerman, G., 185, *187*
Klinger, E., 2–3, 6, 11, 15, 17, 31, *44*, 53, *61*, 99, 101, *106*, 110–115, 117, *119–120*, 128, *132*, 150, *162*, *207*
Klos, D. S., 127, *132*
Knutson, B., 76, *79*
Kopp, D. A., 13, 18, *43*, 196–197, *207*
Krampen, G., 184, *186*
Krantz, D. S., 128, *131*
Kruglanski, A. W., 153, *163*, 205, *208*
Krull, D. S., 31, *44*, 160, *161*
Kuhl, 30
Kuhl, J., 30, *44*, 101, *106*, 136, *144*, 183, *186*

L

Laberg, J. C., 113, *119*
LaFevre, J., *43*
Landman, J., 3, 8, *44*
Larson, J., 113, *120*, 137–138, *144*, 184, *187*, 204, *208*
Larson-Gutman, M. K., 115, *120*
Lassiter, G. D., 2, 38–39, *44*, 153, 155, *162*, 174, *176*
Lawrence, J. W., 19, 37, *43*
Lazarus, R. S., 3, 17, *44*, 54, *61*
Lefcourt, H., 183, *186*

LeFevre, 16
Leggett, E. L., 81, 95
Levensohn, H., 184, 187
Levy, P. E., 52, 61
Lewin, K., 11, 24, 44, 116, 119, 190, 208
Liberman, A., 154, 161
Linville, P. W., 64, 71, 122, 128–129, 132
Lombardi, W., 182, 186
Lord, R. G., 52, 61
Lowe, D. G., 129, 132
Lupfer, M. B., 168, 176
Lyonfields, J. D., 183, 186
Lyubomirsky, S., 37, 45, 113, 119, 138–141, 144, 180, 187

M

Maccoby, E., 184, 187
MacDonald, J., 123, 132
Mackie, D. M., 146, 163
MacLeod, C., 128, 133
Macrae, C. N., 76, 78
MacWhinney, B., 123, 132
Maheswaran, D., 150, 162
Mallone, P. S., 160, 161
Mandler, G., 128, 132
Mann, L., 136, 143
Marrow, A. J., 13, 24, 25, 44
Martin, L. L., 1–2, 4, 6, 11, 13, 18, 22, 24, 27, 29–30, 35, 39–41, 43–46, 49–53, 55–60, 63–66, 69–70, 73–75, 77–78, 81–88, 90–92, 94–95, 97–104, 106, 107–114, 116–118, 119–120, 121–122, 125–128, 130, 135–139, 142–143, 143, 146–152, 154–158, 160–161, 162–163, 165–167, 170–175, 175–176, 177–185, 187, 189–190, 193, 195, 197, 201, 203, 207, 208
Mathews, A., 117, 120, 128, 133
Mavin, G. H., 33, 44
Maxeiner, M. E., 99, 106, 111, 115, 119
McClelland, D. C., 98–99, 106
McDonald, H. E., 18, 44
McDougal, W., 201, 208
McDowd, J. M., 124, 132
McGuire, C. V., 81, 95
McGuire, W. J., 81, 95
McIntosh, W. D., 1–2, 11, 13, 18, 20, 22, 27, 40–41, 45, 109, 119–120, 157, 162, 171–174, 176, 185, 187, 189, 195, 201, 203, 208
McMahon, S. R., 76, 79
McWilliams, J., 125, 131
Mednick, M. T., 92, 95

Mednick, S. A., 92, 95
Melton, R. J., 18, 44
Mendolia, M., 18, 46, 108, 119, 146, 158, 160, 163, 190, 208
Meyer, D. E., 3, 47
Millar, K. U., 21, 24, 45, 66, 71, 171–172, 176
Millar, M. G., 21, 24, 45, 66, 71, 171–172, 176
Miller, G. A., 11, 42, 45, 190, 208
Milne, A. B., 76, 78
Mogg, K., 117, 120
Molinari, V., 68, 71
Moos, R. H., 54, 60
Moretti, M. M., 128, 132
Morgan, M., 67, 71
Morrow, D., 37, 46
Morrow, J., 40, 45, 138–140, 144, 180, 184, 187
Moscovici, S., 170, 176
Moskowitz, G. B., 168, 176
Mowrer, O. H., 114, 120

N

Neale, J., 180, 187
Neill, W. T., 123, 129, 132
Neimeyer, R. A., 143, 144
Neumann, O., 123, 132
Newman, L. S., 168, 176
Nikula, R., 115, 120
Nisbett, R. E., 14, 45, 170, 176, 190, 208
Nolen-Hoeksema, S., 16, 18–19, 26, 37, 39–40, 45, 55, 61, 113, 119–120, 128, 132, 137–141, 143, 143–144, 180, 183–185, 186–187, 204, 208
Nowak, A., 158, 163

O, P

Oseas-Kreger, D. M., 124, 132
Osviankina, 24
Paige, M. S., 74, 79
Park, B., 150, 162
Parker, L. E., 113, 120, 137–138, 144, 184, 187, 204, 208
Pavelchak, M. A., 195, 207
Pennebaker, J. W., 69, 71, 102–105, 106, 128, 132, 137, 144
Pennington, B. F., 125, 132
Perloff, L. S., 3, 45
Peterson, C., 185, 187
Petty, R. E., 81, 90, 95, 145–146, 148, 150–151, 153–155, 157–159, 161–164, 205, 207
Pezzo, M. V., 2, 38–39, 44, 153, 155, 162, 174, 176
Powell, M. C., 113, 119
Powell, T., 125, 131

Powers, W. T., 11, 42, *45*, 98, *106*
Pozo, C., 53, *60*
Pratto, F., 113, *118*
Pribram, K. H., 11, 42, *45*, 190, *208*
Priester, J. R., 146, 154, *163*
Pryor, J. B., 33, *45*
Pyszczynski, T. A., 1, 10, 13, 40, *45*, 140, *144*, 149, *163*, 185, *187*

R

Rabin, P. L., 184, *187*
Rachman, S., 1, 2, 5–8, 10, 13, 16–17, 26, *45*
Rachmiel, T., 180, *187*
Radloff, L., 185, *187*
Reichlin, R. E., 68, *71*
Rhodewalt, F., 156, *161–162*, 197, *207*
Rholes, W. S., 33, 39, *44–45*, 195, *207*
Richardson-Klavehn, A., 171, *176*
Richman, S. A., 146, *163*
Riemann, B. C., 113, *120*
Roback, H. B., 184, *187*
Robins, C. J., 108, *120*
Robinson, L. A., 143, *144*
Roediger, H. L., III, 171, *176*
Roemer, L., 2, 9, 35, *45*
Romer, D., 38, *43*
Roney, 10, *45*
Roney, C. J. R., 201, *208*
Roper, D. W., 128, *133*
Rosenzweig, S., 24, 25, *46*
Ross, M., 14, *46*
Rothkopf, E. Z., 159, *163*
Rotter, J., 184, *187*
Rude, S. S., 37, *46*, 128, *131*
Rush, A. J., 128, *131*, 142, *143*
Rypma, B., 124, 129, *131*

S

Salovey, P., 19, *46*
Saltzberg, J., 180, *187*
Sanbonmatsu, D. M., 113, *119*
Schank, R. C., 65, *71*, 81, *95*
Schaumann, L., 13, 18, *43*, 196–197, *207*
Scheier, M. F., 2, 11, 15–16, 19, 26, 37, 42, *43*, 49–50, 53–54, 56–57, *60*, 98, *105*, 151, *163*, 185, *186*, 190–191, 204–205, *207–208*
Schneider, D. J., 16, 26, 35–36, *46*, 74, 76, 78, *79*, 81, *95*
Schneider, K., 115, *119*
Schneider, S. K., 2–3, 5–7, 37, *46*, 112, *120*
Schneider, W., 31, *46*, 113, 115, *120*
Schneier, W., 159, *162*
Schulz, R. W., 159, *163*
Schumann, D. W., 146, *163*, 159, *162*
Schwartz, M. F., 2, 9, 29, *44*
Schwarz, N., 18, *46*, 81, *95*, 150, *163*
Scott, W. D., 13, 18, *43*, 196–197, *207*
Seiden, A., 185, *187*
Seligman, M., 185, *186*, *187*
Sharp, L. K., 103, *106*
Shavitt, S., 152, *163*, 172, *175*
Shaw, B. F., 128, *131–132*, 142, *143*
Shelby, J. S., 51, *61*
Sherman, S. J., 146, *163*
Shiffrin, R. M., 31, *46*
Shortt, J. W., 74, *79*
Silver, R. L., 1, 3–4, 6–7, 39, *46*, 65, 67, 70, 71–72, *105*, *106*, 127–128, *132*, 179, *187*, 192, 200, *208*
Silverman, C., 185, *187*
Simon, H. A., 52, *61*, 194, *208*
Singer, J. E., 128, *131*
Singer, J. L., 2, 5–6, 19, *46*, 111, *120*
Singh, B. G., 184, *187*
Skowronski, J. J., 168, *175*
Smith, S. M., 146, 150, 153, 155, 158–159, *162–164*
Sorrentino, 10, *45*
Sorrentino, R. M., 201, *208*
Spera, S., 103, *106*
Spielberger, C. D., 90, *95*
Srull, T. K., 8, 17, 39, *46–47*, 182, *187*
Steele, C. M., 156, *163*
Stokam, L. A., 66, *71*
Stokols, D., 128, *131*
Stoltzfus, E. R., 123–124, 129, *131–132*
Stone, A., 180, *187*
Stone, M., 67, *71*
Stoner, P., 18, *44*, 197, *208*
Stones, M. H., 1, 3–4, 6–7, 39, *46*, 128, *132*, 179, *187*, 192, 200, *208*
Strathman, A. J., 146, 151, *163*, 205, *208*
Strauman, T. J., 11, *46*
Susman, J., 105, *106*

T

Tait, R., 65, 67, *71*, 128, *132*
Taylor, D. M., 7, *43*, 66–67, *71*
Taylor, S. E., 2–3, 5–7, 37, *46*, 60, *61*, 65–66, *71*, 112, *120*
Teasdale, J. D., 143, *143*, 185, *186*
Tellegen, A., 204, *208*
Tesser, A., 2, 4, 6, 10–11, 18, 21, 24, *44*, *46*, 49–53, 55–60, 63–66, 69–70, *71*, 73–75,

77–78, 81–92, 94–95, 97–104, 107–114, 116–118, *119*, 121–122, 125–128, 130, 135–139, 142–143, 145–152, 154–158, 160–161, *163*, 165–167, 170–172, 174–175, *176*, 177–185, 189–190, 193, 195, 201, 207, *208*
Thein, R. D., 194, *207*
Thompson, S., 66, *72*
Tipper, S. P., 123–124, 129, *132–133*
Tolman, E. C., 201, *208*
Tomkins, S. S., 100, *106*, 114, *120*
Tredinnick, M. G., 51, *61*

U, V

Uleman, J. S., 8, 11, *46*, 63, *72*, 81, *95*, 168, 170, *176*
Underwood, B. J., 159, *163*
Vaksdal, A., 113, *119*
Vallacher, R. R., 15, *46*, 158, *163*, 169, *176*
Varner, K. R., 123, *131*
Vazquez, C., 128, *131*
Verma, O. P., 184, *187*
von Bertalanffy, L., 11–12, 42, *46*, 105, *106*, 196, *208*

W

Walster, E., 10, *46*
Ward, D. W., 18, *44–45*, 101, *106*, 154, *162*
Warren, W., 159, *162*
Watson, D., 204, *208*
Watt, L. M., 69, *72*
Watts, F. N., 128, *133*
Weber, A. L., 68, *71*
Webster, D. M., 153, *163*, 205, *208*
Wegener, D. T., 146, 150, 154, *163–164*
Wegner, D. M., 15–16, 26, 35–36, *46*, 74, 76–78, *79*, 81, *95*, 127–128, *133*, 151, *164*, 169, *176*

Weintraub, J. K., 2, *43*, 54, *60*
Weissman, M., 185, *187*
Weldon, M. S., 171, *176*
Wells, G. L., 145–146, *163*
Welsh, M. C., 125, *132*
Wenzlaff, R. M., 16, 26, *46*, 76, 78, *79*, 128, *133*
White, L., 74, 76, 78, *79*
White, S. W., 68, *70*
White, T. L., 16, 26, 35–36, *46*, 81, *95*
Wicklund, R. A., 4, 12, 15, 24, *46*, 190, *208*
Williams, C. W., 33, *47*
Williams, J. M. G., 128, *133*
Williams, L. M., 206, *207*
Wilner, N., 19, 22, *44*
Wilson, J. P., 98, *105*
Wilson, T. D., 14, *45*, 170, *176*, 190, *208*
Winter, L., 168, *176*
Winterberger, P., 184, *186*
Wong, P. T. P., 69, *72*
Wood, J., 180, *187*
Wortman, C. B., 70, 72, 105, *106*, 127, *132*
Wyer, R. S., 8, 11, 17–19, 32, 39, *44–47*, 86–88, 90, 92, *95*, 101, *106*, 145, 154, 159, *162*, *164*, 174, *176*, 182–184, *186–187*

X, Y

Xu, G., 160, *161*
Yaniv, I., 3, *47*
Young, J., 31–32, *47*, 113, 115, 118, *120*, 174, *176*

Z

Zacks, R. T., 123–124, 129, *131–133*
Zajonc, R. B., 160, *164*
Zanakos, S., 74, 76, *79*
Zanna, M. P., 156, *162*, 197, *207*
Zeigarnik, B., 11, 24, *47*, 190, *208*
Zentner, M., 37, *46*

Subject Index

A

Accessibility in memory
  of causes of behavior, 32–34
    chronic, 33–34
  of emotional responses, 116–118
  role,
    in rumination, 116–118, 194–196
    in thought suppression, 77–78
Affect and emotion
  positive versus negative, 18, 39–41
  relation to rumination, 17–19, 39–41, 54–56, 114–118, 138–142, 196–198
Attention
  inhibition of, 121–130, 196
  selective, 122–123
Attitude change; see Persuasion
Attitudes
  strength of, 157–158
Attributions
  luck versus skill, 27–30

C

Cognitive dissonance
  role on recurrent thought, 155–157
Current concerns
  theory of, 3–4, 110–118

D

Depression
  and ruminative thinking, 10, 39–41, 127, 138–142
  and stress, 128–129

Distraction
  effect on thinking, 27–30

E

Ego involvement, see also Motivation
  role in thinking, 25–26
Elaboration–Likelihood Model, 145, 148–151, 157–160
Emotion, see Affect and emotion
Expectations
  discrepancies from, in goal seeking, 49–50, 73
Extroversion–introversion
  relation to rumination, 89–90

G

Goals
  blocking of
    attribution for, 27–30
    effect on thinking, 15, 22–24, 31, 50–51, 178–179
  change in progress toward, 11–13, 50–51, 57–59
  conceptualization of, 64–65, 179
  discrepancies from expectations in goal seeking, 49–50, 57–59
  disengagement of, 53–54
  hierarchy of, 13–14, 99–100, 108
  higher order, 13–14, 98–100
  lifetime, 98–100
  nonattainment of, 75–76
  prioritization of, 51–53

215

role, in rumination, 3–4, 11–15, 21–24, 49–53, 97–105, 165–170
unconscious, 165–170, 201
    role of, in rumination, 165–175, 200–201

I

Implicit theories, 32–34, 67–69, 142–143
Impulsivity
    effects of, 92–93
    versus rumination, 87
Individual differences
    action-oriented versus state-oriented, 30–31, 136–138
    in implicit theories, 32–34
    linkers versus nonlinkers, 22–24
    in rumination, 19–20, 22–24, 182–183, 203–205
    in thinking style, 88–91
Inhibition, *see also*, Suppression of thought
    of attention, 121–125
    effects of emotion on, 127–130
    role in rumination, 125–128
    underlying mechanisms, 123–125

L, M

Linkers versus nonlinkers, 22–24, 171–172
Mental models, 67–69
Mood, *see* Affect and emotion
Motivation, *see also* Goals
    self-protective, 25–26

N, P

Need for cognition, 92–94
Persuasion
    attributes of, 146
    role of thought in, 145–161
    and thought content, 146–148

R

Rumination
    and attention, 125–130
    consequences of, 37–41, 155–160
    content of, 14–15, 145–146, 178–179
    definition of, 1, 7, 177–178, 181–182, 191–193
    distraction from, 27–30, 138–140
    effect of
        on depression, 10
        on maintenance of goal-related thought, 38–39
    on negative thought, 39–41
    on other thought processes, 37–38
    effects of goals on, 11–15, 22–24, 31, 49–454, 97–100, 165–175, 193–196
    functionality of, 113–114, 179–180, 198–200
    individual differences in, 19–20, 22–24, 30–31, 182–183, 203–205
    modes of, 8–11
    persistence of, 73–76
    in real world contexts, 65–67, 205–206
    role of
        in affect and emotion, 17–19, 100–102, 114–118, 127–130, 138–142, 196–198
    role of ego involvement in, 25–26
    stopping of, 15–17
    theoretical models of, 2, 11–21, 50–51, 110–118, 189–191
    unintentionality of, 56–57
    versus incubation, 51
    versus problem solving, 136–138
    versus talking and writing, 102–104

S, T

Suppression of thoughts, 35–37, 74–78
    effects of stress and depression on, 128–130
Thought and thinking, *see also* Rumination
    content of, 146–147, 151–152
    dimensions of, 83–88
        intentionality, 83–85
        temporal–situational focus, 83–85
        valence, 85–88
    extent of, 150–151
    flow of, 112–113
    individual differences in, 19–20, 22–24, 88–89
    consequences of, 91–94
    initiation and termination of, 148–150, 153–154
    and meaning of life, 97–105
    physiological bases of, 89–90
    positive versus negative, 9
    recurrence of, 3–6, 152–153
    role of goals in, 4, 11–14, 21–30
    styles of, 83–95, 202–203
        consequences of, 91–94
        dimensions of, 83–88
        individual differences in, 88–90
        personality correlates of, 90–91

suppression of, 35–37
theories of, 3–6, 107–118, 148–150
    commonalities in, 6–8
    comparison of, 11–118
    varieties of, 2–3, 83–88

W, Z

Writing about trauma
    effects of, 103–104
Zeigarnik effect, 24–26, 195